BECOME STRONG
Finish STRONG

Living a "Best-Is-Yet-To-Come" Life

MIKE GARST

Become Strong, Finish Strong

© Copyright 2024 Mike Garst
ISBN: 978-1-962848-05-3

Scriptures are taken from the NEW KING JAMES VERSION® (NKJV): Copyright© 1982 by Thomas Nelson, Inc. Used by permission. All rights reserved.

All rights reserved. No part of this publication may be reproduced or transmitted in any form or by any means without written permission from the publisher.

Interior and cover design: Marji Laine
Editing: Lisa Bell

Published by:
Roaring Lambs Publishing
17110 Dallas Parkway, Suite 260
Dallas, TX 75248

Published in the United States of America.

What people are saying about Become Strong, Finish Strong

Too many people seem to believe their "later years" are a time to throttle back and coast to the finish line. Mike Garst's book, *Become Strong, Finish Strong,* encourages all Christians, regardless of age, to stay focused on doing their Lord's Will for as long as they are on this earth. Discipline, readiness, rigor, integrity, courage, forbearance—all are concepts that resonate throughout this inspiring book.
Lieutenant Colonel Robert H. Van Horn, Jr., U.S. Army (retired).

What a timely book, as I begin approaching this next stage of my life. While so many are out to help pre-retirees with financial planning asking, "Is your financial house in order?" Mike is on a quest to help others with their spiritual planning. He does an incredible job of making you think to ensure your life counts where it matters most. You will enjoy the stories, wisdom and insights as to navigating how you too can finish strong.
Mary Anne (Wihbey) Davis, Owner, Peak Performance Solutions.

As a clinical psychologist, I know that often those truths which are met with the most resistance are the ones most essential to ingest if one wants joyous transformation. The practical applications of God's Word that Mike Garst offers are not sexy or popular in the world view, but drink them in and see what beauty and fulfillment unfolds in your life. Very inspiring and highly recommended!
Shoshana S. Bennett, Ph.D. Clinical psychologist, Author, Speaker

Mike Garst is the real deal! He is a mighty man of God who is living his life for the glory of God and having impact for the Lord and His Kingdom! I am so thankful to God for connecting our hearts some 25+ years ago. It has been incredible to watch Mike go from a fairly nominal church attender to a dedicated follower of Jesus! It has been such a blessing to watch Mike become strong in the Lord, strong enough to care! It is such a joy to see Mike's desire to finish strong for the Lord and for God's Kingdom purposes. If you have an interest in knowing how to live strong in the Lord, if you have a desire to finish strong, Mike's book, Become Strong, Finish Strong, is for YOU! In this book, Mike shares his journey of faith and growth and how God has worked in his life. Mike shares how he has worked to establish spiritual disciplines in his life so he can discern God's guidance and walk in the love, and grace and strength of God as he seeks to fulfill God's will and God's callings on his life. Buckle up and get your heart and your mind ready to go on a journey with Jesus as you read, learn, and grow with Mike so you can BECOME STRONG and FINISH STRONG!

Bud Miller, Pastor

I have known Mike Garst for well over a decade, and as I read his book, I felt like I was watching his life unfold as he consistently and persistently has walked into increasing fullness of being loved by God and loving God. Over the span of our friendship, he has been the most intentional and disciplined and passionate disciple of the risen Lord. This book captures the wisdom and revelation he has learned in his walk. Drink deeply, and you will be more wholehearted toward God and you will love your neighbors as Jesus has loved you. Be challenged… Be discipled… Be encouraged!

Paul Foss, Founder and President of Waterboyz for Jesus

Contents

Introduction 7
Chapter 1: What Would a Strong Finish Look Like?................... 13
Chapter 2: What Do I Believe?.. 21
Chapter 3: What Am I Seeking?... 35
Chapter 4: Am I Called to Become Like Christ? 49
Chapter 5: How Can I Become Like Jesus?............................... 61
Chapter 6: Have I Been Born Again?.. 75
Chapter 7: What is the Devil's Strategy? 91
Chapter 8: What is my Purpose? 111
Chapter 9: What Is the Current State of My Mind?................... 127
Chapter 10: How Do We Develop a Sound Mind?..................... 147
Chapter 11: What or Who Am I Investing In? 167
Chapter 12: Why Should We Invest in People? 183
Chapter 13: What Does an Intentional Life Look Like?.............. 197
Chapter 14: What Are the Dangers of Not Living Intentionally? 213
Chapter 15: Am I Listening to God's Warnings? 229
Chapter 16: Am I Being Faithful? 245
Chapter 17: Am I an Overcomer? 259
Chapter 18: Am I Persevering? 275
Chapter 19: What Will Be My Legacy?..................................... 289
About the Author 293

Mike Garst

Introduction

It's interesting that when most people are young, they have dreams about what they might do with their lives. But as people get older, those early dreams may fade away, and they may settle for much less. By the time adults are approaching what we call retirement age, most of their dreams may have disappeared. But it doesn't need to be this way, especially for anyone who believes Jesus is their Lord and Savior. The prophet Joel wrote, *"And it shall come to pass afterward that I will pour out My Spirit on all flesh; your sons and your daughters shall prophesy, your old men shall dream dreams, your young men shall see visions"* (Joel 2:28).

It should be encouraging for Christians to know they may be able to prophesy, dream, or have visions into their old age. Having this capability should also enable believers to function with God's power in ever-increasing ways, so they can keep living strong to the end of this life on earth. For those of us who are in relationship with Jesus and are well into the second half of our lives, this should be good news. Our best years should always be in front of us.

Unfortunately, this kind of thinking doesn't appear to be the mindset of everyone, even for followers of Christ, in the second half of their lives. Although a few older people may say their best years are in the future, many would probably still say their best years are behind them. Is this you?

For many adults, it appears their purpose in the final years is built around trying to live the "good life," which includes doing all the things they like to do to increase their pleasure, comfort, and security. In other words, they believe their last years are to be fun years when they get to do all the things they have always wanted to do. On the surface, this sounds good, especially to our natural body. But we may need to ask ourselves if we want to experience the peace and joy that comes from bringing glory to God, or at least to help our fellow man, or do we want to please our natural body and stay within its comfort zones in our final years? What do we really want from our final years in the deepest part of our heart?

The reason I'm writing this book is because I believe this is a serious issue each of us needs to face honestly. Because of what God told the prophet Ezekiel, we believers have a serious responsibility to warn people if we believe they are on the wrong path. Otherwise, we will be held accountable for what happens to them. Here is what Ezekiel wrote.

> *"Son of man, I have made you a watchman for the house of Israel; therefore, hear a word from My mouth, and give them warning from Me: When I say to the wicked, 'You shall surely die,' and you give him no warning, nor speak to warn the wicked from his wicked way, to save his life, that same wicked man shall die in his iniquity; but his blood I will require at your hand. Yet, if you warn the wicked, and he does not turn from his wickedness, nor from his wicked way, he shall die in his iniquity; but you have delivered your soul" (Ezekiel 3:17-19).*

God repeated these verses in *Ezekiel 33:7-9*. These verses say the watchman has a responsibility to warn the wicked. Who are the watchmen today? Many people might say it's the leaders of the church, such as the pastors and elders. But I believe anybody who is a disciple of Jesus Christ, who has clearly heard and understood the Word of God, has a responsibility to share it with the people God puts in their lives.

The problem is, of course, nobody likes to deliver warnings people don't want to hear. Jeremiah was not a popular prophet to the Israelites. The Old Testament nation of Israel mistreated him when he shared the truth with them. In a like manner, the watchmen for this generation should not expect to be treated any differently. Nevertheless, God says if the prophet doesn't warn people, they will be responsible for their blood. But if they do warn them, even if they don't repent, they will *"have delivered"* their soul. The consequences are straightforward, and there's only one good choice to be made.

God also told Ezekiel he must warn the righteous when they commit iniquity and that the consequences of obedience and disobedience were the same as for the wicked. This is what Ezekiel wrote.

> *"Again, when a righteous man turns from his righteousness and commits iniquity, and I lay a stumbling block before him, he shall die; because you did not give him warning, he shall die in his sin, and his righteousness which he has done shall not be remembered; but his blood I will require at your hand. Nevertheless, if you warn the righteous man that the righteous should not sin, and he does not sin, he shall surely live because he took warning; also you will have delivered your soul" (Ezekiel 3:20-21 – see also Ezekiel 33:1-6).*

This means the righteous must stay righteous and finish righteously. This is why we must live daily in a right way as if tomorrow depended on it. Based on what King David wrote, all true believers are called to finish our life journey well.

> *"Blessed is the man whose strength is in You, whose heart is set on pilgrimage. As they pass through the Valley of [Weeping] Baca, they make it a spring; the rain also covers it with [blessings] pools. They go from strength to strength; each one appears before God in Zion" (Psalm 84:5-7).*

God is calling us on a journey with Him that will include the valleys of weeping and the mountains of blessings, and His purpose is to strengthen our faith at each spiritual milestone until we appear before Him in Zion. This is consistent with what Jesus said to the seven churches in chapters two and three of the Book of Revelation. Most Christians know about the lukewarm church at Laodicea, which God said He would vomit out of His mouth if they didn't repent. But Laodicea was not the only church that received a strong warning from Jesus. Four of the other churches had issues that required repentance. Plus, they needed to overcome those shortcomings to receive any rewards. Even the two churches that didn't require repentance were told they needed to overcome to receive any rewards. It's hard to believe we can overcome if we don't finish strong. It's also going to be hard for us to finish strong if we don't first become strong.

If my personal observations are close to correct, few people finish this life strong. If this is true, it would be good to know why, so we can make the adjustments needed to finish strong. No one starts out life consciously choosing NOT to live to the fullest. A long-distance runner doesn't want to fade at the end of the race. An athlete knows to win any race, a strong finish will be needed. In every long-distance race I've ever witnessed, the lead runners are sprinting when they cross the finish line. Shouldn't we have this same attitude as we finish our lives here on earth? Doesn't a Christian want to sprint across the finish line and run into the arms of Jesus?

So why don't more people finish strong? As I've thought and prayed about this, I've come up with several important questions that will be the title of each chapter in this book. It's important for us to answer each of these questions honestly, because earnest answers will help us make needed changes in our priorities so we can become strong and finish strong.

One thing you will notice as you are reading this book is that I include many Scripture references (I use the New King James Version). If I've learned one thing in this life, it's that God's Word can speak more effectively into a person's heart than my words. *Hebrews 4:12* states the following.

> *"For the word of God is living and powerful, and sharper than any two-edged sword, piercing even to the division of soul and spirit, and of joints and marrow, and is a discerner of the thoughts and intents of the heart."*

It would be risky and presumptuous for me to try to interpret what I believe any Scripture is saying to you. So, my goal is to share what I think the scriptures are saying, but I want you to be motivated to study and meditate on the verses I've included, so God can speak to you directly through His Word. I will also tie different scriptures together and add my testimony or the testimonies of others between God's Word. The apostle John wrote in *Revelation 12:11* that our testimonies are important.

> *"And they overcame him by the blood of the Lamb and by the word of their testimony, and they did not love their lives to the death."*

Our testimonies are important because they are the evidence Christ has truly come into our hearts and changed us. Without a testimony, we can look like we are religious on the outside but continue to live like the world on the inside. I hope those of you who read this book will do everything you can to discover God's heart and His mission for your lives, so you can live the rest of your lives for His purposes and have a testimony that proves it.

Mike Garst

Chapter 1
What Would a Strong Finish Look Like?

I'm sure we would get a wide range of responses if we asked enough people how they would characterize a strong finish in this life. If you have not given much thought to finishing strong and what that might look like, I want to give you an idea of what I mean.

I believe we will finish our lives strong when life is understood as a mission from God right up to the last breath. This means we will use whatever gifts and resources God has given us to be an ever-increasing river of God's attributes of love, which includes patience, kindness, gentleness, grace, mercy, forgiveness, generosity, encouragement, justice, compassion, and faithfulness, just to name a few. We will model, teach, and train these attributes of God until our last breath. And those we teach and train will also be experiencing an ever-increasing level of peace, contentment, and joy in everything they do. Let me share with you an example of someone who I believe finished strong.

Granny Brand

Granny Brand was a thirty-five-year-old single woman from England when she went to serve as a missionary in India in 1909. She married another missionary there who died when Granny was fifty. Most everybody expected her to go back to live in England at that point, where their two children lived at the time. But she decided to continue being a missionary. When she was approaching seventy, the mission board she was serving under decided it wasn't good for a single woman her age to continue being a missionary there. That ended up being a turning point in her life, because she didn't retire, but continued with her own resources and was essentially freed from all the restrictions the mission board had imposed on her mission work. Nothing could stop her, including a broken hip, falling headfirst off a horse, and several other accidents. And even though she could barely walk after all those injuries, she continued until she died at ninety-five.

Retirement

When you look at Granny Brand's life, you'll realize she never retired but continued pursuing the vision God gave her until her last breath. It seems to me an unhealthy concept of retirement has crept into our way of thinking, especially in developed countries that have some kind of government retirement program. It's unfortunate many people wait until retirement before they finally do what they want. In some cases, this might lead a person to do something that would help their fellow man and glorify God. But it appears many people are focusing the end of their lives mostly on entertainment, comfort, and security only for this life, and nothing beyond it. The apostle Paul wrote about the dangers of focusing on this life. *"If in this life only we have hope in Christ, we are of all men the most pitiable" (1 Corinthians 15:19).*

Now if we don't believe there is anything beyond this life, it might make sense to focus on the things I mentioned above.

If any of you are thinking staying strong to the end isn't possible as you get older and are less able physically to do things, I hope Granny

Brand's story has changed your thinking. Our physical ability isn't nearly as important as our spiritual health and having a purpose that motivates us to live each day for the glory of God. Granny Brand's son, Paul, said about his mom, "This is how to grow old. Allow everything else to fall away, until those around you see just love." [1]

There at least five things I can think of that should never stop growing in this lifetime, regardless of our physical limitations. They are love for God (if you believe there is a God), love for people, wisdom, knowledge, and influence. It appears to me Granny Brand never stopped growing in any of these things. She knew her God-given purpose, and she wasn't going to stop fulfilling it regardless of her health or circumstances. We must have this same kind of commitment to keep fulfilling our mission by continually growing in these areas, so we can finish strong. We must know our God-given purpose and be fully committed to completing it, despite any physical limitations or advice from other people, even those close to us, which doesn't motivate us to continue developing and using our gifts and talents to serve others and honor God.

All Things New

I also want to share an excerpt from a book by John Eldredge called *All Things New*[2]. It will give you another vision of what finishing strong might look like.

> "I want to finish well! I want to return as a hero, as a warrior worthy of the Kingdom... worthy of the King!
> I had this vision... I don't know if it was an actual vision or just my heart's expression. I saw myself, sword at my side, shield slung over my back, my Beauty close at hand, making our way up the main street of the city. I wore the battle gear of war, soiled and torn by long years at the front.

---

[1] Granny Brand Her Story, Dorothy Clarke Wilson, Paul Brand Publishing, Seattle WA, 1976, Page 206
[2] All Things New, John Eldredge, Nelson, Thomas, Inc. Nashville, 2018.

People lined both sides of the street to welcome me, the great cloud, I think. I recognized hundreds of faces, the faces of those whose freedom I fought for. I also realized there were many more... thousands whose faces I didn't know but for some reason I knew they were there in part, because of God using me and my life. Their smiles and tears filled my heart with profound joy. It WAS worth it after all... my life had counted for something... profound joy!

As we made our way up the street toward Jesus and our Father, our friends and fellow warriors stepped into the street with us, and we moved forward as a band of brothers. I saw angels there, the angels who fought for us and with us, walking alongside of us. They were beautiful and fearsome... and yet childlike in a way that made me laugh out loud.

I saw flower petals on the pavement; I saw banners flapping in the breeze. We reached the throne, and we all knelt. Jesus came forward and kissed each of our foreheads. When He came to me, we embraced deeply, freely, like I always knew we would. Time stood still... Everything made sense in a way it never had fully.

Then my Father stepped forward and took me by the shoulders and said, "Well done, my son. Very well done indeed! Welcome home. "As we embraced, a great cheer went up from the crowd."

Don't Waste Your Life

John Piper wrote a book called *Don't Waste Your Life* [3]. I want to include a couple of the sections he wrote because they describe both how to waste your life, and how not to waste your life. Here are some excerpts from his book:

"A Tragedy in the Making"

"You may not be sure that you want your life to make a difference. Maybe you don't care very much whether you make a lasting difference for the sake of something great. You just

---

[3] Don't Waste Your Life, John Piper, CROSSWAY BOOKS, Wheaton IL, 2003, Pages 45-46

want people to like you. If people would just like being around you, you'd be satisfied. Or if you could just have a good job with a good wife, or husband, and a couple of good kids and a nice car and long weekends and a few good friends, a fun retirement, and a quick and easy death, and no hell—if you could have all that (even without God)—you would be satisfied. That is a tragedy in the making."

"An American Tragedy: How Not to Finish Your One Life"

I will tell you what a tragedy is. I will show you how to waste your life. Consider a story from the February 1998 edition of Readers Digest, which tells about a couple who "took early retirement from their jobs in the Northeast five years ago when he was 59 and she was 51. Now they live in Punta Gorda, Florida, where they cruise on a 30-foot trawler, play softball and collect shells." At first, when I read it, I thought it might be a joke. A spoof on the American Dream. But it wasn't. Tragically, this was a dream: Come to the end of your life—your one and only precious, God-given life—and let the last great work of your life, before you give an account to your Creator, be this: playing softball and collecting shells. Picture them before Christ at the great day of judgment: "Look, Lord. See my shells." That is a tragedy. And many people today are spending billions of dollars to persuade you to embrace that tragic dream. Over against that, I put my protest: don't buy it. Don't waste your life.

"These Lives and Deaths Were No Tragedy"

In April 2000, Ruby Eliason and Laura Edwards were killed in Cameroon, West Africa. Ruby was over 80. Single all her life, she poured it out for one great thing: to make Jesus Christ known among the unreached, the poor, and the sick. Laura was a widow, a medical doctor, pushing 80 years old, and serving at Ruby's side in Cameroon. The brakes failed, the car went over a cliff, and they were both killed instantly. I asked my congregation: was that a tragedy? Two lives, driven by one great passion, namely, to be spent in unheralded service to the perishing poor for the glory of Jesus Christ—even two decades after most of their American counterparts had retired to throw away their lives on trifles. No, that is not a tragedy. That is a glory. Those lives were not wasted. And these lives were not lost. *"Whoever loses his life for My sake and the gospel's will save it"* (Mark 8:35)."

Strong Finishers in Scripture

If we look at some of the most well-known men in the Bible, we will see they were in the latter stages of their lives when God did some of His greatest work through them, especially Abraham, Moses, Joshua and Caleb in the Old Testament. Paul and most of Jesus' original disciples also continued to grow stronger and finished strong at the end of their lives. It appears the apostle John wrote the book of Revelation when he was about ninety-nine years old, and it's hard to imagine the Bible without that book. If we are true followers of Christ, we will be Holy Spirit-led people who don't focus on any of the pleasures in this life. Instead, we will be continually stepping out in faith to do the things God is calling, leading, and preparing us to do. This shouldn't surprise any of us who have yielded our lives to Jesus and are being transformed into His likeness. It should be very natural for us to continue growing in our love and faith, because that is what true disciples of Christ do. And if Jesus is living inside us, He promises to change us into His likeness. If we are growing in Christ's likeness, God will make us winsome people who can greatly influence the lives of many others in a way that honors Him.

What I believe all of us need to become is what I call a *Jeremiah 20:9* man or woman.

> *"Then I said, 'I will not make mention of Him, nor speak anymore in His name.' But His word was in my heart like a burning fire shut up in my bones; I was weary of holding it back, and I could not."*

My hope and prayer for those of you reading this book is that you would become *Jeremiah 20:9* men and women, who truly have the Word of God in your hearts like a fire and you would keep that fire burning so you would never become complacent in your faith or your life in general. Then you will be like the apostle Paul who said,

> *"Brethren, I do not count myself to have [laid hold of it] apprehended; but one thing I do, forgetting those things which are behind and reaching forward to those things which are ahead, I press toward the goal for the prize of the upward call of God in Christ Jesus"*
> *(Philippians 3:13-14).*

It is my firm belief any man or woman who has the Word of God in his or her heart, like a fire, will not rely on anything they've done in the past but will keep pressing on to continually strengthen themselves in the Lord. This will enable them to be transformed further into Christ's likeness so they can finish their lives strong in the Lord. They will do this, not because they feel obligated to do so, but because they want to, knowing it will please and glorify their Father in heaven.

I don't know where you are on your spiritual journey, but I have a long-time friend who sent me a text while I was writing this book, after I challenged her to finish strong in the Lord. It was a very honest, yet revealing statement that might represent the thoughts of many people in the world today.

She said, "I really am tired of a lukewarm existence and want to follow Christ and obey. Taking that identity is…well…I don't know yet."

We desperately need more men and women in today's world to grow into mature followers of Christ whose only desire is to glorify and honor God until He takes them home. We need enough believers who have testimonies that can inspire others to follow Christ more closely. Only in this way can we make any gains against all the evil in this world. The government is not able to do it. Only the Church can do it. The early Christians were accused of turning the world upside down. *"But when they did not find them, they dragged Jason and some brethren to the rulers of the city, crying out, 'These who have turned the world upside down have come here too'"* (Acts 17:6).

Can we truthfully say our church is turning the world upside down? Is our church full of Granny Brands going strong to the end and inspiring younger Christians to imitate them?

Dallas Willard wrote something in his book *Living in Christ's Presence* that should strongly challenge each of us.

"If you read the Great Commission, you may not realize it is about world revolution. If you think it is about planting churches, as important as that may be, if you think it is about evangelization, as that is often understood—no, no, it is about a world revolution promised through Abraham, come to life in Jesus and living on in his people up to today. That is what our hearts hunger for, even when we don't know how to approach it or how to go about it." [4]

I believe this is truly what our hearts hunger for, and we will need to be as transparent as possible with each other if we want to remove all the obstacles preventing this from becoming a reality. I hope to stimulate your thinking on what you may need to do differently so you can be a part of this revolution God is calling each Christian to participant in wholeheartedly, so they can become strong and finish strong.

---

[4] Living in God's Presence, Dallas Willard, IVP Books, Downers Grove, IL, 2014, Page 11

Chapter 2
What Do I Believe?

"They profess to know God, but in works they deny Him, being abominable, disobedient, and disqualified for every good work" (Titus 1:16).

We typically judge people by what they do, not by what they say they believe. Yet it's not unusual for us to expect other people to judge us by what we say and not by what we do. Hypocrisy is to say one thing and do the opposite. (The word hypocrite ultimately came into English from the Greek word hypokrites, which means an actor or stage player [Merriam-Webster.com]). Jesus told the Pharisees and teachers of the law they were hypocrites because they taught God's ways but lived contrary to them. And when Jesus talked about the faithful and evil servant at the end of Matthew 24, He said the fate of the evil servant was the same as that of the hypocrites.

"The master of that (evil) servant will come on a day when he is not looking for him and at an hour that he is not aware of,

> *and will cut him in two and appoint him his portion with the hypocrites. There shall be weeping and gnashing of teeth" (Matthew 24:50-51).*

This should provide plenty of incentive for each of us to take an honest inventory of our lives regularly, so we can know if what we say we believe lines up with reality. The apostle Paul told the church in Corinth, *"Examine yourselves as to whether you are in the faith. Test yourselves. Do you not know yourselves, that Jesus Christ is in you?—unless indeed you are disqualified" (2 Corinthians 13:5).*

The first sentence could be restated to say, "See if what you say you believe lines up with what you do." Then Paul followed that by saying they would need to test themselves. We will never know what we would do in any situation until we get put to the test, and our faith is no different. This means if we want to become strong and finish strong, we must regularly put our lives under a microscope and then take the actions needed to become men and women of integrity.

Dallas Willard wrote,

> "Belief is when your whole being is set to act as if something is so… So we do not, in general, control our beliefs or those of others. We never choose to believe, and we must not try to get ourselves or others to choose to believe. That is God's work. We can try to understand and try to help others to understand. And beyond that - God must work." [5]

This means taking an oath and proclaiming anything out loud or in writing will not cause us to believe it. It will only happen when we believe it in our hearts, and it becomes who we are on the inside and outside. So, when we say we believe God or believe in God, but don't do what He commands, then we may believe some things about God, but we don't

---

[5] Renovation of the Heart, Dallas Willard, NAVPRESS, Colorado Springs CO, 2002, Pages 248-249

believe God or believe in Him yet. This is important for us to understand, because our enemy, Satan, is quite satisfied with having people say they believe something which their actions don't reflect. And he will try to keep them thinking they believe it.

Faith and Actions

A genuine faith will always be demonstrated by actions. The second greatest commandment is to love our neighbor as ourselves, and it's hard to see how we can do that without using our hands, feet, mind, or mouth to some degree. Even keeping our mouths closed will take some effort because it will require restraint on our part not to say something we should keep to ourselves. Jesus' earthly, as well as His spiritual, brother James wrote about faith and works in the second chapter of *James*. He summarized it in *James 2:20* when he said,

"But do you want to know, O foolish man, that faith without works is [useless] dead?

Then James followed this by talking about the working faith of Abraham. *"Was not Abraham our father justified by works when he offered Isaac his son on the altar? Do you see that faith was working together with his works, and by works faith was made [complete] perfect? And the Scripture was fulfilled which says, 'Abraham believed God, and it was [credited] accounted to him for righteousness.' And he was called the friend of God. You see then that a man is justified by works, and not by faith only"* (James 2:21-24).

It would have taken a very strong faith developed over time for Abraham to offer his son Isaac on the altar. I can't imagine a new believer being asked or being able to do something anything close to this. In other words, Abraham's faith had gotten to the point where it was in the final stages of development by God because it says at the end of *verse 22, "and by works faith was made [complete] perfect."* The Bible says Abraham is the father of all who believe, so his faith had to get to the point he would willingly sacrifice anything that might stand between himself and God. After waiting so long for a son, and then having Isaac, his only son at that time, be born when Sarah was way past childbearing age could have caused Abraham to see Isaac as more important than God. Yet Abraham withstood that test of faith.

James also wrote about the working faith of Rahab. *"Likewise, was not Rahab the harlot also justified by works when she received the messengers and sent them out another way? For as the body without the spirit is dead, so faith without works is dead also" (James 2:25-26).*

Rahab was one of several non-Israelites in the Old Testament that played an important part in the history of the Israelite people. She lived in Jericho, and before the Israelites crossed over the Jordan to enter the Promised Land, Joshua had sent two men to spy out the land, especially Jericho. They entered Jericho and were staying at Rahab's house when the king of Jericho sent her a message telling her to bring those men out because they were spies. But she had hidden them under some stalks of flax on the roof and told the king, although they had been in her house, they left and went out of the city. Plus, she urged the king to go after them (see Joshua 2:1-8). The next verses tell us why Rahab did this.

> *"Now before they lay down, she came up to them on the roof, and said to the men: 'I know that the Lord has given you the land, that the terror of you has fallen on us, and that all the inhabitants of the land are fainthearted because of you. For we have heard how the Lord dried up the water of the Red Sea for you when you came out of Egypt, and what you did to the two kings of the Amorites who were on the other side of the Jordan, Sihon and Og, whom you utterly destroyed. And as soon as we heard these things, our hearts melted; neither did there remain any more courage in anyone because of you, for the Lord your God, He is God in heaven above and on earth beneath.'" (Joshua 2:9-11).*

Rahab became a traitor to her people, because she realized God was with the Israelites and her only hope of survival was to place her faith in God. Her faith will always be remembered because she became the wife of an Israelite named Salmon and was the mother of Boaz, who was an ancestor of King David, who was an ancestor of Jesus. *"Salmon begot Boaz by Rahab, Boaz begot Obed by Ruth, Obed begot Jesse, and Jesse begot David the king" (Matthew 1:5-6).*

Abraham and Rahab were both excellent examples of people whose actions confirmed what they believed. And the Bible is full of other examples of people who lived out what they believed.

What Do Our Actions Show?

What's the practical application of this? It means if we say we believe we should forgive everybody who hurts us or asks us for forgiveness, but if we don't forgive them, then we don't believe we should forgive everybody who hurts us or asks us for forgiveness. Or if we say we believe we shouldn't lie, yet we only tell the truth when it's convenient or benefits us, then we believe it's okay to lie. Our actions will show what we believe.

Some of us say we believe there are great benefits in reading and knowing God's Word, yet the evidence shows few people make time to read and study it regularly. Therefore, our actions may show we don't believe there are great benefits in reading and knowing God's Word. And since God's Word is consistent with His character, then we may also be saying we have little interest in knowing God any deeper than we think we know Him already.

Some people may also say God and prayer are their top priorities. If this is true, the first thing they do each day should reflect that. In other words, they should do something that shows God is their most important priority. For those who believe this, they typically spend the first part of each day with God in His Word and in prayer.

If we say humility is an important godly character trait, yet are slow to admit when we are wrong, then we are showing we don't believe humility is a necessary godly character trait. Therefore, regardless of what godly character trait we say is important, the evidence of whether it is or not will always be evident in our actions and priorities each day.

What Are Our Current Priorities?

If we really want to get a glimpse of what we believe and, thus, how we might live and finish our lives, we need to honestly examine our current priorities and how we spend our time and money. If we examine people approaching retirement age, we would likely see they are primarily living for financial independence, pleasure, comfort, and security. If true, this means many of us may have very short-term and self-centered desires that focus mainly on work/careers, hobbies, entertainment, vacations, financial investments, insurance policies, or anything else we think will benefit us the most in this life. Our thinking and our priorities might be similar to "The Parable of the Rich Fool."

> *"And He said to them, 'Take heed and beware of covetousness, for one's life does not consist in the abundance of the things he possesses.'*
>
> *Then He spoke a parable to them, saying: 'The ground of a certain rich man yielded plentifully. And he thought within himself, saying, "What shall I do, since I have no room to store my crops?" So he said, "I will do this: I will pull down my barns and build greater, and there I will store all my crops and my goods. And I will say to my soul, 'Soul, you have many goods laid up for many years; take your ease; eat, drink, and be merry.'"'*
>
> *But God said to him, 'Fool! This night your soul will be required of you; then whose will those things be which you have provided?'*

> *So is he who lays up treasure for himself and is not rich toward God" (Luke 12:15-21).*

If eternity in heaven is what we say we are looking forward to, shouldn't we be *"rich toward God,"* and shouldn't our priorities be on the things that will prepare us for eternal life? Eternal life is infinitely longer than the remaining years of our life on earth. If we're hoping to spend eternity with God, shouldn't we get to know Him as intimately as possible, so we are prepared to live continually in His presence? If the church is going to be the bride of Christ, shouldn't we prepare not only ourselves, but encourage and challenge all our brothers and sisters in Christ to be devoted fully to Him alone? And shouldn't our actions and priorities reflect this?

Preparation to Meet the King

It's interesting to read the Book of Esther and see what each of the candidates for queen had to do before they were given a chance to meet with King Ahasuerus for the first time. We aren't given the reason why Esther, who was Jewish, had the opportunity to become the new queen in a non-Jewish nation. We just know the king became very angry with her predecessor, Queen Vashti, because she refused the king's command to come and show her beauty to his guests at a big party he had thrown (see *Esther 1*). So, he removed Vashti as Queen. But once Esther had this opportunity, this is what the Bible says.

> *"Each young woman's turn came to go in to King Ahasuerus after she had completed twelve months' preparation, according to the regulations for the women, for thus were the days of their preparation apportioned: six months with oil of myrrh, and six months with perfumes and preparations for beautifying women. Thus prepared, each young woman went to the king, and she was given whatever she desired to take with her from the women's quarters to the king's palace" (Esther 2:12-13).*

Each of these young women had to go through one year of intense preparation before they had an opportunity to meet with the king for the first time. There were also many candidates, but only one of them would be chosen by the king to be the new queen. Since King Ahasuerus was only an earthly king, we might want to ask ourselves, "How does my preparation to meet the King of the Universe face-to-face compare with what Esther had to do before she could meet her earthly king?" Do we believe meeting God and His Son is worth at least the effort Esther went through to meet her king?

There, of course, is a significant difference between Esther's situation and ours. Esther was hoping to be chosen by the king as one of many candidates. Only one of the young women was going to be the new queen, so her preparation time was critical. We have a huge advantage over Esther because God isn't choosing just one of us, He's called all of us by the gospel and will choose everyone who trusts Him and surrenders their life to Him. Praise God we're not in competition to meet the King of the universe! Nonetheless, we are required to prepare ourselves if we expect to meet King Jesus and His Father. The apostle Paul wrote,

> *"But we are [under obligation] bound to give thanks to God always for you, brethren beloved by the Lord, because God from the beginning chose you for salvation through [being set apart] sanctification by the Spirit and belief in the truth, to which He called you by our gospel, for the obtaining of the glory of our Lord Jesus Christ" (2 Thessalonians 2:13-14).*

According to Merriam-Webster.com, sanctify means "to set apart to a sacred purpose or to consecrate; to free from sin or to purify; or to make productive of holiness or piety." One of the definitions it gives for 'sanctification'" is "the state of growing in divine grace as a result of Christian commitment after baptism or conversion." Sanctification is a continuous state of growing in Christlikeness and preparation for a sacred purpose. That sacred purpose ultimately is to see God face-to-face and live in God's presence for eternity. This is the highest calling any of us have, and it's something we must believe in our heart, so we can have the right priorities that lead us to take the actions necessary to know God so He can transform us into Christ's likeness more each day. But it's also important for God to know us because of what Jesus said.

> *"Not everyone who says to Me, 'Lord, Lord,' shall enter the kingdom of heaven, but he who does the will of My Father in heaven. Many will say to Me in that day, 'Lord, Lord, have we not prophesied in Your name, cast out demons in Your name, and done many wonders in Your name?' And then I will declare to them, 'I never knew you; depart from Me, you who practice lawlessness!'"*
> *(Matthew 7:21-23).*

We are not going to call Jesus *"Lord, Lord,"* unless we think we know Him. This statement, therefore, isn't going to be said by an atheist. It's going to be said by those who are very likely part of a church and believe they are destined for heaven based on the things they've done, including prophesying, casting out demons, and doing wonders in Jesus' name. But Jesus told the *"many"* in this verse to depart from Him, because He didn't know them since they didn't have an intimate relationship with Him. They just knew about Jesus and tried to do things in His name and possibly things for Him. Therefore, we can be deceived into thinking we believe in God and saying we know Him when we may not.

But this should not surprise us because Jeremiah wrote in *Jeremiah 17:9, "The heart is deceitful above all things, and desperately wicked; who can know it?"*

From this verse, we might conclude we have a heart problem, and we can't trust our hearts. But it might be more accurate to say we have a half-hearted problem. Our human tendency is to be half-hearted, yet God wants and will not accept anything less than our whole heart. This means our actions are very likely a reflection of what our whole heart believes. I've heard people defend themselves concerning something evil they have said or done by saying God knows their heart. Their defense indicates they don't believe they need to be accountable for what they say and do as long as they think they believe, which is the definition of hypocrisy. Since Jesus was hard on hypocrisy, we should also be hard on hypocrisy, especially our own.

Wholeheartedness

Half-heartedness comes from having a divided heart. King David was aware of this, and He asked God to, *"Teach me Your way, O Lord; I will walk in Your truth; unite my heart to fear Your name" (Psalm 86:11).*

As long as our heart is divided, it cannot believe something fully. This means we will still have doubts about a particular thing. Jesus and his brother James were both hard on doubters. Jesus said to Thomas, *"Reach your finger here, and look at My hands; and reach your hand here, and put it into My side. Do not be unbelieving, but believing" (John 20:27).*

The second sentence in this verse in the NIV Translation says *"Stop doubting and believe."* James also wrote, *"But let him ask in faith, with no doubting, for he who doubts is like a wave of the sea driven and tossed by the wind" (James 1:6).*

Belief and doubt can't coexist. This is why we must pursue something until we can fully make up our mind about it so our heart will be totally committed to it. Otherwise, we will be double-minded and unstable (see *James 1:8*). Nobody is going to look to us for advice or as a role model if we are like this. Instead, we should want to be like King David. *"I have found David the son of Jesse, a man after My own heart" (Acts 13:22).*

David understood his need to have his heart fully in line with God's heart. This can only happen when we trust God completely for everything we need in our lives. When we do this, we won't need to be concerned about our security, our comfort, or anything else the world is trying to get us to invest in more than God. There are many verses in the Bible that talk about wholeheartedness, and I think it's accurate to say nobody on earth has ever had a significant impact on the world with anything less than a wholehearted effort in whatever they did, good or bad. The greatest commandment is included in the Old Testament and in the New Testament. *"You shall love the Lord your God with all your heart, with all your soul, and with all your strength" (Deuteronomy 6:5).*

The gospels of Matthew, Mark and Luke all reference this verse.

> *"Jesus answered him, 'The first of all the commandments is: "Hear, O Israel, the Lord our God, the Lord is one." And you shall love the Lord your God with all your heart, with all your soul, with all your mind, and with all your strength. This is the first commandment.'" (Mark 12:29-30). (Also see Matthew 22:36-38 and Luke 10:27.)*

God makes it clear in these verses He wants all our heart. If we don't give God all our heart, then we are going to have doubts about God and will not be fully devoted to following Him and obeying His commands. Yet, if we asked a number of people, including professing Christians, if it is possible to love God with all our heart, I suspect many of them would say "no." Yet it's the greatest commandment in both the New Testament and Old Testament. But we would likely say no, because we are thinking about our natural ability to do it, which is why it's easy for us not even to make an earnest effort to love God with all our hearts. But the scriptures tell us, *"The things which are impossible with men are possible with God"* (Luke 18:27). (See also Matthew 19:26, Mark 10:27 and Luke 1:37.)

God could never command us to do something impossible to do. This may be the reason this is the greatest commandment, because everything else hinges on it, starting with the second greatest commandment—to love our neighbor. If we don't believe the greatest commandment, then we are not going to believe the second greatest commandment. Plus, our actions are going to show we don't believe either commandment.

Overcoming Unbelief

We shouldn't be surprised when our actions and words don't always line up with each other. We should also not be overly hard on ourselves when it's something God is still working on in our hearts. Each of us is very similar to the man in the ninth chapter of *Mark* whose son was possessed by a mute spirt that caused him to have convulsions, fall to the ground, and foam at the mouth. The man brought his son to Jesus and asked Jesus to heal him if He could. Jesus said to him, *"If you can believe, all things are possible to him who believes" (Mark 9:23).*

The man's response to Jesus is described in the next verse. *"Immediately the father of the child cried out and said with tears, 'Lord, I believe; help my unbelief!'" (Mark 9:24).*

Our belief is not usually where we would like it to be, and we need God's help to overcome our unbelief. This is why "by grace you have been saved through faith" (*Ephesians 2:8*).

Grace is one of the key components that causes our belief to change and grow when we seek to know the truth. Grace and truth are what Jesus brought to us. *"And of His fullness we have all received, and grace for grace. For the law was given through Moses, but grace and truth came through Jesus Christ" (John 1:16-17).*

Grace is the unlimited number of second chances that enable us to know and believe the truth about God, His Son Jesus, ourselves, and the world when we humble ourselves before God, confess our wrongdoings, and turn from them. Each of us can continually grow into men and woman of integrity who not only know the truth, but believe and act on it. Grace is an incredible gift from God, available to the humble.

Final Thoughts on Belief

It's vital for everyone to understand what we believe will always be reflected by what we do. Our life and our priorities will demonstrate it, including how we spend the money God gives us. But we are all a work in process, so we must be earnest and patient in our pursuit to believe the right things about everything in our life. And when we do this, we will become strong men and women who finish strong, and who will have a godly impact on the world around us.

In the Book of *Joshua* God said to Joshua, *"This day I will begin to exalt [make you great] you in the sight of all Israel, that they may know that, as I was with Moses, so I will be with you" (Joshua 3:7).*

One of the reasons God wants to exalt us is so the people around us may know God is with us. If people believe God is with us, then they are much more likely to listen to us and want to learn from us because God's glory will come through the resurrected life of Jesus to every believer who is being transformed into His likeness. This means we must be authentic in every part of our lives by saying and doing what is right increasingly more. I believe most people are looking to know a man or woman who is the genuine article when it comes to knowing and living by the truth, being honest, being generous, and setting a godly example. They want to know people who say and do what is right consistently. This can only happen if we believe it with all our heart, so our actions and words can demonstrate it more consistently each day of our life. I hope and pray this is the desire of your heart.

Mike Garst

Chapter 3
What Am I Seeking?

Life might be easier if we had a computer readout from our heart telling us the truth about what we truly believe. It would also be easier if that printout told us if our priorities were in line with God's priorities. We might then be able to make the changes needed to get our hearts in line with God's heart and desires for us, especially since our heart is what He is looking at, and since He alone knows our heart better than we do. The following verses talk about God looking at our hearts. *"Then hear from heaven Your dwelling place, and forgive, and give to everyone according to all his ways, whose heart You know (for You alone know the hearts of the sons of men)" (2 Chronicles 6:30).*

> *"If we had forgotten the name of our God, or stretched out our hands to a foreign god, would not God search this out? For He knows the secrets of the heart" (Psalms 44:20-21).*

> *"I, the Lord, search the heart, I test the mind, Even to give every man according to his ways, According to the fruit of his doings" (Jeremiah 17:10).*

See also *1 John 3:20, Acts 1:24-25, Acts 15:8, 1 Corinthians 4:5, 1 Thessalonians 2:4*.

The apostle Paul also told us to do everything from the heart or with all our heart, whether it's in working, serving, believing, remaining true, preaching, or obeying. You can find these verses in *Romans 6:17, Ephesians. 6:7-8, Colossians 3:23-24, Acts 8:36-37, Acts 11:23*.

As much as it cost God to have His Son, Jesus, pay the penalty for everyone's sins, it stands to reason we should give Him all our heart, mind, soul, and strength, especially since we can't give God anything close to what He gave us through His Son. Yet He loves us so much He was willing to give us His all so we could have an opportunity to live together with Him forever. That's a small price to pay in return for the benefits promised to those who love and trust God. This is the reason it's important for us to examine what we are truly seeking in this life. What we believe will eventually spring from what we are seeking, because our understanding will grow as we experience what we are seeking. If we are seeking God and His truth, which are the same thing, we will find it.

Seeking God Wholeheartedly

Jeremiah and the writers of Deuteronomy and Chronicles both said we would find God if we sought Him with all of our heart.

> *"And you will seek Me and find Me, when you search for Me with all your heart" (Jeremiah 29:13).*

> *"But from there you will seek the Lord your God, and you will find Him if you seek Him with all your heart and with all your soul" (Deuteronomy 4:29).*

In *1 Chronicles 28:9*, King David also said to his son Solomon,

> *"As for you, my son Solomon, know the God of your father, and serve Him with a loyal heart and with a willing mind; for the Lord searches all hearts and understands all*

> *the intents of the thoughts. If you seek Him, He will be found by you; but if you forsake Him, He will cast you off forever."*

Jeremiah 29:13 and *Deuteronomy 4:29* talk about seeking God with our whole heart, but *1 Chronicles 28:9* also talks about seeking God with our minds and our thoughts. God cares if we are following Him wholeheartedly or not and about our every thought and desire, because He deeply cares about each of us. But the last part of *1 Chronicles 28:9* says He will reject forever those who forsake Him. Could this mean we can forsake God when we don't seek Him with all of our heart? This is a serious question for all of us to ponder. But the real question may be, "Why would we not seek God with all of our heart?"

God's Responsibility

In any healthy relationship, each person has a responsibility to keep the relationship strong. The following Scripture says God first seeks and shows Himself to us. *"In this is love, not that we loved God, but that He loved us and sent His Son to be the propitiation for our sins"* (*1 John 4:10*).

God not only sought us out and loved us first, He is also responsible for other parts of our relationship with Him that He doesn't expect us to do. Paul said in *1 Corinthians 3:6-7*, *"I planted, Apollos watered, but God gave the increase. So then neither he who plants is anything, nor he who waters, but God, who gives the increase."*

We can't make anything grow—we can only plant and water it, whether it's a child or a garden, or even our faith. God has also created us and given us everything we need. He also paid the price for all our disobedience through the sacrifice of His Son so we can be restored into a right relationship with Him, if we will faithfully and continually confess and repent as needed, and love one another. But we can't do this with a half-hearted effort.

Our Responsibility

Because God made it possible for us to seek Him, we have a responsibility in this relationship. But like any relationship, it works better when both parties are seeking each other. God's sacrifice of His Son to pay the penalty for all our sins and to open the door for an eternal relationship with Him shows He is earnestly seeking us with all His heart. As a result, it stands to reason He would want and expect us to seek Him with our whole heart, especially since He promised we will find Him if we do. Jesus even simplified it for us when He boiled down the Ten Commandments to two: to love God and to love our neighbor.

But we have some other responsibilities in addition to obeying the first and second greatest commandments. We must also put to death the sin in our lives. The apostle Paul wrote in Colossians:

> *"Therefore, put to death your members which are on the earth: fornication, uncleanness, passion, evil desire, and covetousness, which is idolatry" (Colossians 3:5).*

> *"But now you yourselves are to put off all these: anger, wrath, malice, blasphemy, filthy language out of your mouth" (Colossians 3:8).*

I've heard fellow Christians ask God to take a bad habit away from them. But it doesn't appear God works that way. He will teach and train us, and even quicken our spirit to recognize sin once we know it's a sin. But He won't put it to death for us. I'm sure there's a good reason why God does it that way. Have you ever noticed how easy it is to go back to doing something wrong when we don't have to suffer through discipline or punishment for the wrong decisions we make? The children of parents who constantly bail them out of trouble typically repeat the offense and will likely go a step farther down the wrong road. These parents become enablers of bad habits for their children because they don't allow their children to suffer the consequences of poor choices. When we suffer the consequences for bad decisions, we are much more likely to learn from those experiences. For this reason, suffering the consequences of our wrongdoing can encourage us to put sin to death.

We must also put on some things and do some things.

> *"Therefore, as the elect of God, holy and beloved, put on tender mercies, kindness, humility, meekness, longsuffering; bearing with one another, and forgiving one another, if anyone has a complaint against another; even as Christ forgave you, so you also must do. But above all these things put on love, which is the bond of perfection"* (Colossians 3:12-14).

All of us have probably heard at some point in our lives that love is a choice. That's easy to say, but much harder to do. None of us naturally feels like being merciful, kind, humble, meek, patient or forgiving. We do those things because we know they are the right thing to do and what we believe God wants us to do. This is the reason we must first trust God and believe His commands and ways are the right thing to do. Plus, we must do them regardless of how we feel or the cost or benefit to us. It may not be easy to see the benefit upfront, so we must do the right thing knowing the eternal benefit is worth it. And when we obey God's commands and experience the reason obeying His commandments is good for us, God will make our faith grow. Like a muscle that only grows when it is exercised, our faith will only grow when we feed and exercise it.

We also must do the following: *"And let the peace of God rule in your hearts, to which also you were called in one body; and be thankful"* (Colossians 3:15).

Trying to make peace doesn't mean we must compromise what we believe. It just means we try to do what's right in God's eyes by speaking the truth in love and listening to others in order to gain understanding. It is not forcing anyone to do something they don't really want to do, but convincing them with God's truth in a respectful way so they can make that choice willingly. But we can't expect true peace to always happen. We can only do our part. *"If it is possible, as much as depends on you, live peaceably with all men" (Romans 12:18).*

Knowing how to love a person in a way that is right in God's eyes isn't something natural for us, we only learn how to do it as we come to know God's heart and mind. This is the reason we must *"Let the word of Christ dwell in you richly in all wisdom, teaching and admonishing one another in psalms and hymns and spiritual songs, singing with grace in your hearts to the Lord" (Colossians 3:16).*

We come to know God by not only reading His Word, but by meditating on it and doing what it says. Otherwise, we can deceive ourselves. *"But be doers of the word, and not hearers only, deceiving yourselves"* (James 1:22).

This is another way of saying our actions will show what we really believe. We can read instructions about how to do many things in this life, but if we don't follow them, we are going to get a much different result than if we had followed the instructions. We've all acquired things that required "some assembly" (or lots of assembly in the IKEA world) and have experienced the disappointment and frustration that comes from not following the instructions. This is the reason we must seek God through His Word, because the Bible never gets old. His Word includes instructions that still apply to our lives today.

Another part of our responsibility is to make this a life-time effort, because the apostle Paul encouraged Christians to aim for perfection, or Christlikeness, as much as possible. *"Not that I have already attained, or am already perfected; but I press on, that I may lay hold of that for which Christ Jesus has also laid hold of me" (Philippians 3:12).*

Jesus also called us to perfection. *"Therefore, you shall be perfect, just as your Father in heaven is perfect" (Matthew 5:48)*

Perfection is a word that intimidates many of us because we think we are a long way from it. But we must remember, spiritual perfection is increasing maturity in Christ. That means we must be patient, persevere and overcome our unbelief. This will be a life-time journey to our last breath. We will always have an opportunity to grow in our love for God and for people. We just need to be faithful to keep seeking God, confessing and turning from our sins, and learning what is right in God's eyes as we experience all the different ways He loves us. God wants us to learn to trust Him completely, so He can transform us daily into one of His sons or daughters who trust Him completely and do what He requires of us. In *Deuteronomy 10:12-13* God spells out clearly what He asks of us. *"And now, Israel, what does the Lord your God require of you, but to fear the Lord your God, to walk in all His ways and to love Him, to serve the Lord your God with <u>all your heart</u>* [emphasis added] *and with all your soul, and to keep the commandments of the Lord and His statutes which I command you today for your good?"*

In *verse 12,* it first tells us to *"fear the Lord your God."* This doesn't mean we are to be afraid of Him, but it does mean we should greatly revere Him, be in awe of Him, and desire to honor Him above all things. When a person does these things, they take His commands, His ways, and His promises seriously, and do everything they can to please Him. And when they do that, they will be able to do what the next part of *verse 12* says, which is to *"walk in all His ways,"* because they will know He doesn't command us to do anything that would not be good for us.

Next it tells us to *"love Him."* The best way to love God is to trust Him, because we can't love Him if we don't trust Him. How do we think God would respond if we said we love Him, but we don't trust Him? We can't have that kind of relationship with God or with anybody in this world that we claim to love. And if we know and trust God, we should know He is only interested in what is best for us.

In the last part of *verse 12*, we see again that God is looking for our whole heart when He says *"to serve the Lord your God with all your heart."* Why is it so important to love, serve and seek the Lord with all our heart? The answer lies in understanding that we, as believers, are called to be the bride of Christ as a part of His church. We are called into an intimate relationship in which our hearts are to be fully devoted and open to God's heart and to our fellow believers. Would we want a spouse who is only partly devoted to being our spouse? A marriage only works the way God intended it to function when we are fully committed and devoted to the person we marry. This doesn't mean we love them more than anything else, because we know as Christians we are called to love God above all things. But this doesn't mean we can't still be devoted to our spouses and love them wholeheartedly.

Consequences of Wholeheartedness

If we are looking for more reasons to seek God's heart with all our heart, we need to understand why only two of the Israelite men over twenty years old made it into the Promised Land. We see the reason in the following two verses.

> *"Surely none of the men who came up from Egypt, from twenty years old and above, shall see the land of which I swore to Abraham, Isaac, and Jacob, because they have not wholly followed Me, except Caleb the son of Jephunneh, the Kenizzite, and Joshua the son of Nun, <u>for they have wholly followed the Lord</u>." [emphasis added] (Numbers 32:11-12).*

(See also *Deuteronomy 1:35-36, Joshua 14:8-9, 14.*)

God had saved and delivered the Israelites from their life of slavery in Egypt. All they had to do was follow Moses and be obedient to what he told them to do, and they would be delivered into the Promised Land. But only two of the men twenty years and older made it. And these two verses say it was because the rest of the Israelites over twenty years old didn't follow the Lord wholeheartedly. This is a profound verse because it appears there were about six hundred thousand males in the group. Even Moses wasn't included in this group of two, but we know Moses saw the Promised Land from a distance (see *Deuteronomy 34:1-2*), and we know Moses was with Jesus when He was transfigured (see *Matthew 17:1-9, Mark 9:2-13* and *Luke 9:28-36*).

This is a reminder we can miss out on some things in this lifetime if we do anything rash that displeases God, especially once we've developed an intimate relationship with Him like Moses did. And it should serve as a warning that anything less than wholehearted devotion to Christ is not a good place for anyone to be. Therefore, if we recognize we are not following God wholeheartedly, we need to confess and repent as quickly as possible so our heart can know and follow God's heart increasingly more.

When we read through Deuteronomy, we see that God was patient with the Israelites and warned them several times to do everything with all their heart. I've included a couple of those warnings below and listed a few more for your reference.

> *"If there arises among you a prophet or a dreamer of dreams, and he gives you a sign or a wonder, and the sign or the wonder comes to pass, of which he spoke to you, saying, 'Let us go after other gods'--which you have not known--'and let us serve them,' you shall not listen to the words of that prophet or that dreamer of dreams, for the Lord your God is testing you to know whether you love the Lord your God <u>with all your heart and with all your soul.</u>"*
> *[emphasis added] (Deuteronomy 13:1-3).*
>
> *"The Lord your God will make you abound in all the work of your hand, in the fruit of your body, in the increase of*

> *your livestock, and in the produce of your land for good. For the Lord will again rejoice over you for good as He rejoiced over your fathers, if you obey the voice of the Lord your God, to keep His commandments and His statutes which are written in this Book of the Law, and if you turn to the Lord your God <u>with all your heart and with all your soul</u>." [emphasis added] (Deuteronomy 30:9-10).*

(See also *Deuteronomy 11:13-14, 26:16, 30:1-3, 6.*)

We also see from *1 Kings 14:8* and *1 Kings 15:3* below that wholeheartedness was the key to King David's success.

> *"And yet you have not been as My servant David, who kept My commandments and <u>who followed Me with all his heart</u>, [emphasis added] to do only what was right in My eyes;" (1 Kings 14:8*

> *"And he [Abijah] walked in all the sins of his father, which he had done before him; <u>his heart was not loyal</u> [emphasis added] to the Lord his God, as was the heart of his father David" (1 Kings 15:3).*

We also see this message consistently in *1 Kings* and *2 Kings*, as well as *1 Chronicles* and *2 Chronicles,* because each of the kings of Judah and Israel were characterized by whether he did what was evil or right in God's eyes, or if they followed God wholeheartedly or not. The kings that followed David failed or succeeded based on whether they followed God wholeheartedly. Even Solomon, who started so well, didn't finish well, because he didn't continue to follow God wholeheartedly, even after being warned to do so and warning the people to do so.

One of the key reasons it is so important to commit our whole heart to God is spelled out in *2 Chronicles 16:9.*

> *"For the eyes of the Lord run to and fro throughout the whole earth, to show Himself strong on behalf of those whose <u>heart is loyal</u> [emphasis added] to him."*

In any endeavor, we must have the strength and stamina to finish. God is giving us strength and stamina based on our loyalty to Him and whether we have an intimate relationship with Him. If we do, His strength will flow to and through us.

Jesus' Wholehearted Lineage

We can learn who Jesus' ancestors were if we read His genealogy in *Matthew 1:1-16* and *Luke 3:23-38*. But we can also learn something interesting about His genealogy in *Psalm 78:65-68*. It says,

> *"Then the Lord awoke as from sleep, like a mighty man who shouts because of wine. And He beat back His enemies; He put them to a perpetual reproach. Moreover He rejected the tent of Joseph, and did not choose the tribe of Ephraim, but chose the tribe of Judah, Mount Zion which He loved."*

Jacob had twelve sons. Judah was his fourth son, and his mother was Leah, not Rachel, who was Jacob's first love. Judah ended up sleeping with his daughter-in-law, Tamar, thinking she was a prostitute at the time, because she disguised herself. She did this to Judah because he had not given her to his third oldest son Shelah as he said he would after the oldest two sons had been killed by the Lord for the evil they did. She bore twins from that encounter, and one of them was Perez, and through his line David was eventually born (see *Genesis 38:13-30*). In *Psalm 78:70-72* it says,

> *"He also chose David His servant, and took him from the sheepfolds; from following the ewes that had young He brought him, to shepherd Jacob His people, and Israel His inheritance. So he shepherded them according to the integrity of his heart, and guided them by the skillfulness of his hands."*

I'm including this information because of what we read about Caleb.

> *"'Surely not one of these men of this evil generation shall see that good land of which I [promised] swore to give to your fathers, except Caleb the son of Jephunneh; he shall see it, and to him and his children I am giving the land on which he walked, because he [fully] wholly followed the Lord"* (Deuteronomy 1:36 – see also Joshua 14:6-9).

Caleb was a descendant of Judah, and although he was not directly in the lineage to David that ultimately led to Jesus, he was part of the tribe God chose. Why did God choose the tribe of Judah and specifically say, *"Moreover He rejected the tent of Joseph, and did not choose the tribe of Ephraim, but chose the tribe of Judah, Mount Zion which He loved?"*

We don't know for sure why God choose Judah, but since Caleb and Joshua were the only two men of all the tribes over twenty years old that followed God wholeheartedly, Caleb's wholeheartedness may have been the reason. But why Judah and not Ephraim, which is the tribe that Joshua was from? All we know is that *Psalm 78:67* says, *"And did not choose the tribe of Ephraim."* God didn't reject Ephraim, He just didn't choose it. He could only choose one tribe, and maybe He could have chosen Ephraim. All we know is He chose a tribe with a person who followed God "wholeheartedly." Both tribes were mentioned in this passage, and the only other tribe mentioned was specifically rejected. I believe it's worth pondering, especially when it says, *"He chose the tribe of Judah, Mount Zion, <u>which He loved</u> [my emphasis]."*

Final Thoughts on Seeking

I've talked about wholeheartedness in each of these last two chapters because it appears what we believe will largely be a function of what we seek with all our heart. And what we believe will determine how we live our lives and how we finish. One of God's many great promises is we will find Him if we seek Him with all our heart (*Jeremiah 29:13, Deuteronomy 29:4, 1 Chronicles 29:8*). Since God has never failed to deliver on a promise and never can, we have an iron-clad guarantee that we can know God's heart and mind and be in an intimate relationship with Him. The only way this won't happen is if we fail to seek Him with all our heart. This means we are not rolling the dice on our life priorities or how our life will end. Our circumstances aren't guaranteed, but our eternal destiny is clearly in our hands. It only requires that we respond to God loving us first by seeking Him with all our heart. He's eagerly waiting for us to do that.

Mike Garst

Chapter 4
Am I Called to Become Like Christ?

Jesus said,

> "Most assuredly, I say to you, he who believes in Me, the works that I do he will do also; and greater works than these he will do, because I go to My Father" (John 14:12).

This is an astounding verse, because it says if we believe in Jesus, then we will do the things He did and greater things. This may not mean we would do those things as individuals, especially since the church is the body of Christ, but we should certainly be able to do our part as individuals in doing the things Jesus did and greater things.

If we observe what Jesus did, He spent a lot of time healing, driving out demons, teaching, preaching, giving sight to the blind, restoring hearing to the deaf, and enabling the mute to speak. He also raised some people from the dead. But probably the most important thing about Jesus was He only did what His Father told Him to do. John wrote what Jesus said concerning this.

> "But that the world may know that I love the Father, and

> *as the Father gave Me commandment, so I do"*
> *(John 14:31).*

This means becoming like Jesus will enable us to hear God's voice and know what God wants us to do throughout each day just as Jesus did. Can you imagine being able to know what God wants you to do every moment of the day? Is this possible for not just some Christians, but for all Christians? It's a challenging question, but it's a question I believe every professing Christian must be able to answer.

The Call

The apostle Paul wrote, *"For God did not call us to uncleanness, but in holiness. Therefore he who rejects this does not reject man, but God, who has also given us His Holy Spirit" (1 Thessalonians 4:7-8).*

The first thing to note is God does the calling, and He calls us to a holy life. This can be intimidating to anybody who is not yet a believer in Jesus or just new to the faith. But this is no different from somebody who enlists in the army because he wants to be a good soldier. He doesn't go in the army expecting he is a good soldier already, but that he will be trained to be a good soldier. The only difference might be that Christians are being called to be more like a "Ranger" in the army, which is the highest level an army soldier can reach. But even those aspiring to be a "Ranger" know they must go through a lot of training.

It's been said God doesn't call the "qualified" but qualifies those who are called. The apostle Paul reminded the Corinthians they were far from qualified when God called them, so no one could boast about their qualifications (see *1 Corinthians 1:26-31*). God wants us to understand upfront He is not only doing the calling, but He will be involved in the teaching and training. He is essentially saying He is going to be your Personal Trainer. That should blow us away if we think about it long enough. But it's the reason He expects us to become like Christ. We have the Perfect Trainer who *"in all things God works for the good of those who love him, who have been called according to his purpose" (Romans 8:28).*

This is the greatest news possible because we have a Personal Trainer who isn't going to give up on us, but will keep encouraging us to go on, no matter what is going on in our lives at any time.

1 John 4:17 also tells us believers will become like Jesus. *"Love has been perfected among us in this: that we may have boldness in the day of judgment; because as He is, so are we in this world."*

Not only does this verse say we are like Jesus in this world, but it will give us confidence to be bold about it. This boldness and confidence will come from knowing we are being changed on the inside, and as a result, our priorities, compassion, patience, and many other things in our life will not only be noticeably different to us, but to those who know us well enough to see those changes in us. John also wrote, *"He who says he abides in Him (Jesus) ought himself also to walk just as He walked" (1 John 2:6).*

If we are connected to Jesus and walking as He did, then we should be doing the things He did. Because each of us is gifted differently, we aren't all going to be doing the same things, but each of us can do extraordinary things only possible when the power of God is working in and through us as part of the body Christ. We won't do everything possible immediately, we will only be able to do them more and more as we are taught, trained, and grow in our faith. This is what Paul said to the church at Thessalonica when he wrote, *"We are bound to thank God always for you, brethren, as it is fitting, because your faith grows exceedingly, and the love of every one of you all abounds toward each other" (2 Thessalonians 1:3).*

When our faith grows, our love will also grow. And if both of those are growing, then we are going to become more and more like Christ.

John also wrote, *"Beloved, now we are children of God; and it has not yet been revealed what we shall be, but we know that when He is revealed, we shall be like Him, for we shall see Him as He is" (1 John 3:2).*

When gold or silver is heated up to the point all the impurities are driven out, it will be clear and like a mirror. If we look in a mirror, we see a reflection of ourselves. In the same way, when all the impurities have been driven out of us, we will reflect Jesus. Therefore, as we learn and train to be disciples, we, like any student, will be tested by God to see if we are doing the things Jesus did. These tests and trials are meant to expose any impurities still in our heart so we can confess and turn from them. These are the areas of unbelief, ignorance, pride, selfishness, and anything else in us that is not yet a reflection of Jesus Christ or God, His Father.

Perfection

Paul also wrote in *Colossians 1:28-29, "Him we preach, warning every man and teaching every man in all wisdom, that we may present every man perfect in Christ Jesus. To this end I also labor, striving according to His working which works in me mightily."*

Being perfect or mature doesn't mean we won't be able to sin, it just means we should be confessing our sin as quickly as possible and turning from it so we sin less and less. Therefore, one of the ways to measure our perfection or maturity in Christ is to examine how quickly we agree with God when He confronts us about anything.

Christlikeness is also Godlikeness since the Father and Son are alike. The apostle Paul wrote in *Colossians 3:9-10, "Do not lie to one another, since you have put off the old man with his deeds, and have put on the new man who is renewed in knowledge according to the image of Him who created him."*

God is also our creator, and His purpose has always been to have us resemble Him. But He also knew from the beginning it would take the sacrifice of His perfect, obedient Son, to make it possible since our sinful nature makes it impossible for us to meet God's requirement of holiness and righteousness through our own efforts.

Paul also wrote, *"Therefore, if anyone is in Christ, he is a new creation; old things have passed away; behold, all things have become new" (2 Corinthians 5:17).*

If we combine *Colossians 3:9-10* and *2 Corinthians 5:17,* they say we are a new creation when we are in Christ, and Christ is in us. This means we cannot retain any of our old self in any way or form. It must die and be replaced by our new self, which is being molded into Christlikeness in every area of our life, not just in some parts. Jesus talked about this with the old and new wine and the old and new cloth.

> *"No one puts a piece of unshrunk cloth on an old garment; for the patch pulls away from the garment, and the tear is made worse. Nor do they put new wine into old wineskins, or else the wineskins break, the wine is spilled, and the wineskins are ruined. But they put new wine into new wineskins, and both are preserved" (Matthew 9:16-17).*

If I try to blend the old with the new, it will be ruined. In other words, I can't become a hybrid of the old and new and expect I will have any real likeness to Jesus. In fact, we will be worse off trying to be a hybrid because of what Jesus said to the church in Laodicea in *Revelations 3:15-16. "I know your works, that you are neither cold nor hot. I could wish you were cold or hot. So then, because you are lukewarm, and neither cold nor hot, I will vomit you out of My mouth."*

An atheist is at least honest with God when he says he doesn't believe, whereas those who profess to believe, but live as if they don't, are trying to straddle the fence, which isn't acceptable in God's kingdom since it is hypocrisy.

The apostle Paul also talked about being "made complete" in *2 Corinthians 13:9* when he wrote, *"For we are glad when we are weak and you are strong. And this also we pray, that you may be made complete."*

He also repeated it again in *2 Corinthians 13:11, "Finally, brethren, farewell. Become complete."*

The words "complete," "perfect," or "mature" can easily be interchanged in these verses because they imply Christlikeness. It's hard to read the epistles Paul wrote that make up much of the New Testament without recognizing Paul believed God wanted all believers to become mature, Christlike disciples, and he was never satisfied with anything less. It's one of the main reasons Paul didn't hesitate to confront anybody or any church that wasn't living in line with the whole truth of the gospel.

The verses I've referenced up to this point consistently support the call to become like Christ. And God's Word is essentially a promise that will come to pass. *"Not a word failed of any good thing which the Lord had spoken to the house of Israel. All came to pass" (Joshua 21:45* – See also *Joshua 23:14*).

But we must be in Christ, and Christ must be in us, and we must be fully connected to Jesus just like Jesus is fully connected to His Father.

The Cost

Before Jesus died on the cross, He said to His disciples, *"If anyone desires to come after Me, let him deny himself, and take up his cross daily, and follow Me" (Luke 9:23).*

One of the reasons we may not think we are called to be like Christ is because we don't like the cost. It's much easier to become a "church member" in today's world, because not every church has set the right standard on what it takes to be a follower of Christ. Jesus laid out the cost in *Luke 14:26-33*. The first thing this cost includes is *"If anyone comes* to Me and does not hate his father and mother, wife and children, brothers and sisters, yes, and his own life also, he cannot be My disciple" (Luke 14:26).

It's interesting Jesus started with the family. The word *"hate'* in this verse may appear to be overly hard. But I believe it means pleasing our family can't be a higher priority than pleasing God in our life. Jesus was obedient to His earthly parents when He was growing up (see *Luke 2:51*), and we are commanded to honor our parents (see *Deuteronomy 5:16, Exodus 20:12, Matthew 19:19, Mark 10:19, Luke 18:20,* and *Ephesians 6:2*). But after we grow up, we must follow God's calling for our life and not what our parents or grandparents want us to do. Many a young adult has displeased their parents when they chose to follow what they believed was God's call on their life. And this includes parents who are professing Christians that raised their children in the Christian faith.

The cost also includes *"And whoever does not bear his cross and come after Me cannot be My disciple" (Luke 14:27).*

We must teach and train ourselves to say "no" to any natural desires that keep us from following Jesus wholeheartedly each day. This isn't a part-time call. It's a serious battle we must face every day, because we will always have natural desires in this life. But they will become increasingly powerless as Christ is formed in us.

These two verses precede the next four verses for a reason. They may be telling us these two things are the most important two issues (i.e., self-denial and bearing the cross) every person must consider if they want to be a disciple of Christ. Knowing these two things, we must now decide if we understand the full cost and whether we want to pay it or not.

> *"For which of you, intending to build a tower, does not sit down first and count the cost, whether he has enough to finish it—lest, after he has laid the foundation, and is not able to finish, all who see it begin to mock him, saying, 'This man began to build and was not able to finish'? Or*

> *what king, going to make war against another king, does not sit down first and consider whether he is able with ten thousand to meet him who comes against him with twenty thousand? Or else, while the other is still a great way off, he sends a delegation and asks conditions of peace.*
> *(Luke 14:28-32).*

Men and women have decided not to follow Christ just to please their family, or in some cases to inherit the family business or future. Others have decided they can't deny certain material things they think they must have in this life. In some cases, this can be titles and positions. *"Nevertheless, even among the rulers many believed in Him, but because of the Pharisees they did not confess Him, lest they should be put out of the synagogue; for they loved the praise of men more than the praise of God" (John 12:42-43).*

We can believe many things about Jesus, about His Father, including what Jesus did for us, but still not be willing to surrender our lives to Him. This is why Jesus' last sentence on the cost summarized it well. *"So likewise, whoever of you does not forsake all that he has cannot be My disciple" (Luke 14:33).*

Jesus said there can't be anything more important in our lives than knowing and obeying God through His Son Jesus. The great paradox of the gospel is the gift of salvation will cost us everything. All our self-interests must die. Dietrich Bonhoeffer wrote in his book, *The Cost of Discipleship* [6], "When Christ calls a man, He bids him to come and die." Dietrich not only talked about what cheap grace is, he referenced many verses in the Bible that talk about the cost. Many of the things Jesus said in the four gospels were about the cost of following Him. He also talked extensively about what would disqualify us. In addition to that, Jesus talked often about what life was like in the kingdom of God, and that we

---

[6] The Cost of Discipleship, Dietrich Bonhoeffer, Simon & Schuster, New York NY, 1959, Page 11

should be living here on the earth as if we were living in the kingdom of heaven. *"Your kingdom come. Your will be done on earth as it is in heaven" (Matthew 6:10).*

This means we can't live like the rest of the world lives each day. We must live the way Jesus lived during His brief time on earth. And it will be costly as Jesus said in *Luke 14:26-33*. This is also the reason Jesus said, *"For whoever desires to save his life will lose it, but whoever loses his life for My sake will save it. For what profit is it to a man if he gains the whole world, and is himself destroyed or lost?" (Luke 9:24-25).*

If we hold on to any of the things this life that are temporal, it will disqualify us from the kingdom of God.

Jesus also talked about the cost when he was in a crowd with children. *"Then Jesus called a little child to Him, set him in the midst of them, and said, 'Assuredly, I say to you, unless you are converted and become as little children, you will by no means enter the kingdom of heaven.'" (Matthew 18:2-3).*

Jesus often said things that were counter-cultural. Children are naturally selfish, but that obviously isn't the quality Jesus was talking about in these two verses. Children are quick to forget and forgive. They are also teachable, humble, and have no prejudices. These are essential character traits for Christians, so they can keep learning and growing in Christlikeness.

When given a chance to talk about our faith, we must also be ready to do that. *"For whoever is ashamed of Me and My words, of him the Son of Man will be ashamed when He comes in His own glory, and in His Father's, and of the holy angels" (Luke 9:26).*

We have an opportunity in this world to boast about God and tell others about our Father in a way that should make others want to know Him. When we fail to do that, it demonstrates we don't believe God is worthy to be talked about or praised in the presence of other people. And it will be costly to us.

Once we count the cost and decide we are willing to pay that price, we can't turn back. *"But Jesus said to him, 'No one, having put his hand to the plow, and looking back, is fit for the kingdom of God'" (Luke 9:62).*

This is the most important decision we will ever make. We are choosing either life or death. This is what Joshua was choosing when he said,

> *"And if it seems evil to you to serve the Lord, choose for yourselves this day whom you will serve, whether the gods which your fathers served that were on the other side of the River, or the gods of the Amorites, in whose land you dwell. But as for me and my house, we will serve the Lord" (Joshua 24:15).*

We lie to people if we tell them following Jesus has no cost. It would be better if we challenge people who are thinking about following Jesus to really ponder their decision by counting all the costs so they can be sure they know what they are committing to. This is what Ernest Shackelford did when he supposedly put an ad in the London newspaper, *The Times,* to recruit men to go to the South Pole in 1900.

> "Men wanted for hazardous journey. Low wages, bitter cold, long hours of complete darkness. Safe return doubtful. Honour and recognition in event of success."

Whether this was true or not has been debated. Either way, this ad better represents the cost to follow Christ.

Glory to God alone

Another important part of the call and the cost is that everything we do must be for the glory of God. If we must have some of the glory, then we can't really be a disciple of Christ. This is what Jesus said about the

Pharisees and the Teachers of the Law.

> *"But all their works they do to be seen by men. They make their phylacteries[7] broad and enlarge the borders of their garments. They love the best places at feasts, the best seats in the synagogues, greetings in the marketplaces, and to be called by men, 'Rabbi, Rabbi'" (Matthew 23:5-7).*

These religious leaders were glory-seekers. They wanted to be noticed and admired by men. Disciples of Christ want to only bring glory and honor to God in everything they say and do. The apostle Paul told the Corinthians, *"Therefore, whether you eat or drink, or whatever you do, do all to the glory of God" (1 Corinthians 10:31).*

If God doesn't get the glory in everything we say and do, then either we are trying to get the glory or somebody or something else is getting the glory. God is a jealous God, and He will not share His glory. *"I am the Lord, that is My name; And My glory I will not give to another, Nor My praise to carved images" (Isaiah 42:8* – see also *Isaiah 48:11).*

Final Thoughts on the Call to Become Like Christ

I've shared some scriptures with you in this chapter I hope will convince you we are called to become like Christ. It's clearly a high calling, and it comes with a cost. But it's a different kind of cost in that we don't have to pay anything because Jesus paid it all. Instead, we must put our selfish nature and pride to death and surrender control of our lives to God and trust Him to lead us.

---

[7] A phylactery is small square leather box containing slips inscribed with scriptural passages and traditionally worn on the left arm and on the head by observant Jewish men and especially adherents of Orthodox Judaism during morning weekday prayers. *Merriam-Webster Dictionary,* https://www.merriam-webster.com/dictionary/phylactery. Accessed Sep 15, 2022.

Mike Garst

Chapter 5
How Can I Become Like Jesus?

If you read the previous chapter and are convinced the call to become like Christ is true, then you are probably wanting to know some more details about what your responsibility is in this process. Hopefully you were encouraged when I said God was going to be your Personal Trainer. And even though you may still be thinking about that statement, the thought of having God as our Personal Trainer should intrigue us at least a little bit. Before we do that though, let's start by looking at what it takes to become proficient at anything.

Training to be a Doctor

Let's assume somebody believes they are called to be a doctor. To do this, they need to pursue extensive education and training. First, they must do well enough in their high-school studies to get into a college that offers a medically related curriculum, commonly known as "pre-med." Once they get into a college, they are going to go to classes, listen to the instructor, do their homework assignments, and study so they can get good enough grades to get them into medical school. And once they get into med school, they need to still go to classes, do well in those classes, and eventually do practical training under the guidance of a competent and experienced doctor.

After they have studied and trained for a while, then they will at some point began to treat patients, but will still be under the direction of an experienced physician who will keep teaching and training them. They will continue to learn from practical experience, and they will continue to study as they strive to become a better doctor, and possibly start their own practices. Finally, once they become a good, experienced doctor, they will start teaching and training others. Nobody who wants to become a doctor sets out to be mediocre. Everybody wants to be a great doctor. None of us want to go to a mediocre doctor! In the same way, who would want to go to a mediocre Christian for advice or help?

Training and Discipline

Practically speaking, there isn't really any difference in what it takes to become a mature Christian than what it takes to become a good doctor, because the gospels refer to the followers of Jesus as disciples. Disciples of Christ weren't given the name "Christians" until later when the apostle Paul was in Antioch. *"And the disciples were first called Christians in Antioch" (Acts 11:26).*

During the time Jesus was on earth in a physical body, a disciple was somebody who was learning and training to become like their master. Jesus said this in the gospels of *Matthew* and *Luke*.

> *"A disciple is not above his teacher, nor a servant above his master. It is enough for a disciple that he be like his teacher, and a servant like his master"*
> *(Matthew 10:24-25).*

> *"A disciple is not above his teacher, but everyone who is perfectly trained will be like his teacher" (Luke 6:40).*

Luke 6:40 also tells us the key to becoming like Jesus. He told His disciples everyone who is *"perfectly trained"* will be like his teacher. A "perfectly trained" doctor needs to go through the basic process I described previously to become proficient. If you look at any profession, a person who aspires for excellency will need to go through a similar process. Becoming a great athlete at any level also requires many hours of training and study. We don't typically think of athletic training as requiring study, but to become the best at any sport, we must understand how to use and take care of our bodies effectively and how to properly take care of and use the athletic equipment in the sports that require it. This will require that we read the instructions or listen to an instructor who will teach us these things.

The apostle Paul also emphasized training and discipline.

"Do you not know that those who run in a race all run, but one receives the prize? Run in such a way that you may [win] obtain it. And everyone who competes for the prize [exercises self-control] is temperate in all things. Now they do it to obtain a perishable crown, but we for an imperishable crown. Therefore, I run thus: not with uncertainty. Thus, I fight: not as one who beats the air. But I discipline my body and bring it into subjection, lest, when I have preached to others, I myself should become disqualified" (1 Corinthians 9:24-27).

Paul says athletes go into training so they can get a perishable crown, but spiritual training is for an imperishable crown. This means we should put just as much or more effort into training for an imperishable crown. Are we approaching our spiritual training with this understanding?

A soldier must also go through long and intense training to become a good soldier. This is at least a one- to two-year full-time process, and this is just to get him or her ready for the first battle. It takes months and even years of practical experience beyond this to become a truly good and reliable soldier who can be counted on in the heat of a battle.

Paul also says in *1 Corinthians 9:27* he is doing it so he would not be disqualified for the prize after preaching to others. He apparently didn't look at his salvation as a onetime event, but as a continuous process in which he was responsible for doing his part to live out his faith, so God could make it grow. This is consistent with what he also wrote in *Philippians 2:12-13*.

> *"Therefore, my beloved, as you have always obeyed, not as in my presence only, but now much more in my absence, work out your own salvation with fear and trembling; for it is God who works in you both to will and to do for His good pleasure.*

It's interesting the words *"work out your own salvation"* were used in this verse. The words *"exercise your own salvation"* could be substituted, because it implies we need to continue living out our faith, and we can never reach a point where we can stop being faithful to God in this life. The apostle Paul made this clear when he said,

> *"Not that I have already attained, [obtained it] or am already perfected; but I press on, that I may lay hold of that for which Christ Jesus has also laid hold of me. Brethren, I do not count myself to have [laid hold of it] apprehended; but one thing I do, forgetting those things which are behind and reaching forward to those things which are ahead, I press toward the goal for the prize of the upward call of God in Christ Jesus"*
> *(Philippians 3:12-14).*

Paul's attitude was to keep moving forward and forget the past, regardless of how mature he'd become in his faith. This is because grace and faith are never based on what we've done in the past; only what we are doing presently.

> *"We then, as workers together with Him also plead with you not to receive the grace of God in vain. For He says: 'In an acceptable time I have heard you, and in the day of salvation I have helped you. Behold, now is the accepted*

> *time; behold, now is the day of salvation.'"*
> *(2 Corinthians 6:1-2).*

Although God won't forget the things we've done by faith in the past, He expects us to continue living out our faith each day going forward.

> *"For God is not unjust to forget your work and labor of love which you have shown toward His name, in that you have ministered to the saints, and do minister. And we desire that each one of you show the same diligence to the full assurance of hope until the end, that you do not become [lazy] sluggish, but imitate those who through faith and patience inherit the promises"*
> *(Hebrews 6:10-12).*

If we stop physical training, we will eventually get out of shape, meaning we will lose strength and stamina. And if we don't adjust our calorie intake, we will gain weight. We don't normally think of our faith in terms of strength or stamina, but we are growing in spiritual strength and stamina or endurance when we are growing in our faith. Therefore, if we stop exercising or working out our faith, we will lose spiritual strength and endurance. When our physical bodies stop exercising, our muscles atrophy. In the same way, if we stop exercising our spiritual bodies, our spiritual body will get weaker.

Training is required to develop the ability to do anything worthwhile, and becoming like Christ is no exception. It is especially vital in teaching believers what is right and wrong. *Hebrews 5:13-14* says,

> *"For everyone who partakes only of milk is unskilled in the word of righteousness, for he is a babe. But solid food belongs to those who are [mature] of full age, that is, those who by reason of [practice] use have their senses exercised to discern both good and evil."*

In other words, each of us must be trained to distinguish good from evil. It's not something we automatically know just because we profess to be followers of Christ. It's no different from teaching children what's right and wrong. It takes time to teach a child right from wrong. No child learns even close to what he or she needs to know by the time he or she becomes a teenager. Children are still learning even as they get well into their teenage years. Even as adults, we need to continue learning, because God designed us to be lifelong learners.

The apostle Paul told Timothy, *"But reject profane and old wives' fables, and exercise yourself toward godliness" (1 Timothy 4:7).*

This verse also implies godliness requires training or exercising our faith. Paul went on in *1 Timothy 4:8* to say, *"For bodily exercise profits a little, but godliness is profitable for all things, having promise of the life that now is and of that which is to come."*

Rewards of Discipline

Training ourselves to be godly will not only help us in this life but also eternal life. The scriptures talk about the rewards in heaven, so it should motivate us to know what they are, so we can know what we are training for. The *second* and *third* Chapters of *Revelation* tell us some very specific rewards (see below). If you add up all the rewards for overcoming promised to each of the seven churches these letters were written to, they are overwhelming. Therefore, it stands to reason it would require some effort on our part to develop a strong and enduring faith since the rewards are so great.

> *(Ephesus) "To him who overcomes I will give to eat from the tree of life, which is in the midst of the Paradise of God" (Revelation 2:7).*

> *(Smyrna) "He who overcomes shall not be hurt by the second death" (Revelation 2:11).*

> *(Pergamum) "To him who overcomes I will give some of*

the hidden manna to eat. And I will give him a white stone, and on the stone a new name written which no one knows except him who receives it" (Revelation 2:17).

(Thyatira) "And he who overcomes, and keeps My works until the end, to him I will give power over the nations— He shall rule them with a rod of iron; They shall be dashed to pieces like the potter's vessels—as I also have received from My Father; and I will give him the morning star. (Revelation 2:26-28).

(Sardis) "He who overcomes shall be clothed in white garments, and I will not blot out his name from the Book of Life; but I will confess his name before My Father and before His angels" (Revelation 3:5).

(Philadelphia) "He who overcomes, I will make him a pillar in the temple of My God, and he shall go out no more. I will write on him the name of My God and the name of the city of My God, the New Jerusalem, which comes down out of heaven from My God. And I will write on him My new name" (Revelation 3:12).

(Laodicea) "To him who overcomes I will grant to sit with Me on My throne, as I also overcame and sat down with My Father on His throne" (Revelation 3:21).

Great rewards not only require great faith, they also require great discipline. *Hebrews 12:11* tells us discipline will be painful, but it will also be worth it. *"Now no [discipline] chastening seems to be joyful for the present, but painful; nevertheless, afterward it yields the peaceable fruit of righteousness to those who have been trained by it."*

Any kind of serious training requires discipline, because nobody is naturally going to do spiritual training, just like nobody naturally wants to go to the gym and do regular exercise to get in shape. If I want to work out to lose weight, or lift weights to gain strength, or run to improve my lung capacity and physical endurance, then I need to make a commitment to do these things regularly. The reason I would do this is I've decided the benefits are worth the pain and suffering my body is going to experience as I go through this training. But my flesh is going to fight me all the time and try to talk me out of going to the gym. Without discipline, I would not be able to continue the training. But anybody who stays the course of going to the gym to lose weight, gain strength, or improve their endurance capacity, may eventually look forward to going to the gym. It might even become a habit they won't want to give up.

In the same way, nobody is going to naturally develop the discipline to have a good spiritual growth plan unless they first believe the benefits are worth it. This is why it's important for each believer to really know the truth about the need to grow in their faith. *2 Timothy 3:16-17* gives us some reasons why we need to be trained. It says, *"All Scripture is given by inspiration of God, and is profitable for doctrine, for reproof, for correction, for [training, discipline] instruction in righteousness, that the man of God may be complete, thoroughly equipped for every good work."*

This indicates men and women of God are to become mature followers of Christ who are thoroughly prepared to do every good work or deed God wants to do through them. It's not just pastors, elders, and other leaders of the church who are the men and women of God. All believers must know the scriptures so they can share, defend, obey, and teach them. If we love and trust our Father in heaven with all our heart, mind, soul, and strength, shouldn't it be natural for us to want to tell others how awesome He is? And shouldn't we want to know the truth as much as possible, so we don't misrepresent God or His Son in anything we say or do?

Teaching and Modeling

Titus 2:1-5 also gives us some reasons for why both men and women need to grow in their faith and to know the truth as much as possible. It says,

> *"But as for you, speak the things which are proper for sound doctrine: that the older men be sober, reverent, temperate, sound in faith, in love, in patience; the older women likewise, that they be reverent in behavior, not slanderers, not given to much wine, teachers of good things—that they admonish the young women to love their husbands, to love their children, to be discreet, chaste, homemakers, good, obedient to their own husbands, that the word of God may not be blasphemed."*

Every role we serve throughout our life as a believer in Christ must be done in a way that honors and glorifies God, because others can learn from us and will be always watching us. We do this so *"that the word of God may not be blasphemed"* as Titus 2:5 says above. We don't want to model Christ incorrectly, because that would be proclaiming a false gospel. In the first chapter of Galatians, the apostle Paul had some strong words about preaching any gospel that wasn't correct when he said,

> *"But even if we, or an angel from heaven, preach any other gospel to you than what we have preached to you, let him be accursed. As we have said before, so now I say again, if anyone preaches any other gospel to you than what you have received, let him be accursed"*
> *(Galatians 1:8-9).*

Paul didn't want us to miss the serious consequences of preaching a false gospel, since he repeated what he said.

It's also important that we are trained properly. If we don't have an effective spiritual training plan, we will not get the results we want. For example, if basketball players only practice dribbling and shooting but not passing, setting screens, rebounding or playing defense, they will be at best mediocre. And if they don't do enough conditioning, they won't have the stamina to play very long. They could practice countless hours on just dribbling and shooting, but they would still only be a mediocre basketball player. A good coach teaches basketball players to develop all the skills they need to excel. Plus, a good student of basketball would study and try to learn every facet of the game, including watching great college and professional players play.

In the same way, good spiritual coaches, mentors, and peers are needed to help a person grow in their faith so they can not only do the right kind of training but also get feedback on how they are doing. Paul wrote, *"And the things that you have heard from me among many witnesses, commit these to faithful men who will be able to teach others also" (2 Timothy 2:2).*

This was consistent with Jesus's commission.

> *"Go therefore and make disciples of all the nations, baptizing them in the name of the Father and of the Son and of the Holy Spirit, teaching them to observe all things that I have commanded you; and lo, I am with you always, even to the end of the age. Amen" (Matthew 28:19-20).*

It Takes Time

I read somewhere it takes ten thousand hours of training to become an expert at anything worthwhile. So, it stands to reason a Christian probably needs to spend ten thousand hours in godliness training to become a mature disciple of Christ. If a person spends one hour a day training in godliness, it would take them over twenty-seven years to reach ten thousand hours of godliness training. The results of surveys that ask Christians how much time they spend reading and/or studying their Bibles each day indicate very few Christians read their Bible more than fifteen minutes a day. At that rate, it would take one hundred and four years before a person could spend ten thousand hours reading and studying their Bible. Now, godliness training obviously includes more than just reading and studying the Bible. It includes putting into practice what a person learns through their reading and studying. This makes it very difficult to measure how many hours a believer spends in spiritual training. But if it was possible to measure how many hours a day a follower of Jesus spends in spiritual training, and they spent on average two hours a day, then it would take them about thirteen and a half years to reach ten thousand hours of training.

If we look at Jesus' disciples as an example, it appears they spent time with Him for about three years. If we don't count sleeping in the presence of Jesus as part of their training, and we assume they spent about sixteen hours a day in training over those three years, they would have spent about seventeen-thousand five hundred hours training with Jesus. Plus, most, if not all, of them had spent some years in the spiritual training every child went through just being part of a Jewish family. We also know Peter and John didn't have much education or formal religious training based on what the religious leaders said about them. *"Now when they saw the boldness of Peter and John, and perceived that they were uneducated and untrained men, they marveled" (Acts 4:13).*

We can probably also assume that the other disciples were also not educated and trained formally in the Jewish faith. Yet, it appears Jesus' disciples had at least ten thousand hours of training. Based on that, and the fact they had Jesus as their Personal Trainer for the last three years of their training, it seems to confirm every follower of Christ should have a minimum of ten thousand hours of training to become a mature disciple of Christ.

Training Children

If it is true most adult Christians don't spend more than fifteen minutes a day reading the Bible and praying, it stands to reason they are probably not spending much time training their children. Yet the apostle Paul wrote in *Ephesians 6:4,*

"*And you, fathers, do not provoke your children to wrath,*

> *but bring them up in the training and admonition of the Lord."*

How many of us can honestly say we were brought *"up in the training and admonition of the Lord?"* Yes, some parents seriously take on the responsibility of doing their children's spiritual training in their homes. But how many of us are depending more on our local church to do this training, which may take place one to two times a week? Since children learn to do what their parents do, not what they say, real training must take place in the home where they live seven days a week. This appears to have been the case based on what Paul wrote about Timothy's mother and grandmother. *"When I call to remembrance the genuine faith that is in you, which dwelt first in your grandmother Lois and your mother Eunice, and I am persuaded is in you also"* (2 Timothy 1:5).

This was further confirmed in *2 Timothy 3:14-15.*

> *"But you must continue in the things which you have learned and been assured of, knowing from whom you have learned them, and that from childhood you have known the Holy Scriptures, which are able to make you wise for salvation through faith which is in Christ Jesus."*

There are some studies which indicate if we don't get people to place their faith in Christ when they are young, the chances of getting them to do it when they are older decrease significantly. And even though some of us didn't come to faith in Christ at an early age, we probably still had a lot of exposure to Christianity when we were younger. This means our spiritual training can never start too soon, and may increase our chances of taking training more seriously when we place our faith in Christ.

Final Thoughts on Becoming Like Christ

There are no shortcuts to becoming like Christ. Miracles have their place in the scriptures and in our lives, but just as it takes hard work to have strong marriages or to raise children to be mature, responsible adults, there are no easy ways to make mature Christians who resemble Christ. Yet God's Word guarantees it can be done if we do our part to stay connected to Him. And when we do, we will be able to lead others to Christ and help them grow into Christ's likeness.

Just as nobody will eat a half-baked cake, neither will anybody follow a half-baked Christian. Jesus had followers because He was who He said He was. And people will follow us if we are devoted followers of Christ who resemble Him. The apostle Paul was not shy about asking his followers to imitate him. We should not be shy about asking our followers to imitate us. If we are not reproducing devoted disciples of Christ, and we've claimed to be a Christian for a long time, there is something wrong. In other words, a mature follower of Christ without anybody following him or her is an oxymoron.

Mike Garst

Chapter 6
Have I Been Born Again?

Have you ever watched the television show, *Extreme Makeover*? Have you seen the joy and the tears the homeowners have when they enter their home that doesn't look anything like the home they were living in before the radical change? Can you imagine having your soul and spirit go through the same kind of extreme makeover that resulted in a new life overflowing with grace, peace, joy, mercy, love, and hope?

The good news is this can be more than a dream. It's expected and possible for Christians, as I've talked about in the previous two chapters. Yet, even though we are called to seek God wholeheartedly and enter into serious spiritual training, there is still a mystery about the new birth that must take place in us.

Mystery of New Birth

This new birth is so important in salvation that Jesus said in **John 3:3,** *"Most assuredly, I say to you, unless one is born [from above] again, he cannot see the kingdom of God."*

He went on in *John 3:5-7* to say,

> *"Most assuredly, I say to you, unless one is born of water and the Spirit, he cannot enter the kingdom of God. That which is born of the flesh is flesh, and that which is born of the Spirit is spirit. Do not marvel that I said to you, 'You must be born again.'"*

Jesus made it clear that unless we are born again, or born from above, we would not see or enter the kingdom of God. If we want to be strong and finish strong in this life, we need to see the kingdom of God, because a correct view of God's kingdom is what gives us a godly purpose and clarifies our calling in this life on earth.

It is important to talk about this, because even though a Christian may say they are born again, it may have been based on an event in their life or even an emotional experience. A true new birth radically changes your priorities and desires, and enables you to use your gifts and talents to bless people all the days of your life.

Jesus said in *John 3:8*, *"The wind blows where it wishes, and you hear the sound of it, but cannot tell where it comes from and where it goes. So is everyone who is born of the Spirit."*

Now we might argue we can tell which direction the wind is coming from by measuring it with the right instrument. But Jesus was more likely talking about where the wind originally comes from or how it's created and how it changes direction and speed all the time. Meteorologists can predict wind speeds and directions to some extent by measuring barometric pressures, but they can't predict when the barometric pressure is going to change. They only can predict what's going to happen when it does change. The same thing is true for hurricanes and tornadoes. Meteorologists can see patterns developing, but they don't know when an actual tornado or hurricane will be created. Twice in the book of Jeremiah and once in the book of Psalms it says,

> *"When He utters His voice, There is a multitude of waters in the heavens: 'And He causes the vapors to ascend from*

*the ends of the earth. He makes lightning for the rain, He
brings the wind out of His treasuries.'"
(Jeremiah 10:13, 51:16).*

*"He causes the vapors to ascend from the ends of the
earth; He makes lightning for the rain; He brings the wind
out of His treasuries" (Psalm 135:7).*

These verses imply God is the creator of all weather and in control of it, and the wind comes out of His *"treasuries."*

If you combine these verses with what *John 3:8* says, it appears our spiritual birth also comes out of God's *"treasuries."* In other words, it's a mysterious new birth that must come from God somehow. So how does spiritual birth begin? *James 1:18* says, *"Of His own will <u>He brought us forth by the word of truth</u>,* [emphasis added] *that we might be a kind of firstfruits of His creatures."*

This means we must, at a minimum, read or hear God's Word for spiritual birth to occur. This is consistent with what the apostle Paul wrote in *Romans 10:17. "So then faith comes by hearing, and hearing by the word of God."*

It's also similar to what Peter wrote in *1 Peter 1:23. "Having been born again, not of [perishable] corruptible seed but [imperishable] incorruptible, through the word of God which lives and abides forever."*

In the Parable of the Sower in *Matthew 13, Mark 4,* and *Luke 8,* God's Word is referred to as seed. Before a physical birth can begin, the male sperm must first attach itself to the female egg. This conception, which is a uniting of these two things, is the first step in the physical birth process. Since God's Word is a seed, it must unite itself with something in us. This may be a union of our spirit with God's Word.

How much of God's truth must we believe before this spiritual conception can take place? We know from *Romans 10:9-10*

"that if you confess with your mouth the Lord Jesus and

> *believe in your heart that God has raised Him from the dead, you will be saved. For with the heart one believes unto righteousness, and with the mouth confession is made unto salvation."*

This indicates we must read and trust God's Word to the point we believe Jesus was raised from the dead, that He is Lord of our lives, and we will openly acknowledge or confess this to others in order to be saved. Yet this is only a starting point. There must also be a significant change of priorities in a person's life that will be noticed by the person who has been born again as well as the people close to him or her. Without the evidence of change in a person's life, he or she may be able to do some ministry but will do it without a heart change.

Ministering Without Being Born Again

There's a great example of this in the book *The Ways of God*[8] by Henry Blackaby and Roy Edgemon. The authors wrote briefly about the Shantung Revival in China, which includes a story of a man realizing he had not been born again, even though He was a "successful evangelist who was preaching the gospel." Here's what they wrote.

A Lutheran missionary nurse from Norway was one of the believers seeking God among those gathered at Shantung. Her name was Marie Munson. Anybody she met would face the question, "Have you ever been born again by the Spirit of the living God?" And if one of them said, "Oh, yes. I have been born again," she would look them straight in the eye and say, "Tell me the clear evidence that this transaction has taken place."

It is recorded that she made no exceptions on the mission field. There was a Chinese evangelist who for ten years had been preaching the gospel. Marie Munson took him aside and asked, "Have you ever been born

---

[8] The Way's of God, Henry T. Blackaby & Roy T. Edgemon, Broadman & Holman Publishers, Nashville TN, 2000, Pages 151-152

again by the Spirit of God?"

He said, "Why certainly. I am preaching the gospel. I have been for ten years. And people have been saved."

Marie said, "You didn't hear my question. I asked if you have ever been born again by the Spirit of God."

And he answered, "But I am a preacher of the gospel." In Matthew 7:22, that's the kind of answer that some people gave in a parable about the judgment.

So, she asked him again, "Can you tell me clearly the evidence that you have been born again by the Spirit of the Living God?"

The evangelist walked away in anger. But the next day, he returned, an absolutely broken servant of God. "I was angry with you over what you asked me. But the question haunted me. Last night I asked myself, 'Have I ever been born again by the Spirit of the Living God? What evidence is there in my life that this has ever taken place?'"

He continued. "I began to look through my life, and everything that I saw that ought to have been there was missing. There was never a time when the old passed away. There was never a time when everything became new," he said, turning to the diminutive missionary nurse. ' I want you to know that last night I cried out to God and was born again for the first time by the Spirit of the Living God. Now I know that He is my Lord." Then he said, "For ten years I have lived under false pretenses and I have taken the support and the offerings of the people of God. I am going to stand and tell the people of God that I have done this. From now until the end of my ministry, I will never again take a cent from any of God's people." The evangelist played an integral part as God brought revival to Shantung. Ten times as many people came to faith in Jesus Christ from the born-again evangelist than responded in the previous years when he was preaching truth from an unchanged heart. Now he had an eternal relationship with the eternal ways and truth of God.

If an evangelist who had been preaching the gospel for ten years can do it without being born again, then it's possible for many people to think they are born-again Christians without experiencing a new birth. You'll note two key things that the evangelist said:

"There was never a time when the old passed away. There was never a time when everything became new."

"Now I know He is my Lord."

From the story about the evangelist, the evidence of a changed life was not there. The old had not passed away, and there was never a time when everything became new. But once the evangelist knew Jesus was his Lord, his life changed.

It's very easy to say we believe something, but it's another thing to do it. An example of this kind of belief can be illustrated in the true story about Blondin, a famous acrobat who used to do stunts over Niagara Falls. He did some amazing feats, including riding a bicycle on a tightrope over Niagara Falls. One day he said he was going to push a wheelbarrow across on the tightrope, and he asked the audience watching if they believed he could push the wheelbarrow across the tightrope with a person in it. They all raised their hands and enthusiastically said they believed he could do it. But when he asked for volunteers to sit in the wheelbarrow, he wasn't able to get one person to volunteer. They were satisfied with saying they believed provided they didn't have to do anything to prove it.

Actions Are More Important Than Words

There's a short parable in *Matthew 21:28-31* where Jesus talked about the responses of two sons who were asked by their father to do something. This is what Jesus said.

> *"But what do you think? A man had two sons, and he came to the first and said, 'Son, go, work today in my vineyard.'*
>
> *He answered and said, 'I will not,' but afterward he*

> *regretted it and went.*
>
> *Then he came to the second and said likewise. And he answered and said, 'I go, sir,' but he did not go.*
>
> *Which of the two did the will of his father? They said to Him, 'The first.' Jesus said to them, 'Assuredly, I say to you that tax collectors and harlots enter the kingdom of God before you.'"*

One conclusion you might take from this parable is our actions are much more important than our words. But there's also an important point fundamental to the gospel and the kingdom of God. The son who said "no" initially was expressing disobedience to his father with his words, but changed his mind to do what pleased the father. This is why God gives us grace, which is a chance to be convicted, confess, and repent when we realize we are not doing what is pleasing to God. *1 **Peter** 5:5* says, *"God resists the proud, but gives grace to the humble."*

We will not receive grace without first humbling ourselves before God. Humility is a critical part of being born again because we won't be able to receive and retain God's Word without humility. Nor will we be able to receive His grace. Without each of these things, the new birth cannot happen. But with them, we can be born anew, and over time there will be increasing evidence this change is real.

Forming Christ in Us

The apostle Paul wrote in *Galatians 4:19*,

> *"My little children, for whom I labor in birth again until Christ is formed in you."*

From this verse, we might conclude Jesus must be formed in our spiritual bodies and it's a process that takes time. In a physical birth, a fetus must continue to grow after the conception takes place in the womb of the female. This means it must continue to receive nourishment. This is why our spiritual bodies need to be fed after there's a spiritual conception, or what is often called a conversion. If a fetus is not fed, it's not going to grow, and will eventually die and result in a miscarriage. Can a spiritual miscarriage happen? In *Hosea 13:13*, it says, *"The sorrows of a woman in childbirth shall come upon him (Ephraim). He is an unwise son, for he should not stay long where children are born."* The NIV translation says, *"Pains as of a woman in childbirth come to him, but he is a child without wisdom; when the time arrives, he doesn't have the sense to come out of the womb."*

In this chapter of Hosea, God is expressing His anger against Israel, and Ephraim is part of Israel. Israel is rebelling against God, even after all He's done for them since delivering them out of Egypt. In verse thirteen, the primary reason for God's anger is a lack of wisdom or common sense. God had been delivering them from evil things, but they kept turning back to them. So, what would happen to a person who turned to God's Word and believed the basic things it takes for Christ to be conceived in him or her, but then went back to the old ways of living? It would be like a drowning man being rescued and pulled into a boat and then jumping back into the water.

Or imagine a homeless person, who gets set up in an apartment and lined up with a job, but he or she still chooses to go back to a homeless way of life. Or when the prisoner is finally set free and a short time later purposely commits a crime to go back to the life he or she knew in prison. *Proverbs 26:11* describes this well. *"As a dog returns to his vomit, so a fool repeats his folly."*

It's hard to understand why anyone would do any of these things, but we know they happen. Habits control our actions, and that's why we need the power of the Holy Spirit, knowledge of what's in the scriptures, an active church or small group, and mentors to help us make this successful transition into the life God has ready and waiting for us to experience. This will not only make us strong in the Lord, but will enable us to finish strong in the Lord.

Isaiah also wrote something similar in *Isaiah 26:17-18*.

> *"As a woman with child Is in pain and cries out in her [sharp pains] pangs, When she draws near the time of her delivery, So have we been in Your sight, O Lord. We have been with child, we have been in pain; We have, as it were, [given birth to] brought forth wind; We have not accomplished any deliverance in the earth, nor have the inhabitants of the world fallen."*

The NIV translation may help to clarify these two verses as well.

> *"As a pregnant woman about to give birth writhes and cries out in her pain, so were we in your presence, Lord. We were with child, we writhed in labor, but we gave birth to wind. We have not brought salvation to the earth, and the people of the world have not come to life."*

I don't know what God's timeline on spiritual birth looks like, but I know God looks at time much differently than we do. He isn't time bound, but is more process-bound, meaning we can't go from one stage to the next until the stage we are in is complete. Just as a butterfly starts out as a worm before it is transformed into a beautiful butterfly in a cocoon, it cannot come out of the cocoon until it's ready. If we try to open the cocoon, the butterfly will die. This is similar to what happens to a baby bird in an egg. The baby bird must break out from the inside and will do so when it's developed to the point it's ready to come out.

It appears to me our spiritual birth can be like these examples. Plus, we must remember a bird doesn't fly right away, and neither does the butterfly. The timeline and the process for each are naturally different, and neither happens in an instant. The process a baby bird must go through before it flies takes more time than a butterfly. The physical growth process for humans is much longer, and spiritual growth never stops, since growing into Christ's likeness appears to take a lifetime. Even Jesus and His cousin John had to grow spiritually as the following verses indicate.

> *"So the child (John) grew and became strong in spirit, and was in the deserts till the day of his manifestation to Israel." Luke 1:80.*

> *"And the Child (Jesus) grew and became strong in spirit, filled with wisdom; and the grace of God was upon Him." Luke 2:40.*

> *"And Jesus increased in wisdom and stature, and in favor with God and men." Luke 2:52.*

Evidence of Spiritual Birth

The apostle John wrote several times about the evidence we should see when a person is born again. In *1 John 2:29*, he wrote, *"If you know that He is righteous, you know that everyone who practices righteousness is born of Him."*

Therefore, anybody who has been born again will consistently and earnestly make doing what is right in God's eyes their top priority, regardless of the cost. This also means they will quickly confess and turn from anything the Holy Spirit convicts them of that isn't right in God's eyes. King David did this when the prophet Nathan confronted him concerning the murder of Uriah in *1 Samuel 15:13*. *"So David said to Nathan, 'I have sinned against the Lord.' And Nathan said to David, 'The Lord also has put away your sin; you shall not die.'"*

A person who is born again will not persist in doing what is wrong. *1 John 3:9* confirms this because John wrote, *"Whoever has been born of God does not sin, for His seed remains in him; and he cannot sin, because he has been born of God."*

This can be a challenging verse for most of us, including believers, because it appears to indicate we can't sin at all. But this is most likely talking about willful sin. We all have impurities in our heart we are not aware of yet, but the Holy Spirit will expose them to us as we earnestly follow Jesus by denying ourselves and picking up our cross daily so we can do what is right in God's eyes. When our unknown sin is exposed by the Holy Spirit, John tells us, in *1 John 1:9, "If we confess our sins, He is faithful and just to forgive us our sins and to cleanse us from all unrighteousness."*

This is one of the fundamentals of Christianity we all benefit from when we are sincerely following Jesus, because confession cleanses *"us from all unrighteousness,"* and thus makes us righteous and blameless in God's eyes. In addition to this, *1 John 2:1-2* says,

> *"My little children, these things I write to you, so that you may not sin. And if anyone sins, we have an Advocate with the Father, Jesus Christ the righteous. And He Himself is the propitiation for our sins, and not for ours only but also for the whole world."*

Whenever a believer sins, God doesn't see it initially, because it first must go through Jesus. It's as if Jesus blocks it from God, at least temporarily, to give us a chance to confess and repent. Even though *1 John 1:9* doesn't say confess and repent, we know from *2 Corinthians 7:12, "For godly sorrow produces repentance leading to salvation, not to be regretted; but the sorrow of the world produces death."*

Repentance is a necessary part of our salvation that will also lead to the production of good fruit in a person. That fruit will resemble what Paul called the fruit of the Spirit in *Galatians 5:22-23*, which is *"love, joy, peace, longsuffering, kindness, goodness, faithfulness, 23 [meekness] gentleness, self-control."*

When a Christian is consistently producing this kind of fruit in their lives, we can be confident they have been born from above. Whereas, when we observe a professing Christian doing what appears to be right some of the time, but at other times doing what is wrong and not taking the steps to confess and repent when they are confronted about their wrongdoings, we may have good reason to question whether they have been born again. This can happen when people do what appears to be good in God's eyes with the wrong motive.

New Birth and Knowing God

1 John 4:7-8 says everybody who loves has not only been born of God but also knows God. *"Beloved, let us love one another, for love is of God; and everyone who loves is born of God and knows God. He who does not love does not know God, for God is love."*

The difference between knowing about God and knowing God is the same as knowing something about a person versus knowing a person. When we know a person, we know his or her story in detail, and we know what's important to that one. We would even have a good idea of what he or she might do in any situation. This is the kind of relationship God wants with us, and why we must be born again for it to be possible.

1 John 5:1-4 goes on to say everyone born of God will obey His commands and overcome the world.

> *"Whoever believes that Jesus is the Christ is born of God, and everyone who loves Him who begot also loves him who is begotten of Him. By this we know that we love the children of God, when we love God and keep His commandments. For this is the love of God, that we keep His commandments. And His commandments are not burdensome. For whatever is born of God overcomes the world. And this is the victory that has overcome the world—our faith."*

When obeying God's commands is a burden to us, it's an indication we have not been born of God yet, because His commands are always for our good, and anybody born of God knows that. Even when they know that following God's commandments might be painful, they still do so because they know it pleases God and will ultimately be best for them.

Another evidence of the new birth is the confidence it gives a person concerning God's protection. *1 John 5:18* says, *"We know that whoever is born of God does not sin; but he who has been born of God keeps [guards] himself, and the wicked one does not touch him."*

When somebody has been born of God, he or she knows the devil cannot touch him or her, but he can only deceive them. That is why a person born of God will do everything possible to protect his or her heart and know God's truth to recognize the lies of the devil. They will also understand Christians are in a war, and the earth is Satan's kingdom. This knowledge is critical for all born-again believers so they know to whom they belong and whom they must serve and follow throughout each day.

We Can't Speed Up the Process

There are many ways to try and convert people to Christianity using a variety of doctrines in the world. It's unfortunate most of them revolve around trying to talk people into the kingdom of God. But Jesus had some hard words for the scribes and Pharisees when He said "Woe to you" eight times in Matthew 23. It's particularly interesting what He said in *Matthew 23:15. "Woe to you, scribes and Pharisees, hypocrites! For you travel land and sea to win one proselyte, and when he is won, you make him twice as much a son of hell as yourselves."*

Jesus not only told the scribes and Pharisees they were sons of hell, but anyone they traveled far to reach and convert would be twice as much a son of hell as they were. This should get our attention! It's a strong reminder we must understand what our role is in sharing the gospel with others and what God's responsibility is. We can sow the seed and water when needed, but only God can make it grow (see *1 Corinthians 3:6*).

We must also know we can't push people to Christ. They can only be drawn by God, as Jesus said in *John 6:44-45*.

> *"No one can come to Me unless the Father who sent Me draws him; and I will raise him up at the last day. It is written in the prophets, 'And they shall all be taught by God.' Therefore everyone who has heard and learned from the Father comes to Me."*

Jesus repeated this in *John 6:65*. *"And He said, 'Therefore I have said to you that no one can come to Me unless it has been granted to him by My Father.'"*

There are many verses in the Bible that tell us to wait on God, and since God is the only One who can make anything grow, we must wait and trust in God's process and timing for the new birth to occur, especially if we are hoping and praying for the people we know to experience this new birth.

Final Comments on the New Birth

As we grow older and our physical bodies start breaking down and falling apart, the only real hope we have for the future is our spiritual body. We all know our physical body is going to die one day. We can spend a lot of time trying to keep it alive and strong, but the return on our investment is going to have decreasing benefits. Yet everything we invest in our spiritual bodies is going to have an eternal reward. One of the reasons the new birth is so important is because we will be increasingly more sensitive to the need to feed our spiritual body to keep it growing and healthy, so we can live a meaningful life in which our peace, joy, patience, kindness, gentleness, self-control, love, faithfulness, and goodness continually increases. This will not only enable us to become strong in this life, but finish strong so we can be ready to live in the kingdom of God forever.

Mike Garst

Chapter 7
What is the Devil's Strategy?

One of the best-kept secrets in this world is we are born into a spiritual war. This is something to really think about since many people, including professing Christians, don't realize this war is taking place. Can you visualize a battle going on and people walking around in the middle of it while missiles are flying overhead and not being aware of it? Yet that is what is happening in this spiritual war. Most often, the people who aren't aware of it don't see any of the casualties laying all around them.

The good news is Christ has already won the war. The victory has been assured to us if we believe in the necessary death and resurrection of God's Son, Jesus Christ, to pay the penalty for our sins, and then do our part to trust and obey God and the gospel of Christ. Therefore, it's important to realize we still need to be overcomers, because our enemy the devil, who's crafty and deceiving, is going to do everything he can to get us not to trust God and not obey the whole gospel of Jesus. He's attempting to steal something that is rightfully ours by trying to get us to believe his lies.

Beginning of the War

It's important to have a right understanding about how this war started, the nature of both sides, and the weapons we have available for the fight. First, let's examine some scriptures in *Revelation 12* and *13* that talk about this war and where it started.

> *"Now a great sign appeared in heaven: a woman clothed with the sun, with the moon under her feet, and on her head a garland of twelve stars. Then being with child, she cried out in labor and in pain to give birth. And another sign appeared in heaven: behold, a great, fiery red dragon having seven heads and ten horns, and seven diadems on his heads. His tail drew a third of the stars of heaven and threw them to the earth. And the dragon stood before the woman who was ready to give birth, to devour her Child as soon as it was born. She bore a male Child who was to rule all nations with a rod of iron. And her Child was caught up to God and His throne. Then the woman fled into the wilderness, where she has a place prepared by God, that they should feed her there one thousand two hundred and sixty days" (Revelation 12:1-6).*

The twelve stars may represent the twelve tribes of Israel, or Jacob's twelve sons. The Child is Jesus since He was to rule all the nations with a rod of iron. The woman appears to be His earthly mother, Mary. We will see in verse *nine* (below) that the dragon is Satan. It's not clear what is meant in verse *five* when it says the Child was caught up to God and His throne. It may mean God protected Jesus during the time His family fled to Egypt to get away from Herod. This would make sense since it says the woman fled into the wilderness about three and a half years. The next few verses then talk specifically about the war in heaven.

> *"And war broke out in heaven: Michael and his angels fought with the dragon; and the dragon and his angels fought, but they [were not strong enough] did not prevail, nor was a place found for them in heaven any longer. So*

> *the great dragon was cast out, that serpent of old, called the Devil and Satan, who deceives the whole world; he was cast to the earth, and his angels were cast out with him" (Revelation 12:7-9).*

From this, we can conclude the devil was leading one side of this war in heaven and lost. As a result, he and his angels were cast out. Verse *ten* gives more information about both sides of this war:

> *"Then I heard a loud voice saying in heaven, 'Now salvation, and strength, and the kingdom of our God, and the power of His Christ have come, for the accuser of our brethren, who accused them before our God day and night, has been cast down.'" (Revelation 12:10).*

From this verse we can see the other side of this war is the *"Kingdom of God."* The devil is identified as the *"accuser,"* that is, one who accused the subjects in the kingdom of God daily.

Revelation 12:12 gives us some more information about the devil, as well as what this means to heaven and to the inhabitants on earth

> *"Therefore rejoice, O heavens, and you who dwell in them! Woe to the inhabitants of the earth and the sea! For the devil has come down to you, having great wrath, because he knows that he has a short time" (Revelation 12:12).*

From this, it appears the heavens are rejoicing because evil has been thrown out of it. On the other hand, the inhabitants of the earth are now going to experience the devil's *"great wrath,"* and his time is short. What's a short time since Jesus was crucified and resurrected from the dead over two thousand years ago? Based on this, people on the earth have been experiencing the devil's wrath that long. But we must remember time in God's eyes is much different than time in our eyes. *"But, beloved, do not forget this one thing, that with the Lord one day is as a thousand years, and a thousand years as one day" (2 Peter 3:8* – see also *Psalm 90:4.*).

The most important thing we need to know from *Revelation 12:12* is this. *"For the devil has come down to you, having great wrath."* This means the devil isn't coming against the inhabitants of the earth with a half-hearted effort; he's going to be intensely focused. This is why we can't be half-hearted Christians. We know what happens in any game of sports when one team is focused and diligently practicing to play against their opponent, and the other team only prepares half-heartedly. We should not expect a different result when the stakes are infinitely higher. The good news is we are guaranteed to win this battle if we trust the Lord and stay connected to Him, which will enable us to prepare ourselves properly to fight with the right weapons.

The next verses in *Revelation 12:13-16* seem to be talking about the devil's pursuit of Mary and baby Jesus after His birth. It appears the devil went after Mary with every resource he had, but God protected her and His Son. One of the ways He did this was by giving Joseph dreams.

> *"An angel of the Lord appeared to Joseph in a dream, saying, 'Arise, take the young Child and His mother, flee to Egypt, and stay there until I bring you word; for Herod will seek the young Child to destroy Him'"*
> *(Matthew 2:13).*

Later, after Herod died, God told Joseph in a dream to come back to Israel. This is a reminder God will protect everybody who belongs to Him, even though Satan now has a new target. *"And the dragon was enraged with the woman, and he went to make war with the rest of her offspring, who keep the commandments of God and have the testimony of Jesus Christ" (Revelation 12:17).*

Therefore, the devil will be making war against those who love and trust God. This is why we must know what we are committing to when we say we are going to surrender control of our lives to Jesus.

In *Revelation 13:3-8,* we are introduced to a beast, who was also given power by the dragon (the devil) to make war and blaspheme God and His name. We are told again the saints are the target. *"It was granted to him to make war with the saints and to overcome them. And authority was given him over every [people] tribe, tongue, and nation" (Revelation 13:7).*

If you are a saint, and the scriptures tell us every believer is a saint, then Satan is making war against you. This is why every Christian needs to put on the full armor of God, so he or she can win the war, along with fellow believers.

Why the Devil is Active

One of the reasons it appears God has allowed Satan to still be around is because our faith must be tested before we really know if it is genuine. Therefore, it appears God allows Satan to be one of the ways our faith gets tested. In the book of Job, God encouraged Satan to test Job's faith. He twice asked Satan, *"Have you [set your heart on] considered My servant Job, that there is none like him on the earth, a blameless and upright man, one who fears God and [turns away from] shuns evil?" (Job 1:8, 2:3).*

In this first conversation, Satan told God if He would take His hand of protection and blessing away from Job, he would *"surely curse You to Your face!" (Job 1:11).* But God responded by saying, *"Behold, all that he has is in your [hand] power; only do not lay a hand on his person" (Job 1:12).*

Job lost much of his livestock, many of his servants, and all his sons and daughters. This clearly indicates Satan, although he may not be able to lay a hand on us, can still do a lot of damage to our possessions, to people working for us, and our family. The second time Satan came to God, He commended Job when He said, *"And still he holds fast to his integrity, although you incited Me against him, to [consume] destroy him without cause" (Job 2:3).*

But Satan then said to the Lord, *'Skin for skin! Yes, all that a man has he will give for his life. But stretch out Your hand now, and touch his bone and his flesh, and he will surely curse You to Your face!' And the Lord said to Satan, 'Behold, he is in your hand, but spare his life.'" Job 2:4-6.*

I don't think anybody would want to be the subject of this conversation God had with Satan, especially when God gave Satan permission to attack Job's health.

But Satan wasn't allowed to take Job's life. As you may know, Satan did afflict Job physically, but Job passed the test and ended up doubly blessed. Yet we must also not conclude from the book of Job all afflictions come from Satan. The Psalmist said in *Psalm 119:75,"I know, O Lord, that Your judgments are right, and that in faithfulness You have afflicted me."*

And a few verses before, in *Psalm 119:71,* it says, *"It is good for me that I have been afflicted, That I may learn Your statutes."*

This means both Satan and God can afflict us. The difference is Satan will afflict us to try and get us to question God's goodness and fairness. But God afflicts us to discipline us, so we can learn His ways and He can strengthen our faith. The good news is Satan can't take our life if we belong to God. The bad news is he may be allowed to inflict some damage. This is why we must pray and ask God to show us if there is something we need to either confess and turn from or to learn when we are facing a challenging trial, since we don't typically know the root cause of the test.

The Devil as an Angel of Light

Satan's strategy is not only to afflict believers, he also wants to deceive believers. In *2 Corinthians 11:13-14*, Paul writes, *"For such are false apostles, deceitful workers, transforming themselves into apostles of Christ. And no wonder! For Satan himself transforms himself into an angel of light."*

An angel of light is going to look like somebody who cares for us and only wants to do what is best for us. This may be the hardest deception to guard against, because Satan won't be trying to get us to do something obviously wrong. He may be attempting to get us not to obey God by tempting us to choose another way that looks good on the surface, but is really disobedience. Therefore, we need to start thinking about how *"an angel of light"* might operate, and learn how we must respond.

Satisfy Your Physical Body First—Jesus' First Temptation

We can start by looking at the encounter Jesus had with Satan in the desert when Jesus *"was led up by the Spirit into the wilderness to be tempted by the devil" (Matthew 4:1).*

This didn't appear to be a gentle leading, but more compelling, because *(Mark 1:12)* says, *"Immediately the Spirit [sent Him out] drove Him into the wilderness."*

Next it says, *"And when He had fasted forty days and forty nights, afterward He was hungry. Now when the tempter came to Him, he said, 'If You are the Son of God, command that these stones become bread.'" (Matthew 4:2-3).*

Since Jesus had access to God's power, the devil was trying to get Him to use that power to get what His physical body wanted at that moment. But God doesn't give us power to only satisfy the needs and wants of our natural body. Satisfying our natural body's needs whenever it wants something doesn't glorify God. It may even separate us from Him, at least temporarily. Jesus responded by saying, *"It is written 'Man shall not live by bread alone, but by every word that proceeds from the mouth of God.'" (Matthew 4:4* – See also *Luke 4:4*).

Jesus knew this from *Deuteronomy 8:3*, and His response shows us how we must always respond in any given situation when our natural body wants to be satisfied first. Yes, our physical body needs food to stay alive, but our spiritual body also needs spiritual food, and Jesus is showing us spiritual food is more important than physical food for our body. This also appeared to be the case for Moses when he went up on Mount Sinai, because in *Exodus 34:28* it says, *"So he (Moses) was there with the Lord forty days and forty nights; he neither ate bread nor drank water. And He wrote on the tablets the words of the covenant, the Ten Commandments."*

Jesus appeared to be following the precedent Moses already set by confirming if we first take care of our spiritual body, God will take care of our physical body.

Test God—Jesus' Second Temptation

The next strategy Satan used was trying to trick Jesus into testing God, because he took Jesus

> *"up into the holy city, set Him on the pinnacle of the temple, and said to Him, 'If You are the Son of God, throw Yourself down. For it is written: "He shall give His angels charge over you," and, "In their hands they shall bear you up, lest you dash your foot against a stone."'"*
> *(Matthew 4:5-6* – See also *Luke 4:9-11).*

The devil was quoting from *Psalm 91:11-12* and was taking Scripture out of context. He still uses this strategy today when he tries to get people to use verses out of context to get what they want and not necessarily what God wants. The devil doesn't want what God wants, since he's the deceiver and accuser. Sometimes people use Scripture out of context intentionally, and at other times, it's due to ignorance. It's interesting this occurred after the first temptation, because it also shows why man cannot live on bread alone but on every word that comes from the mouth of God. It's when we know only some of God's Word someone can take it out of context and deceive us. Jesus responded by saying, *"It is written again, 'You shall not [test] tempt the Lord your God.'"* (Matthew 4:7 – See also *Luke 4:12*).

Jesus quoted this from *Deuteronomy 6:16,* showing Jesus knew the whole Word of God and not just parts of it. One of the reasons this is so important is because God's Word can appear contradictory at times. But it is true and consistent; it's just that we have to know the whole, so we can better understand the parts.

Sometimes one verse can take precedent over another verse. For example, Jesus tells us to be His disciple we must hate our wife and family. *"If anyone comes to Me and does not hate his father and mother, wife and children, brothers and sisters, yes, and his own life also, he cannot be My disciple"* (Luke 14:26).

But Paul wrote, *"Husbands, love your wives, just as Christ also loved the church and gave Himself for her"* (Ephesians 5:25).

Exodus 20:12 also says, *"Honor your father and your mother."*

Paul also wrote to Timothy, saying, *"But if anyone does not provide for his own, and especially for those of his household, he has denied the faith and is worse than an unbeliever"* (1 Timothy 5:8).

When you take all these scriptures together, God is telling us not to love our wife, our parents, or anyone or anything else more than God, but to still take care of them.

Luke also wrote in *Acts 19:5-6,*

> *"When they heard this, they were baptized in the name of the Lord Jesus. And when Paul had laid hands on them, the Holy Spirit came upon them, and they spoke with tongues and prophesied."*

Some doctrines say all true believers speak in tongues, but Paul also wrote in *1 Corinthians 12:29-31,*

> *"Are all apostles? Are all prophets? Are all teachers? Are all workers of miracles? Do all have gifts of healings? Do all speak with tongues? Do all interpret? But earnestly desire the best gifts. And yet I show you a more excellent way."*

This implies not everybody has the same gifts, and tongues is just one of the gifts. Many scriptures can be taken out of context, which is why we must know all Scripture well enough not to be deceived.

You Can Have It Now—Jesus' Third Temptation

For the next temptation, Satan *"took Him up on an exceedingly high mountain and showed Him all the kingdoms of the world and their glory. And he said to Him, 'All these things I will give You if You will fall down and worship me'"* (*Matthew 4:8-9* – See also *Luke 4:5-7*).

It seems Satan was trying to get Jesus to believe he could offer Him more than God could offer Him and offer it sooner. Satan still uses this strategy on us to make us think we can have more and have it sooner by not trusting or waiting on God. We don't think of this as worshiping Satan, but that is what we do when we don't trust or wait on God's timing. Jesus of course didn't fall for this either and said to Satan, *"Away with you, Satan! For it is written, 'You shall worship the Lord your God, and Him only you shall serve.'"* (*Matthew 4:10* – See also *Luke 4:8*).

Jesus was quoting from *Deuteronomy 6:13.*

In the first two temptations, it wasn't as obvious Satan was tempting Jesus with something evil, whereas it seems obvious in the third temptation, since Satan was trying to get Jesus to worship him. But Satan doesn't necessarily ask us to worship him; he just tries to get us not to trust God or wait on Him, which is the same as worshiping Satan. Jesus said, *"He who is not with Me is against Me, and he who does not gather* with Me scatters abroad" (Matthew 12:30).

We are either with Jesus or against Him. There is no middle ground, but Satan tries to get us to think there is. He does that by trying to get us to choose any option that looks good or reasonable versus what God is commanding or leading us to do.

It's interesting Satan came into the scene early in both the garden with Adam and Eve and in Jesus' ministry. Since Jesus knew the scriptures, He knew what Satan did in the garden with Eve.

> "Now the serpent was more cunning than any beast of the field which the Lord God had made. And he said to the woman, 'Has God indeed said, "You shall not eat of every tree of the garden"?'" (Genesis 3:1).

Satan's first approach was to get Eve to question God's Word. And Eve's first response was good, because she said, *"We may eat the fruit of the trees of the garden; but of the fruit of the tree which is in the midst of the garden, God has said, 'You shall not eat it, nor shall you touch it, lest you die.'"* (Genesis 3:2-3).

But Satan said, *"You will not surely die. For God knows that in the day you eat of it your eyes will be opened, and you will be like God, knowing good and evil"* (Genesis 3:4-5).

Satan was able to convince Eve God was withholding something from her, so when she *"saw that the tree was good for food, that it was [a desirable thing] pleasant to the eyes, and a tree desirable to make one wise, she took of its fruit and ate. She also gave to her husband with her, and he ate"* (Genesis 3:6).

We can probably assume the fruit always looked good, but then it looked better because it was not only pleasing to the eye. Eve was deceived into thinking she would gain wisdom God didn't want her to have. This is another strategy still used by Satan today. Sometimes we can resist something initially even though it looks good to us. But if Satan can get us to see more benefits, we will gain by partaking of it, then it becomes easier to ignore our initial resistance. Nothing is said about Adam in this whole conversation except *"She also gave some to her husband, who was with her, and he ate it" (Genesis 3:6).*

Since it says he was with her, it appears he witnessed this whole conversation. If he did, then he had plenty of opportunity to rebuke or correct Eve, but he didn't. He apparently went along with her reasoning, although the Apostle Paul wrote, *"And Adam was not deceived, but the woman being deceived, fell into transgression" (1 Timothy 2:14).*

I don't understand yet the reason Adam doesn't get any blame in this Scripture (although he was held accountable), but it's clear they both took the bait, and both ate of the fruit, which led to *"Then the eyes of both of them were opened, and they knew that they were naked; and they sewed fig leaves together and made themselves coverings" (Genesis 3:7).*

Up until that point, Adam and Eve had not felt shame, but it's clear from this verse God opened their eyes, so they both could know they did something wrong, and thus experience shame and feelings of guilt. Even if Adam wasn't deceived, he felt the shame and guilt of sin, which is also a reminder our sin can lead others to sin.

An Angel of Light in Today's World

Now let's fast-forward two thousand years from Jesus' temptations and think about how Satan might appear as an angel of light in today's world. An angel of light isn't going to tempt us with anything obviously wrong. When we look at the first two temptations of Jesus, we see Satan started the temptation by saying, *"If You are the Son of God."* When he tempted Eve, he also brought God's name into the conversation early. We could conclude Satan likes to bring God into the conversation but gives us a corrupt view of Him. Because of this, and because of all the division in many churches around the world, it seems Satan's primary strategy is to either water down or distort the gospel so people can think they know the truth, when in fact they have been deceived into following a gospel that is not God's whole truth.

Because of this, we should expect Satan is going to spend of lot of his efforts on trying to distort or corrupt the Word of God. For this reason, Jesus and many of the writers of the books in the Bible included verses about false prophets and teachers. One of the main reasons they did this was because false prophets and teachers were causing division in the church. Paul wrote to Timothy,

> *"If anyone teaches otherwise and does not consent to wholesome words, even the words of our Lord Jesus Christ, and to the doctrine which accords with godliness, he is proud, knowing nothing, but is obsessed with disputes and arguments over words, from which come envy, strife, reviling, evil suspicions, useless wranglings of men of corrupt minds and destitute of the truth, who suppose that godliness is a means of gain. From such withdraw yourself"* (1 Timothy 6:3-5).

Jesus also told us what would happen to a divided house or kingdom. *"Every kingdom divided against itself is brought to desolation, and every city or house divided against itself will not stand"* (Matthew 12:25).

It appears Satan has been relentless in trying to bring division into the church and in watering down or perverting the gospel through *"angels of light"* masquerading as televangelists, pastors, politicians, political parties, entertainers and celebrities, social media "influencers," and many other platforms that claim to be representing Christ. For this reason, it would be helpful for us to think of Satan as a false prophet or teacher. One of the more serious warnings also came from the apostle Paul in *Acts 20:29-30* when he wrote, *"For I know this, that after my departure savage wolves will come in among you not sparing the flock. Also from among yourselves men will rise up, speaking [misleading] perverse things, to draw away the disciples after themselves."*

There are probably many reasons why Satan would spend so much time attacking the church and the gospel, but it makes sense he would primarily try to get us to listen to our natural bodies and stimulate our pride. For example, our physical body doesn't like discomfort, so one of Satan's strategies as an angel of light is to get us to stay in our comfort zones. Yet the gospel isn't about being comfortable. It requires instead that we regularly examine and get out of any comfort zones hindering our walk with God. In fact, we are called to suffer with Christ, as the following scriptures say.

> *"The Spirit Himself bears witness with our spirit that we are children of God, and if children, then heirs—heirs of God and joint heirs with Christ, if indeed we suffer with Him, that we may also be glorified together"*
> *(Romans 8:16-17).*

> *"For to you it has been granted on behalf of Christ, not only to believe in Him, but also to suffer for His sake, having the same conflict which you saw in me and now hear is in me" (Philippians 1:29-30). (Read also 2 Thessalonians 1:3-5, and 2 Timothy 3:12.)*

These verses confirm one of the costs of following Jesus will be suffering, although it probably doesn't appear to many people outside the church that Christians in the USA are suffering much. They may experience persecution from people if they take a less popular stand on some controversial issues in today's world. And they may lose their jobs if they talk too much about God while they are at work in some companies. Yet, if we visited countries where Christianity is illegal, we would see identifying yourself as a Christian could cost your freedom, your family, your job, and even your life. This should cause us to wonder if Christianity in America has been watered down through *"angels of light"* to the point where suffering is very limited.

Therefore, it's perfectly logical Satan would want to present a gospel that doesn't require suffering, so our natural bodies can reject any call to suffer. That is why we must not be deceived by any doctrine that focuses on the gift of salvation, but doesn't talk about the cost of following Jesus. This is also why we must question any doctrine that doesn't require Jesus to be Lord of our life. When Jesus isn't our Lord, it's much easier to say "no" to following Him everywhere and obeying all His commands. Our natural body and pride will resist doing anything that requires us to first humble ourselves to Jesus' lordship.

Jesus also said,

> *"Enter by the narrow gate; for wide is the gate and broad is the way that leads to destruction, and there are many who go in by it. [How narrow] Because narrow is the gate and [confined] difficult is the way which leads to life, and there are few who find it"* (Matthew 7:13-14).

Satan, as an angel of light, wants you to believe the road that leads to life is wide, safe, and comfortable. Satan is also going to take out all the "ifs" and warnings in the gospel. All the "ifs" and warnings remind us of our responsibility. Satan wants us to believe God has all the responsibility, and we can't mess up. But this is the kind of doctrine that would take the "fear of God" out of anybody who believes this, because they would believe they are saved no matter what they do or by some of the things they have done in Jesus' name. But Jesus said,

> *"Not everyone who says to Me, 'Lord, Lord,' shall enter the kingdom of heaven, but he who does the will of My Father in heaven. Many will say to Me in that day, 'Lord, Lord, have we not prophesied in Your name, cast out demons in Your name, and done many wonders in Your name?' And then I will declare to them, 'I never knew you; depart from Me, you who practice lawlessness!'"* (Matthew 7:21-23).

Satan's watered-down gospel reminds me of what I read about the third president of the United States, Thomas Jefferson. It's documented he didn't believe in the miracles Jesus did in the New Testament or in His resurrection, so he cut them out of his Bible. It became known as the "Jefferson Bible." In the same way, Satan tries to cut out parts of the Gospel, so you only need to be concerned about the easy parts. Satan would be perfectly content with a church building full of members who aren't serious about discipleship, but only appearances. It might be appropriately titled "The Great Deception Gospel," which would fit perfectly with who Satan is.

An angel of light is also going to try to comfort our natural body when we have trouble forgiving others who have hurt us. Paul talked about this in *2 Corinthians 2:10-11*.

> *"Now whom you forgive anything, I also forgive. For [indeed, what I have forgiven, if I have forgiven anything, I did it for your sakes] if indeed I have forgiven anything, I have forgiven that one for your sakes in the presence of Christ, lest Satan should take advantage of us; for we are not ignorant of his devices."*

(Read also *Matthew 18:34-35* and *Mark 11:25-26.)*

Needless to say, the devil's gospel would not include these verses. His gospel would justify bitterness and resentment when it's too hard for us to forgive. He would encourage us to believe God understands, or as I've heard some people say, "I forgive them, but I won't forget what they did." God's forgiveness includes forgetting our sin, so we must also forget as the following scriptures tell us.

> *"As far as the east is from the west, so far has He removed our transgressions from us" (Psalm 103:12).*

> *"Indeed it was for my own peace that I had great bitterness; but You have lovingly delivered my soul from*

the pit of corruption, for You have cast all my sins behind Your back" (Isaiah 30:17).

(Read also *Isaiah 43:25, Isaiah 44:22, Jeremiah 31:34,* and *Jeremiah 50:20.*)

Forgiveness is at the heart of the gospel, and God didn't spare His Son any suffering to make forgiveness possible for us. The cost was high for God, and it's high for us, because we must also forgive as Christ forgave us. An angel of light is going do all he can to water this part of the gospel down, so we can forgive on our terms and not God's.

Final Thoughts on the Devil's Strategy

The devil is crafty and deceptive, and we are never going to get the truth from him. This is why it's important for each of us to know God's truth, so we can quickly recognize anything that's not true. If we don't know or live by the truth, we are not only going to live a very unproductive life in God's eyes, we are also going to miss out on all the peace and joy we could experience if we did know and live by the truth. In the seven letters to the seven churches in *Revelation Chapters 2* and *3*, four of the letters talk about Satan. See *Revelation 2:9-10, Revelation 2:13, Revelation 2:24,* and *Revelation 3:9.*

In two of those four letters, *Revelation 2:9* and *3:9*, it says some church members are a synagogue of Satan. In the same way, Satan can be working in our churches today. This can be intimidating for new believers, which is why they need mature believers to help them understand how to recognize false prophets and false teachers. This is also why it's important for any church to have a sound doctrine and a serious discipleship process that produces mature disciples, who, in turn, make other mature disciples who know the gospel and live by it. Each of us is in the most important battle of our lives; the fight that will determine our eternal destination, which is why we must put on the full armor of God and know how to use it.

Twice in the first letter to Timothy, Paul wrote about how people had departed or turned aside from the faith. Any doctrine that says we can't fall away is not a true doctrine. The letters Paul, Peter, James, Jude, and John wrote all have clear warnings in them. And they wouldn't have been included if they weren't true. Below are two of those verses.

> *"Now the Spirit expressly says that in latter times some will depart from the faith, giving heed to deceiving spirits and doctrines of demons" (1 Timothy 4:1).*

> *"For some have already turned aside after Satan" (1 Timothy 5:15).*

Paul wrote specifically about the danger of giving a new convert or novice in the faith more responsibility than they were ready for in *1 Timothy 3:6*. *"Not a [new convert] novice, lest being puffed up with pride he fall into the same condemnation as the devil."*

Satan is a master at getting us to puff up ourselves with pride when we get promoted beyond our maturity level and start thinking too highly of ourselves. Paul didn't spare any words when he said a person like this would fall under the same condemnation as the devil. Because of the enemy's relentless attack through deception and lies, Paul was always concerned about the strength of each of the churches that started in the different cities where he shared the gospel. He knew they would face trials and persecution that would test their faith. Paul even sent Timothy to Thessalonica one time to find out how they were doing when he couldn't endure it any longer. *"For this reason, when I could no longer endure it, I sent to know your faith, lest by some means the tempter had tempted you, and our labor might be in vain" (1 Thessalonians 3:5).*

No matter how mature we grow in our faith, we can never let down our guard. Paul warns everyone in his letter to the Ephesians we are not to give an opportunity or place to the devil. *"Be angry, and do not sin: do not let the sun go down on your wrath, nor give [an opportunity] place to the devil" (Ephesians 4:27).*

Satan is persistent and always looking for an open door or window into our souls, so we must also steadfastly guard our hearts and regularly examine our faith. And if we hold firmly to God and live by His truth, our perseverance will overcome Satan's relentless attacks.

Mike Garst

Chapter 8
What is my Purpose?

Most of us know when we wake up in the morning and have specific tasks we want to do, our day will normally be much more fulfilling when we accomplish what we set out to do. But any time we don't have much to do and piddle the day away, it can make us feel empty and useless. It's the difference between having a purpose and not having a purpose on any given day.

From the beginning, God created human beings to have a purpose. The first part of *Proverbs 29:18* says, *"Where there is no [prophetic vision] revelation, the people cast off restraint;"*

This implies if we don't have a vision from God, we will lack self-control and do whatever feels right at the moment. We would be like the uncontrolled sailboat that goes wherever the wind blows it. But the original *King James Version* says the consequences of not having a vision are even more dangerous. *"Where there is no vision, the people perish."*

This translation says if we have no vision, we will have no real life or good purpose for our life. Knowing that should motivate us, but how do we get a vision from God?

I think the answer to that question is simple, but getting that answer is going to be hard. It's simple because it only requires that we hear and recognize God's voice. But to hear God's voice, we need to invest time and effort into developing an intimate relationship with Him, so we can hear and recognize His voice. This is why we must first seek God and be taught and trained, so we can believe the right things about Him and experience a new birth that lives by the Spirit.

Visions in the Bible

Throughout the scriptures, the Bible tells us about different people who had visions from God. And the most important thing about each of these people is they had to know and experience God before they were able to receive a vision.

Some of these visions from God came in dreams. But not every dream is a vision. Some people had dreams in the Bible that were not visions. Sometimes the dreams were warnings from God or God announcing a judgment. And often it required a godly person to interpret the dream.

Abimelek was warned in a dream not to touch Abraham's wife Sarah (see *Genesis 20:3-6*). The chief cupbearer and baker each had dreams while in prison with Joseph in which God told them their fate, although Joseph had to interpret their dreams for them (see *Genesis 40*). Pharoah also needed Joseph to interpret his dreams (see *Genesis 41*). We can probably assume Pharoah's dreams were also a vision from God for Joseph, because he not only was able to share God's interpretation of the dream, but it gave Joseph a new purpose for his life for at least the next fourteen years. After all, he went from being in prison to being put second in charge of Egypt, because he not only told Pharaoh the interpretation of the dream; he recommended what Pharaoh should do in response to the dream.

If we want to know some of the reasons visions from God are so important to us, we can read about Jacob's dream in *Genesis 28:10-21*, which is the first real vision anybody in the Bible received. It gives three important elements in a God-given vision.

Jacob saw a stairway going from heaven to earth with angels descending and ascending on it. Above the stairway was the Lord and He said to Jacob, *"I am the Lord God of Abraham your father and the God of Isaac; the land on which you lie I will give to you and your descendants" (Genesis 28:13).*

God then said Jacob's descendants would be like the dust of the earth and spread out in every direction and *"in you and in your seed all the families of the earth shall be blessed" (Genesis 28:14).*

Every godly vision we have will enable us and our descendants to be a blessing to many people on the earth. If our vision doesn't have this potential effect, it probably isn't from God. The next verse gives us the next two important elements in a God-given vision. *"Behold, I am with you and will keep you wherever you go, and will bring you back to this land; for I will not leave you until I have done what I have spoken to you" (Genesis 28:15).*

God does not just give us a vision and leave us on our own to carry it out. He is going to be with us to guide us and protect us until it has been accomplished. Another way we can know a vision is from God is when it's way bigger than what we could accomplish on our own. We need to know God will be with us because we don't have the wisdom, power, resources, or the influence to bring it to fruition without Him. If our vision isn't God-sized, and if He's not required to carry it out, then it's not a God-given dream.

God gave Moses his vision through a burning bush in the desert (see *Exodus 3*). It had all three of the elements I just discussed in Jacob's vision. He was to lead the people to the Promised Land so they could inherit many blessings in the land. It was God-sized, because Moses was going to be leading about six hundred thousand men and their families. And God was going to be with Moses. Moses knew how important it was for God to be with them when he said to God after the golden calf incident (see *Exodus 32*), *"If Your Presence does not go with us, do not bring us up from here" (Exodus 33:15).*

Moses wanted no part of the journey if God wasn't involved. And that is the attitude we must have about any God-given vision we have.

There are other stories in the Bible about people with God-given visions. And every one of them includes, to some extent, each of the three elements I've talked about.

My Vision from God

I want to share a vision God gave me in the summer of 2017, which has all three of the elements I've talked about that should be in God-given vision. I also believe it's a great visual of the gospel of Jesus Christ, and it may help you recognize any vision God has given you.

The vision God gave me started a few years earlier when my very close friend, Pastor Bud, shared a vision God gave him, which I've drawn on the next page.

In the top left corner are some of the many attributes of God. To the right of that are the ways we connect with God such as prayer, Bible-reading, worship, Scripture meditation, and obedience. When we do this, we enable God's attributes to flow through us increasingly more to all the people in our life. I connected with that vision, although I sensed God wanted to show me more about what it meant.

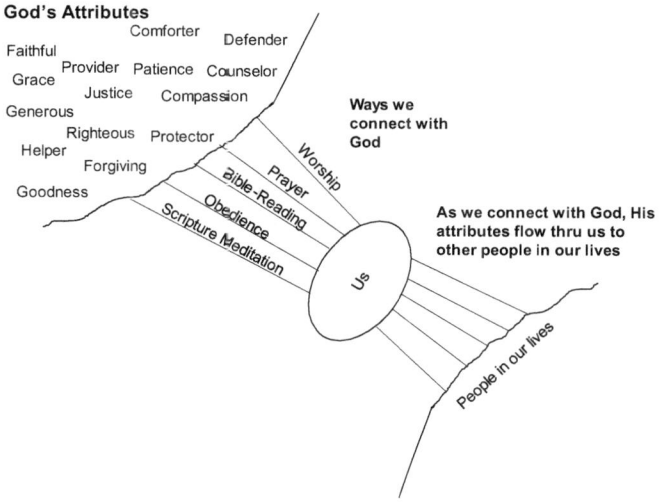

In June, 2017, my wife Susie and I took a trip to Colorado, a place we both love because of the beautiful, majestic Rocky Mountains. We went specifically to visit a few places, see a few people we knew in Colorado, and to stay a few days in a large cabin close to the Great Sand Dunes. The cabin was built by several brothers in Christ from my church home in Carrollton, Texas when I lived there. The cabin, which is called the Zapata Cabin, took about twelve years to complete by these brothers who would take long weekends every month or so to drive eleven or twelve hours from Dallas to the cabin location, bringing most of the building materials with them. They worked on building it a couple of days and then drove back to Dallas. It's an amazing story of patience and perseverance, because somebody tried to burn it down shortly before it was completed. But by the mercy and grace of God, the fire was discovered and put out before too much damage was done.

  I had been to Hooper, Colorado, which is about twenty miles away from the cabin about ten years prior to visit my good friend and brother in Christ, Bill, who was a pastor for a church there at the time. He had shown the cabin to me during that visit when it was a little over half done, and I wanted to stay there sometime.

A few months before Susie and I went on our trip, a friend, and one of the owners, of the cabin told me they were looking for people to stay at the cabin more often, so I jumped at the chance to go. Little did I know the journey we took to get to the cabin enabled God to show me some of what I believe He wanted me to see. After we flew to Denver, we rented a car to visit some friends in the Denver area, spent a night outside Colorado Springs, and then went to see the Royal Gorge. After that, we traveled to the Zapata Cabin. What surprised me on our drive there was the name of the river that ran along the side of the road. It was the Arkansas River, and I didn't realize it started in Colorado until then.

One of the places I visited after getting to the cabin was a place called Zapata Falls (which is where the name of the cabin came from), only a few miles away. The water from Zapata Falls comes from the snow melting on the mountains. In June, most of the snow still left is on the top of the mountains, so we got to see snow-capped mountains most of us have seen in pictures. I realized the water in the creek flowing about fifty yards away from the Cabin came from Zapata Falls. I didn't try to follow that creek, but assumed it flowed into another stream of water that eventually fed into the Arkansas River. Later in the trip, as we traveled back toward Denver, I continued to notice the creeks and rivers running along several of the roads in the mountains. Those were the last thoughts I had of that experience until about six weeks later when I flew to Germany to help lead a couple of Baseball Camps for Jesus I had been doing all but two years since 2001. God had touched my heart at that first camp, and I knew I was supposed to keep going back. Because most of my ancestors are from Germany, that should not have surprised me. From the book of Nehemiah in the Bible, we know Nehemiah went back to build up the walls of Jerusalem in his home country. Therefore, it wouldn't be much of a stretch to think God would want me to go back to

Germany to help rebuild the church there.

If you've ever flown to Europe, you know you typically leave the USA in the afternoon or early evening, and you arrive in Germany in the morning, which is about midnight or later USA time. Many people typically get very little sleep on the plane, and the best thing to get adjusted to the earlier time zone in Germany is not to take a nap after you get there. Instead, try to stay awake. Except for dozing off a few minutes in the car from Hamburg to Aurich, the town where we held the first baseball camp, I didn't sleep much. Therefore, I was looking forward to getting a good night's sleep that first night at my host home. To my surprise, God put a vision on my heart at 3:00 AM that I knew I had to get up and draw. It was such a powerful vision I couldn't go back to sleep.

The River of God

In the vision, God brought to my mind the snow-capped mountains in Colorado and the creeks and rivers flowing from them, along with the vision my friend Bud shared with me a few years earlier. The illustration on the next page shows the first part of the vision, and I'll walk you through the rest of the vision in the next few pages.

Mike Garst

Snowed Capped Mountains Represent God's Attributes of Love
Blue lines represent God's attributes of love as streams of water flowing to a river that represents us

First, there are many mountain peaks thirteen thousand to fourteen thousand feet high in Colorado. God showed me these snow-capped mountain peaks represented His attributes of love in the vision, or the different ways God shows His love to us. This includes His mercy, grace, forgiveness, patience, kindness, compassion, comfort, goodness, gentleness, justice, righteousness, discipline, joy, peace, encouragement, faithfulness, help, generosity, provision, counsel, protection, teaching, and training. Then I saw tiny streams running from each of these snow-covered mountaintops into creeks, and the creeks into rivers like the Arkansas River, which flows all the way to the Mississippi River that flows into the Gulf of Mexico. See illustration on the next page.

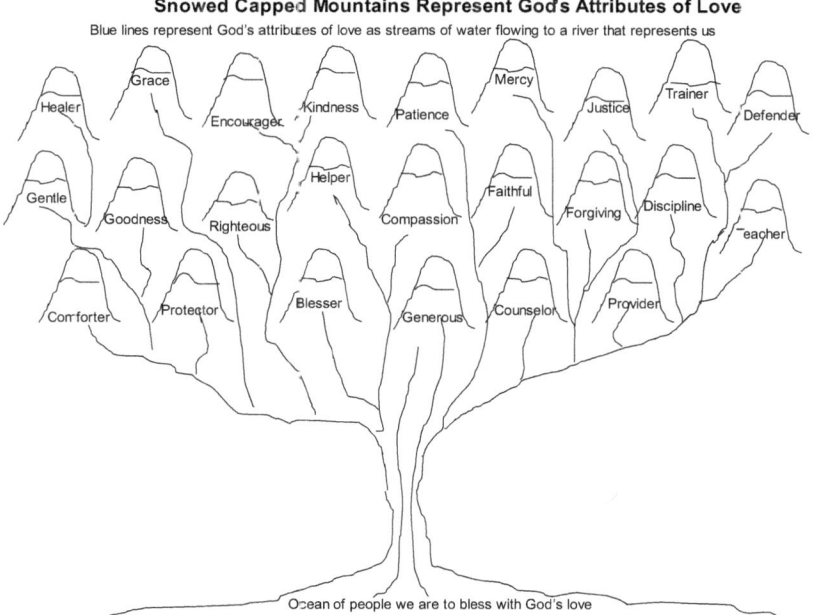

Snowed Capped Mountains Represent God's Attributes of Love
Blue lines represent God's attributes of love as streams of water flowing to a river that represents us

Ocean of people we are to bless with God's love

God then revealed to me we are that river. In *Genesis 1:26-27,* God said, *"Let Us make man in Our image, according to Our likeness; .... So God created man in His own image; in the image of God He created him; male and female He created them."*

From the beginning, God created us in His image and likeness, and He blessed Adam and Eve so they could bless others. We were created to be a river of God's love, meaning the grace that flows to us from God is supposed to flow through us to all the people in our lives, along with all the other attributes of God's love. That is our basic purpose, and it is the primary way we can be a blessing to all the people in our lives. Yet God created each of us differently, with various gifts and talents, so we could use those gifts and talents in unique ways to help us be that river. God didn't want us all to be exactly alike in appearance or gifting. He wanted us to each be unique as much as possible. This enables each of us to better understand and connect with certain people because of our experiences in life, especially the people we encounter daily.

One of the reasons the picture of the snow-covered mountaintops is so important is because most people don't really know what God's love looks like. When I asked the youth at the Baseball Camps to help me identify God's attributes of love, they had a difficult time naming or even describing them. I believe this is because we talk a lot about God's love, but we fail to put it into the appropriate words that help us understand how we experience it. We live in a world that uses the word "love" in many ways, but the world's definition of love is very self-centered in many cases. It includes the many things that make our flesh happy, but not necessarily our soul. Yet our flesh is not going to inherit eternal life. Only our soul and spirit will receive this blessing. After I helped the youth at the camps identify some of the attributes of God's love, I asked them if those were the attributes of a good God. They were quick to agree they were. Who would think a God with all those attributes of love wasn't good? Those are all the attributes of love we wished our parents and other key people in our lives had while we were growing up.

The next question I asked was, "Is this God trustworthy?"

Again, all the youth in the groups I was with said, "Yes!"

Resisting God

Another important thing I did in the early part of 2017 was to read a book, *Resisting Happiness* by Matthew Kelly, recommended to me by one of my brothers in Christ where I work, Steve, who is also in one of my small groups. Matthew said when we resist God, we resist happiness, which means we are resisting His love. This is another way of saying we don't trust God, including all His attributes being shown in the picture of the snow-capped mountains.

For example:

- We become impatient because we don't trust God to be patient.
- We're greedy and selfish because we don't believe God is generous.
- We don't help others because we don't trust that God will help us.
- We slander, gossip, and manipulate because we don't believe God is just.
- We don't give people another chance because we don't believe God is gracious.
- We're not merciful because we don't believe God is merciful.
- We self-medicate because we don't believe God can heal us.
- We're not faithful because we don't trust that God is faithful.
- We defend ourselves because we don't believe God will vindicate us.

There are many more examples, but hopefully you can see everything I listed shuts off the flow of God's love through us as the result of us not trusting God for some basic need we have. I've listed many of the things we do when we resist God's love or don't trust Him in the illustration on the next page. What God was showing me was sin is essentially resisting God's love and not trusting Him. All the things I showed in the drawing on the next page that keep God's love from flowing through us are the opposite of one of His attributes of love. When we resist God's love, it's impossible to serve and show love to others. Whether we are angry, selfish, greedy, lying, cheating, arrogant, insensitive, or any of the other ways we show we don't trust God, it is physiologically impossible for us to love other people at the same time.

God then showed me when we resist any of His attributes of love, we essentially become a big valve that shuts off the flow of His river of love through us. As a result, the people in our lives we were designed to bless with God's love can't experience it through us. As a result, it's going to be very difficult for us to receive a vision from God that blesses other people. The bad news every one of us is born with innate tendencies that lead us to resist God's love. Nobody is exempt. But there is good news for all of us!

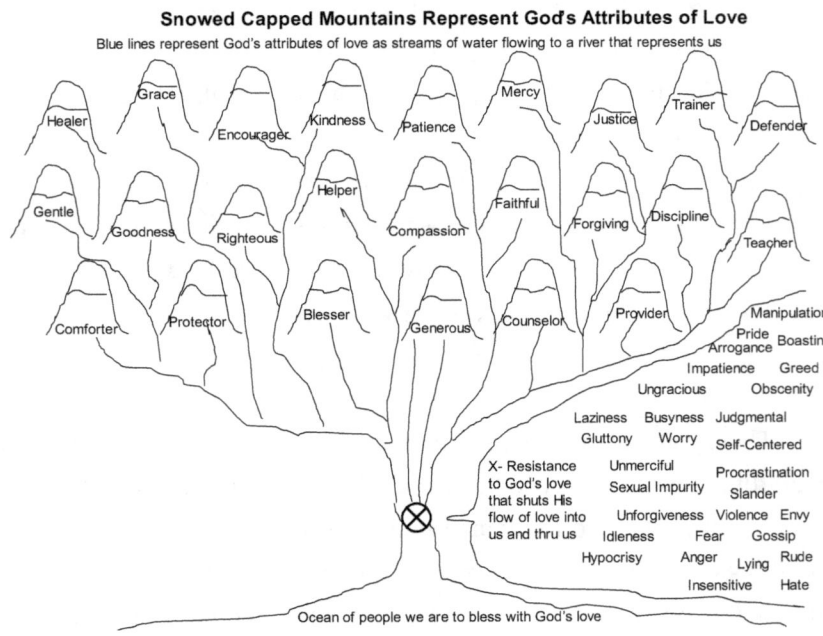

Overcoming Resistance to God

In the next part of the vision God gave me, He showed me how to overcome our resistance to His love. This is where Christianity is set apart from every other form of religion in the world. Paul wrote in *Romans 5:6*, *"For when we were still without strength, [at the right time] in due time Christ died for the ungodly."*

Without Christ, we are powerless to show God's love, but every other religion in the world believes we are not powerless, and we can defeat all the things I just listed as part of our sin nature with our strength alone. But the foundation of Christianity is God had to sacrifice His perfect sinless Son on the Cross and raise Him from the dead to make us right with God and make His strength available to those who believe that and trust in Him.

Many people in the world don't believe Jesus' blood needed to flow from the cross for us to be forgiven. They believe God will forgive us just because He's a forgiving God. Yet the writer of the book of Hebrews said, *"And according to the law almost all things are [cleansed] purified with blood, and without shedding of blood there is no [forgiveness] remission"* (Hebrew 9:22).

God is a holy God, and the kingdom of heaven is a holy place with not even a tiny corner of evil in it. We can't spend eternity with God unless we are spotless and holy like God. We become spotless and holy when we trust Jesus as our Lord and Savior, believing He had to die by shedding His blood on the cross for our sins, that He rose from the dead, and that we must then surrender our lives completely to Him. This is the only way we can overcome our resistance to God and enable His attributes of love to flow through us. The closed valve (see illustration on the next page), which I represented as an "X," essentially turns to a "T" that represents trusting God. This opens the valve and enables His love to flow through us increasingly more as we keep trusting Him more and more.

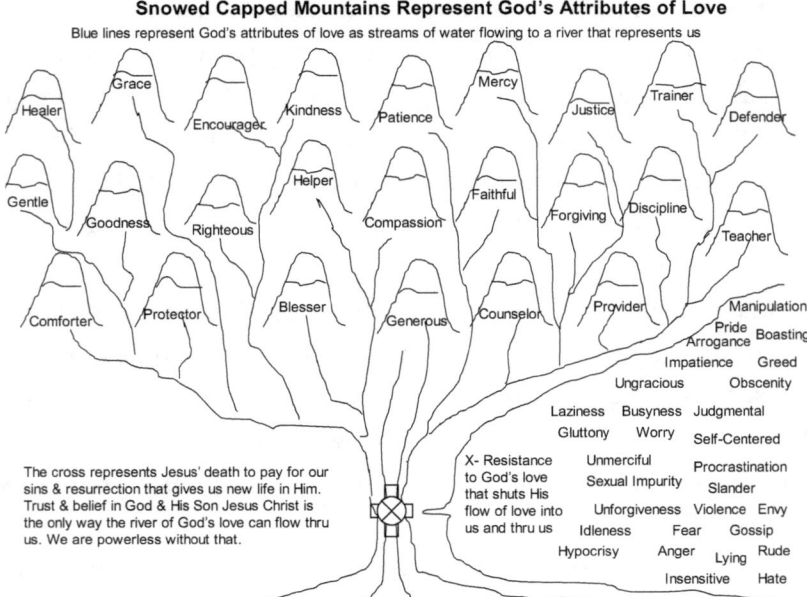

Final Thoughts on Purpose

When I read Dorothy Clarke Wilson's book *Granny Brand: Her Story*, it said the vision God had given Granny and her husband Jesse early on when they felt the call of God to take the gospel to five unreached and uncivilized mountain ranges in India was "If thou canst believe, thou shall see the glory of God. [9]" Granny thought of that vision often, especially after Jesse's death, to keep her going to the end of her life. And interestingly, the number of mountain ranges grew from five to seven by the end of her life.

If you have been struggling with having a vision and knowing the purpose for your life, I hope and pray this chapter has helped you not only to see a visual of the gospel of Jesus, but also to understand each of us is being called to become an ever-increasing river of God's attributes of love

---

[9] Granny Brand Her Story, Dorothy Clarke Wilson, Paul Brand Publishing, Seattle WA, 1976, Pages 117 and 153

in everything we say and do to all the people in our lives, using the unique gifts, talents and resources He gives each of us. We each can do this, not with our strength alone, but only with God's strength that comes to us and flows through us because of Christ's resurrected life in us.

Whether we know it or not, we are in ministry all the time just like Jesus—at home, at the place(s) we work, wherever our recreational activities take us, when we are on vacation, when we are interacting with neighbors, and whatever else we do or wherever else we go. Everyone we encounter each day should experience whatever attribute of God's love they need during the time we are interacting with them. If they need us to show kindness, we show kindness. If they need understanding, we need to give them understanding. If they need forgiveness from us, we forgive them when they confess and repent. If they need grace, we give them grace. If they need us to be patient, we are patient. If they need compassion, we are compassionate. When people experience God's love through us, they are much more likely to want what we have at some point in their lives if they don't trust God yet. And having an intimate relationship with Christ that continually grows is what enables us to hear God's voice, to hear what He is speaking to us, and to recognize and understand the vision He gives us.

When anyone has this foundation, God will open doors of opportunity for them to minister to those people they are uniquely designed and prepared to reach. It will keep them going strong all the way to their last breath.

The vision of the river of God I've talked about in this chapter and the doors of ministry that have opened for me in Germany have set the course for me for the rest of my life. I'm convinced God ultimately wants another Reformation in Germany that is much deeper and more effective than the first one that started in 1519 with Martin Luther. And God is using sports like baseball to bring young people together, so they can

Mike Garst

learn more about Him and experience Him during the Baseball Camps.

At the time of this writing, God has worked through me to start three Baseball Camps. The first two had their fifteenth and eighth camps respectively in the summer of 2023. The third camp started in the summer of 2022 and had its second camp in the summer of 2023. All indications are each will continue to grow.

God is also leading and encouraging me to start other camps through people I've built relationships with through the Baseball Camps I've attended since 2001. These camps are not just an event with a local church; they involve the whole community. It's exciting to be part of something that eventually could sweep through all of Germany and even all of Europe. I'm honored God would use me in any way to make this happen, and I don't see an end to my part in helping bring it to fruition, no matter how old I get. Like Granny Brand, even if my friends need to carry me to these camps, I'm going to be a part of them until my last breath. I may not see this second Reformation in my lifetime, but I'm confident God will be pleased if I do my part to enable it to happen someday in His perfect timing. My prayer is each of you will trust God completely so you can receive a vision from Him that will encourage you to finish your life strong in the Lord.

Chapter 9
What Is the Current State of My Mind?

What if somebody said you were only using 10% of the resources available to you, and unless you made a radical change in your priorities and the way you live, you would never use more than that? I hope that would get my attention. Since it would be rare for anyone not to want to use all the resources available to them, the real question is why would any of us only use a small percentage of our resources? And if our mind is the most powerful resource we have, why would we not use as much of it as possible?

Scientists tell us the human brain has two million megabytes of capacity, and studies have shown very few people use more than 10-15% of their brain's capacity. Even if this underestimates how much of our mind's full potential we are using by 50-100%, it would still indicate we are using no more than 20-30% of what's possible.

This should be especially disturbing to Christians who have been commanded to *"love the Lord your God with all your heart, with all your soul, with all your mind, and with all your strength" (Mark 12:30).*

This verse indicates we are to love God with 100% of our mind's capacity. Or, at the very least, we should be moving in that direction. If we are not using very much of our brain's potential, it would be worth some effort to determine why. Then we could make the necessary adjustments to use this valuable resource more effectively. Anything we do as Christians to love God with more of our mind should increase our faith, our testimony, and our effectiveness in sharing and showing the love of God to all the people in our lives each day. It would be hard to argue the world doesn't need to witness God's love around us more every day. It's also difficult to believe we could really finish this life as strong as possible if we were not continuously developing and using as much of our minds as possible.

Parable of the Talents

Jesus used the Parable of the Talents in *Matthew 25* to show what the kingdom of heaven is like. Three servants were given talents by a man in this parable. It says, *"And to one he gave five talents, to another two, and to another one, to each according to his own ability;"* (*Matthew 25:15*).

The man didn't give each servant the same number of talents, but gave to each according to his ability. The first two servants used their talents and received the same commendation. *"His lord said to him, 'Well done, good and faithful servant; you have been faithful over a few things, I will make you ruler over many things. Enter into the joy of your lord.'"* *(Matthew 25:21, 23)*.

Let's read what was written about the servant who received one talent.

> *"Then he who had received the one talent came and said, 'Lord, I knew you to be a hard man, reaping where you have not sown, and gathering where you have not scattered seed. And I was afraid, and went and hid your talent in the ground. Look, there you have what is yours.'"*

Notice the servant called the man "Lord," which indicated he had authority. Yet the servant was not only afraid of the man who gave him the talent, he hid the talent in the ground. The man's response to the servant is harsh. Here is what he first said.

> *"But his lord answered and said to him, 'You wicked and lazy servant, you knew that I reap where I have not sown, and gather where I have not scattered seed. So you ought to have deposited my money with the bankers, and at my coming I would have received back my own with interest.'" (Matthew 25:26-27).*

It's bad enough to be called wicked or lazy, but to be called both would put us in very bad company. Since this is a parable, the "lord" in this verse is God. As such, God is saying this to everyone who doesn't use the talent(s) given to them. Now some might argue God is only talking about money in this parable. But it would be hard to argue it would be okay to waste any physical or mental talent God gives us, especially our minds.

Why would it be wicked for us not to use our mind? The second part of this verse says the servant knew God reaps and gathers where He has not sown or scattered. This can be a puzzling verse initially for us, but it appears to be saying even though God sows seed, He also expects us to sow some seed, too. And even though the servant knew this, he chose not to do it. Why would any of us not do something we know God expects us to do? Could it be because we believe:

a) God isn't good or trustworthy, and wouldn't give us talents worth developing?
b) God wouldn't teach or train us, or provide any resources to help us develop or use our mind?
c) God wouldn't be patient or gracious with us while we are trying to develop and use our mind?

These are only a few of things we might be showing about our belief in God if we don't use what God gives us. When we don't believe or know God, we will end up like this servant and think God is demanding but unfair, and we could never please Him. It would be the equivalent to thinking God was more like the Egyptian slave masters who demanded the Israelites make as many bricks each day without straw as they had when the straw was provided (see *Exodus 5*).

Why was this servant also called *"lazy"*? *Verse 27* gives us at least some of the reason. Knowing what God expects and then choosing not to use the talent God gave him, he should have at least given it to somebody else to use and increase. It wouldn't take much effort to take money to the bank and ask them to invest it. And even though we can't give our mind to somebody else to use, notice what it says in the next two verses.

> *"So take the talent from him, and give it to him who has ten talents. For to everyone who has, more will be given, and he will have abundance; but from him who does not have, even what he has will be taken away" (Matthew 25:28-29).*

Have you noticed how some people seem to have exceptional abilities when it comes to using their minds? These verses imply God will take gifts and talents from people who don't use them and give them to other people who will use them. When it comes to spiritual gifts, the apostle talks about them in *1 Corinthians 12*. At the end of the chapter, he summaries them. *"And God has appointed these in the church: first apostles, second prophets, third teachers, after that miracles, then gifts of healings, helps, administrations, varieties of tongues" (1 Corinthians 12:28).*

Even in the church, you will find some people functioning in multiple gifts while others are only using some of them. This could be due to the maturity of a person, or it could be because of a wrong understanding of what's expected of them. Regardless, when somebody isn't using their gifts, it appears God will give those gifts to someone in the faith who is using and developing the talents given to them. The old adage, "If you don't use it, you'll lose it" is definitely true in this parable. But we now have a new truth we need to remember, which is "If you use it, it will not only grow, but you will get what others don't use."

What are the consequences of not using the gifts and talents God gives us? *"And cast the unprofitable servant into the outer darkness. There will be weeping and gnashing of teeth" (Matthew 25:30).*

In other words, the servant was thrown into Hell. He not only lost his talent, he lost his soul. God expects us to make good use of what He gives us. The consequences are serious and eternal!

Laziness

God has promised in the Old Testament and New Testament He can be found. It just requires that we seek Him wholeheartedly. The only reason we don't do something wholeheartedly is because we are either lazy or we don't believe it's important to do (often referred to as apathetic). When we are lazy, we don't want to put in the effort required to do something, or we are looking for the easiest way to do something or not to do it at all. We all have this tendency. If we don't realize we have a natural drift toward laziness in us, we really don't know ourselves. It's a part of the sin nature in everybody. The Book of Proverbs addresses laziness more than any other book in the Bible. Here are a few of the verses.

> *"The desire of the lazy man kills him, for his hands refuse to labor" (Proverbs 21:25).*

> *"The lazy man says, 'There is a lion outside! I shall be slain in the streets!'" (Proverbs 22:13 & 26:13).*

> *"I went by the field of the lazy man, and by the vineyard of*

> *the man devoid of understanding; and there it was, all overgrown with thorns; its surface was covered with nettles; its stone wall was broken down. When I saw it, I considered it well; I looked on it and received instruction: a little sleep, a little slumber, a little folding of the hands to rest; So shall your poverty come like a prowler, and your need like an armed man" (Proverbs 24:30-34).*

Laziness is a serious enemy of a sound mind that will kill you, as *Proverbs 21:25* says. It looks for excuses not to do something, as *Proverbs 22:13* and *26:13* tell us. *Proverbs 24:30-34* gives a good visual of what a lazy man's home and property will look like. Verse *thirty* tells us a lazy man and a man devoid of understanding will have the same fate. This makes sense, because a man of understanding would know the consequences of being lazy and would develop the discipline to form the habits that would help him reach his goal. In this case, it would be knowing God with all his heart, mind, and soul.

The Mind Is a Talent

Our minds are our most precious resource. It's one of the key things that separates us from animals. Our minds enable us to do countless things animals will never be able to do. Even though Jesus compared us to sheep, we can still insult human beings when we talk about how smart some animals are, as if they were as smart or smarter than people. The big difference, though, is not what an animal or human can do in a particular moment, it's the fact the human mind's capability and capacity can grow because it can learn new things. Humans can read, hear, and see. Plus, their minds can process all of it. As a result, they can comprehend and grow in knowledge and wisdom. Even Luke made sure we knew Jesus as a man had to grow in wisdom: *"And the Child grew and became strong in spirit, filled with wisdom; and the grace of God was upon Him" (Luke 2:40).*

Because we are also spiritual beings, we have access to God and His wisdom, as well as many of His attributes. Our mind can be used to do incredibly wonderful things that can have a very positive impact on many people. But the mind can also be used to do incredibly destructive things that can have a very negative impact on many people. God will reward those who rightly use this incredible gift of the mind, and He will rightly punish those who don't. But He leaves the choice in our hands.

Sound Mind

You may be wondering how people will ever know how much of their mind's capacity they are using, or how we can ever know if we are loving God with all our minds. Before discussing that, let's explore what it takes to have a "sound mind."

The apostle Paul wrote to Timothy. *"For God has not given us a spirit of fear, but of power and of love and of a sound mind" (2 Timothy 1:7).*

It's interesting to see the different words used in place of *"sound mind"* in other translations. The New International Version (NIV) says *"self-discipline,"* and the English Standard Version (ESV) says *"self-control."* The German "Hoffnung Fur Alle" translation uses a word that translates to *"level-headedness."* Apparently, the original Hebrew or Greek word used here could not be directly translated to just one English word, which is not unusual in the Hebrew or Greek language. But if you think about it, it would be hard to have self-discipline, self-control, or level-headedness without a sound mind and vice versa.

We need self-discipline so we can use our time wisely to feed our minds with the truth. We need self-control and level-headedness to live by the truth and not function on emotions or information that is not true. This would be much easier to do if our minds were filled only with the truth. Yet all of us have read, heard, seen, experienced, and believed things not in line with God's truth. This can cause our minds to have a mixture of God's truth and lies. When we believe anything not in line with God's truth, we will essentially function with an unsound mind. This is because all our words and actions will be the result of what we first believe in our minds and then believe in our hearts. For example, if we are taught to strike back when we are hit by somebody else, this will become our natural response all the time. Or if somebody says words to us that hurt our feelings, and we've learned to retaliate with hurtful words, that will become our natural response. But neither of these would be in line with God's truth or ways.

The best definition I can find in the Bible of a sound mind is:

> *"Finally, brethren, whatever things are true, whatever things are noble, whatever things are just, whatever things are pure, whatever things are lovely, whatever things are of good report, if there is any virtue and if there is anything praiseworthy—meditate on these things. The things which you learned and received and heard and saw in me, these do, and the God of peace will be with you"*
> *(Philippians 4:8-9).*

As you can see, Paul tells us to meditate on all the things he wrote in verse *eight*. It would be good for all of us to not only meditate on this verse so we could know what is says, but to do so until we've memorized it. If a person only functioned based on what these two verses say, they would not only have a sound mind, they would become more like Christ.

The one thing about Jesus that isn't talked about very much is He had a sound mind. He was also perfect and *"increased in wisdom and stature, and in favor with God and men" (Luke 2:52).*

This gives us good reason to believe He was using 100% of His mind. There were no evil thoughts in Jesus' mind. He knew and functioned only on the truth. He was tempted by the devil three times while in the desert, but He never gave in to any of those temptations. He was always able to speak the truth in those situations (see *Matthew 4:1-11* and *Luke 4:1-13*). Because Jesus can now live in us via the Holy Spirit, and we can be transformed into His likeness, we can have the mind of Christ. *"Who has known the mind of the Lord so as to instruct him? But we have the mind of Christ" (1 Corinthians 2:16).*

This indicates anyone who professes faith in Christ is deceiving themselves anytime they say they can't memorize scriptures or do what is right. Jesus studied and memorized Scripture and referenced it all the time. Even at twelve years old, *"all who heard Him were astonished at His understanding and answers" (Luke 2:47).*

Plus, He always did what was right because He did what His Father wanted Him to do. If He's living in us, we will also be able to know the truth like Jesus and do what is right. The reason we wouldn't is that we are either being too lazy to learn and train ourselves to do what is right, or we are putting other things less important in God's eyes ahead of it. We would be consciously not using the talent given to us, thus letting it go to waste.

Corrupt Mind

The apostle Paul wrote to Timothy about men who were teaching false doctrines. He said they were *"useless wranglings of men of <u>corrupt</u> [my emphasis] minds and destitute of the truth, who suppose that godliness is a means of gain. From such withdraw yourself" (1 Timothy 6:5).*

Paul also wrote to Timothy, *"Now as Jannes and Jambres resisted Moses, so do these also resist the truth: men of corrupt minds, disapproved concerning the faith;" (2 Timothy 3:8).*

A corrupt mind is not only destitute of the truth, it also resists it! What is interesting about the truth is it's not complex. *"But I fear, lest somehow, as the serpent deceived Eve by his craftiness, so your minds may be corrupted from the simplicity that is in Christ" (2 Corinthians 11:3).*

We don't need to have great intelligence to follow Christ; we just need to trust He's just and righteous, and obey His simple commands. Peter and John were uneducated, but they trusted Jesus. *"Now when they saw the boldness of Peter and John, and perceived that they were uneducated and untrained men, they marveled. And they realized that they had been with Jesus" (Acts 4:13).*

If our mind is corrupt, it will also lead to a corrupt heart. Then the words from our mouth will also be corrupt. As Jesus said, *"A good man out of the good treasure of his heart brings forth good; and an evil man out of the evil treasure of his heart brings forth evil. For out of the abundance of the heart his mouth speaks" (Luke 6:45).*

God will not be pleased with any corrupt words that come out of our mouths. Instead, as Paul wrote, *"Let no corrupt word proceed out of your mouth, but what is good for necessary edification, that it may impart grace to the hearers" (Ephesians 4:29).*

Our words are to help build people up, which includes speaking truth in love to them so they may be challenged and encouraged. Every word from our mouth is important because of what Jesus said. *"But I say to you that for every idle word men may speak, they will give account of it in the day of judgment. For by your words you will be justified, and by your words you will be condemned" (Matthew 12:36-37).*

This is why it's so important to confess and repent of anything we say that doesn't glorify or honor God, so He can forgive us and forget what we said.

Our Mind Versus Computers

It's interesting our mind functions similar to a computer in many ways. When a computer's operating system and software programs are working correctly, it produces results as designed. But what happens to a computer when the operating system or software is corrupt? It can no longer function as it was designed to operate. What is also interesting to think about is our reaction to software that is corrupt versus a mind that is corrupt. I don't know of anybody who continues to use a computer with a corrupt operating system or software in it, because it either won't work at all, or it won't work correctly. Instead, they replace it with new software as soon as possible so they can have a reliable computer system. Yet, when we take information into our minds that isn't true (i.e., corrupt), we are much more likely not to do anything about it initially. We either don't think or realize it's a serious problem, or we don't understand it's going to eventually cause us to respond in a way that will not be right in God's eyes, but likely will bring unnecessary stress or trouble into our lives.

It only takes one little corrupt spot in a computer program to corrupt the whole program. Like one rotten apple can spoil the whole barrel, we only need to believe one lie to make our thinking corrupt. This is why it's so important to live in a community that values the truth so much it quickly rebukes and corrects anything not in line with God's truth. This is essentially what the church is called to do. And when the church doesn't do this, the whole church will become corrupt. Paul wrote to the Galatians, *"A little leaven leavens the whole lump" (Galatians 5:9* – See also *1 Corinthians 5:6*).

In the same way, a little corruption will corrupt everything. This is why God was not only angry with Achan when he took some of the devoted things in Jericho after the Israelites had destroyed the city, but he was angry with all the children of Israel since He specifically told them through Joshua that everything in the city was to be devoted to the Lord (see *Joshua 6:17-19*).

"But the children of Israel [acted unfaithfully] committed

> *a trespass regarding the accursed [devoted] things, for Achan the son of Carmi, the son of [Zimri] Zabdi, the son of Zerah, of the tribe of Judah, took of the accursed things; so the anger of the Lord burned against the children of Israel" (Joshua 7:1).*

This disobedience, or corruption, was not only costly to Achan, but to his entire family and other Israelites. *"And the men of Ai struck down about thirty-six men, for they chased them from before the gate as far as Shebarim, and struck them down on the descent" (Joshua 7:5).*

Joshua confirmed this later. *"Did not Achan the son of Zerah [acted unfaithfully] commit a trespass in the [devoted] accursed thing, and wrath fell on all the congregation of Israel? And that man did not perish alone in his iniquity" (Joshua 22:20).*

Our natural thinking will question why God was so severe in His judgment on Achan and his family. But God is holy and expects complete obedience to His commands (i.e., no corruption), and all the Israelites knew upfront not to take the *"accursed (devoted) things."* Achan's action was willful disobedience. The writer of Hebrews wrote about willful disobedience. *"For if we sin willfully after we have received the knowledge of the truth, there no longer remains a sacrifice for sins, but a certain fearful expectation of judgment, and fiery indignation which will devour the adversaries" (Hebrews 10:26-27).*

You must also wonder how Achan was able to take the *"accursed (devoted) things"* without anybody seeing him do it, or without his family knowing about it. This means we must always speak up if we see anything that looks corrupt in the body of Christ, especially since we could suffer the consequences of other people's sin.

The writer of Hebrews wrote, *"Therefore, since we are receiving a kingdom which cannot be shaken, let us have grace, by which we may serve God acceptably with reverence and godly fear. For our God is a consuming fire" (Hebrews 12:28-29).*

It's a very serious commitment to follow Christ, one that requires we *"serve God acceptably with reverence and godly fear."* This is why our minds must be purified from any corruption, so we can live by grace and quickly confess and repent when the Holy Spirit exposes any lies we've believed. We know that God will forgive if *"My people who are called by My name will humble themselves, and pray and seek My face, and turn from their wicked ways, then I will hear from heaven, and will forgive their sin and heal their land" (2 Chronicles 7:14).*

What Is Truth?

We live in a time when many people believe truth is relative, meaning what is true for us may not be true for them, and it's okay. But by definition, truth is factual, so it can't be an opinion. What we experience doesn't define the truth; it is only facts about things that happened to us. This is why the Bible was not written to reflect what people understood or experienced. It was written based on facts about God and the events covered in the Bible. Some people claim many things in the Bible didn't happen. Yet, I'm not aware of anybody having proved they didn't. Regardless, if there is a God, He will hold us accountable to the truth. *"For He is coming, for He is coming to judge the earth. He shall judge the world with righteousness, And the peoples with His truth" (Psalm 96:13).*

Our eternal destiny will be dependent on the truth. If the atheists are right, then we have nothing to look forward to except to die and decay. If the Bible is true, we have either an eternity of indescribable peace and joy to look forward to, if we know the truth and live by it fully, or we have Hell to look forward to.

Paul writes, *"To the pure all things are pure, but to those who are defiled and unbelieving nothing is pure; but even their mind and conscience are defiled" (Titus 1:15).*

This is an interesting verse to take apart. *"To the pure all things are pure"* could possibly be written to say, "Those who believe the truth only want to live by the truth." The second part of the verse might be written to say, "Those who act corruptly determine what is true for them and live according to it." It's another way of saying we do what we believe in our minds and hearts, which may or may not be based on God's truth.

If we go back to the example of the computer program, we know if a software program has more than one corrupt area, we must fix all of them to get the software program to function soundly. It's the same way in our minds. If we believe in our minds many things that are not true, we will not be able to have a sound mind until we purge out all those untruths and replace them with the truth. This is why it can take a long time to get a sound mind if our minds are full of lies we've believed over the years. This is also why it's important to raise children in the truth. Otherwise, their minds can be filled with so many lies it may take a long time for them to "unlearn" the lies and replace them with the truth that will enable them to function soundly. This could be the reason it's so hard for some people to realize they need Jesus as their Lord and Savior, and why we must be so patient with them. As our minds become more and more corrupt, our hearts will resist the truth and become like the seed that fell on hard ground in the Parable of the Sower. *"Satan comes immediately and takes away the word that was sown in their hearts" (Mark 4:15).*

We can hear the truth, but unless our hearts and minds are humble enough to receive it, think about it and act on it, it can disappear quickly.

Benefits of a Sound Mind

Jesus didn't do anything not guided by God and His truth. He was continually connected to God, so He was always doing what God was leading and showing Him to do as the following verses say.

"Then Jesus answered and said to them, 'Most assuredly, I

say to you, the Son can do nothing of Himself, but what He sees the Father do; for whatever He does, the Son also does in like manner. For the Father loves the Son, and shows Him all things that He Himself does; and He will show Him greater works than these, that you may marvel.'" (John 5:19-20).

"I can of Myself do nothing. As I hear, I judge; and My judgment is righteous, because I do not seek My own will but the will of the Father who sent Me" (John 5:30).

(See also *John 6:38, John 8:28-29,* and *John 18:37-38.*)

The reason Jesus was perfect was because He never did anything that wasn't the will of God. As we become more like Jesus and develop a sound mind, we will also start to experience the benefits of only doing what is the will of God. Since it may not be very clear yet what this might look like, it may be helpful at this point to better characterize how a sound mind functions compared to an unsound mind. An unsound mind can have a tendency toward any of these behaviors: selfishness, pride, lying, impatience, lack of discipline, disorganization, anger, moodiness, depression, unforgiveness, rudeness, insensitivity, laziness, fear, anxiety, indecision, slander, greed, hypocrisy, judgmentalism, manipulation, violence, boasting, injustice, unfaithfulness, gossip, people-pleasing, and envy.

A sound mind is incapable of doing these things since it will only be guided by the truth. A sound mind will trust God completely for everything in every circumstance. The fruit of the Spirit (see *Galatians 5:22-23*) will become more and more prevalent. A more sound mind will also be a healthier mind, and a healthier mind will also be the best way to have a healthy body. We can invest in a lot of things in life, but the investment that will give us the best return is whatever we do to invest in having a sound mind.

The apostle Peter also gave us a good list of things we need to add to our faith, which are also good investments into our minds.

> *"But also for this very reason, giving all diligence, add to your faith virtue, to virtue knowledge, to knowledge self-control, to self-control perseverance, to perseverance godliness, to godliness brotherly kindness, and to brotherly kindness love. For if these things are yours and abound, you will be neither barren nor unfruitful in the knowledge of our Lord Jesus Christ. For he who lacks these things is shortsighted, even to blindness, and has forgotten that he was cleansed from his old sins"* (2 Peter 1:5-9).

If you looked at what qualities each of these things would develop in a person, the following are some that come to mind.

- Faith—trustworthiness, openness, encouragement, courage
- Virtue—purity, righteousness, justice, submission
- Knowledge—wisdom, optimism, understanding, discipline
- Self-control—self-discipline, organization, balance
- Perseverance—hard work, faithfulness, loyalty
- Godliness—humility, mercy, grace, sensitivity, calmness, truthfulness, righteousness, justice, purity
- Brotherly kindness—helpfulness, consideration, kindness, gentleness, encouragement
- Love—patience, kindness, submissiveness, truthfulness, compassion, gentleness, goodness

As an employer, if you had to choose between two prospective employees, and one had more of the qualities listed with an unsound mind and the other had more of the qualities of the sound mind, it's obvious which prospect you should hire. But employers will hire people with unsound minds if they look more at technical knowledge and experience in a given field of expertise, and they don't look as much for a sound mind. It wouldn't be hard for anybody to look at these two lists and understand why the person with more of the qualities of a sound mind would be a much more productive employee. Employers would expect employees like this to create a more productive work environment that would then improve the productivity of the employees around them. They would also understand why a person with the unsound mind would not only be very unproductive, but why they would likely decrease the productivity of the people around them.

This is one of reasons each of us must be earnest seekers of the truth, who not only know the truth but also live by the truth, so we can have sound minds that allow us to live productive and effective lives that positively impact the other people during our time here on earth. This is especially important where we work because we spend much of our lives at our jobs where we are working with other people.

Peter wrote, *"But the end of all things is at hand; therefore be serious and watchful in your prayers" (1 Peter 4:7).*

Our minds are only capable of praying seriously and watchfully when our minds are at peace with God, and that means we must fill our minds with the truth about God, understand the truth about ourselves, and agree with God about those truths. I can relate to this because as a new Christian, it was more difficult to pray. Not only did I have difficulty in knowing what to pray, my mind was constantly wandering off to think about things going on in my life from a worldly perspective. But the more I came to know God, the easier it became to focus on Him when I prayed.

Curses of an Unsound Mind

What are the consequences of not having a sound mind or not continuing to grow in knowledge and wisdom? Moses wrote about the blessings of obedience and the curses of disobedience in *Deuteronomy 28*. It's interesting most of the chapter addresses the curses. The first fourteen verses cover the blessings, and then the next fifty-four verses cover the curses. Verses *twenty-eight* and *sixty-five* specifically address what can happen to our minds if we don't obey God's truth.

> *"The Lord will strike you with madness and blindness and confusion of heart" (Deuteronomy. 28:28).*

> *"And among those nations you shall find no rest, nor shall the sole of your foot have a resting place; but there the Lord will give you a [anxious] trembling heart, failing eyes, and anguish of soul" (Deuteronomy 28:65).*

Both dementia and Alzheimer's appear not only to be increasing in the USA, they are both showing up in people at a younger age. This could be an early warning there is an increase of unsound thinking.

Paul also wrote in the end of *Romans 1* what will happen to our minds if we reject God's truth.

> *"And even as they did not like to retain God in their knowledge, God gave them over to a debased mind, to do those things which are not fitting; being filled with all unrighteousness, sexual immorality, wickedness, [greed] covetousness, [malice] maliciousness; full of envy, murder, strife, deceit, evil-mindedness; they are whisperers, backbiters, haters of God, violent, proud, boasters, inventors of evil things, disobedient to parents, [without understanding] undiscerning, untrustworthy, unloving, unforgiving, unmerciful; who, knowing the righteous judgment of God, that those who practice such things are deserving of death, not only do the same but also approve of those who practice them"*
> *(Romans 1:28-32).*

These verses describe much of the dysfunction going on in the world around us. There's nothing good about having an unsound mind. In verse *twenty-eight,* it says God gave them over to a debased mind. A debased mind is a corrupt mind. It can't think right and is incapable of doing what is right in God's eyes. It will lead to a miserable life that will finish badly.

Final Thoughts on the State of My Mind

I've written this chapter on the premise our mind is our most valuable resource, and as such, we should make every effort to know the truth about God and about ourselves. This should also lead us to do everything we can to expose and acknowledge the lies we believe so we can confess them, turn from them, and replace them with the truth, so we can have a sound mind that always responds in a right way in God's eyes. When we do this, we will experience God's blessings increasingly more and not experience the curses of an unsound mind. I'll talk more about how we can develop a sound mind in the next chapter.

Mike Garst

Chapter 10

How Do We Develop a Sound Mind?

"But you have not so learned Christ, if indeed you have heard Him and have been taught by Him, as the truth is in Jesus: that you put off, concerning your former conduct, the old man which grows corrupt according to the deceitful lusts, and be renewed in the spirit of your mind, and that you put on the new man which was created according to God, in true righteousness and holiness" (Ephesians 4:20-24).

Hopefully the previous chapter has encouraged you to examine the current state of your mind and inspired you to want to make any changes that will help you to know and live by the truth increasingly more so you can have a sound mind. In this chapter, I will focus on ways to help you do that.

First Steps in Developing a Sound Mind

If we want to develop a sound mind, the apostle Paul gave us a good starting point. *"And do not be conformed to this world, but be transformed by the renewing of your mind, that you may prove what is that good and acceptable and perfect will of God"* (Romans 12:2).

We renew our mind by bringing into it each day new information that is true to replace corrupt information. New truth includes anything we don't know yet in our heart. This is one of the reasons we must continue to read and meditate on Bible verses until they get into our mind and heart. As many Christians have discovered, we can get something new out of verses we've read hundreds of times. This is why it's important to read the Bible over and over, so God can reveal His deeper truths to us. When we do this, we will be better able to test and approve Gods' good, acceptable, and perfect will. Another reason we must read the Bible is because God said to Isaiah, *"For My thoughts are not your thoughts, nor are your ways My ways," says the Lord. "For as the heavens are higher than the earth, so are My ways higher than your ways, and My thoughts than your thoughts" (Isaiah 55:8-9).*

We don't think like God until we get to know Him. His truth must be built into our minds as we read or listen to it over and over. And once we get something into our mind, there is still another step needed to take advantage of it. We must act on it. When we do this, we are giving ourselves a chance to demonstrate what we say we believe. Once our actions line up with what we say we believe, it then goes to our heart where it can permanently reside. James wrote, *"But be doers of the word, and not hearers only, deceiving yourselves" (James 1:22).*

Not doing what the scriptures say shows we don't believe it to be true yet. Knowledge for the sake of knowledge doesn't do us any good if we don't apply it to our lives. Paul wrote to Timothy about this. *"Gullible women loaded down with sins, led away by various lusts, always learning and never able to come to the knowledge of the truth" (2 Timothy 3:6-7).*

This is why it's also important to learn not only what is true, but what can benefit us for eternity. For example, we can learn tons of trivia, but it may only be of value to us if we were able to get on the television show *Jeopardy*. But winning money by knowing trivia isn't going to make us successful if we don't have the wisdom, self-control, and vision to use that money wisely. The world has seen countless examples of people who received large sums of money in various ways but either lost it all foolishly or spent it on worthless things. But if we learn new information about things that are true and relevant to our day-to-day lives, it enables us to be more effective in everything we do, including developing healthy relationships with all the people in our lives.

Knowledge alone also won't benefit us if that knowledge isn't consistent with God's truth and ways. The world is full of hackers who have great knowledge about how computers work, but they are using that knowledge to steal from other people and causing great financial damage to companies whose systems become corrupt because of what the hackers do. Hackers wouldn't do that if they believed God's truth and ways, because they would know they are being destructive and hurting other people, which is never acceptable in God's kingdom. Truth and knowledge working together is the most powerful thing we can ever have in this life. It provides us the offensive weapons as well as the defensive weapons we need to battle all the evil so prevalent in the world and to lead people to the truth.

God's Truth Purifies

Peter wrote, *"Since you have purified your souls in obeying the truth through the Spirit in sincere love of the brethren, (1 Peter 1:22).*

There are several important truths in this verse. This verse could possibly be written, "Since you have purified your minds in obeying the truth through the Spirit." God's Word is God's truth, and it is essentially a purifying agent. When the apostle Paul and Barnabas went to the Jerusalem Council to tell them the Gentiles were also believing in Christ, Paul said, *"So God, who knows the heart, acknowledged them by giving them the Holy Spirit, just as He did to us, and made no distinction between us and them, purifying their hearts by faith" (Acts 15:8-9).*

When we combine this with the verses below, we see further confirmation of how and why God's Word purifies our hearts and our minds. *"Faith comes by hearing, and hearing by the word of God," (Romans 10:17).*

> *"For the word of God is living and powerful, and sharper than any two-edged sword, piercing even to the division of soul and spirit, and of joints and marrow, and is a discerner of the thoughts and intents of the heart" (Hebrews 4:12).*

God's Word, along with the Holy Spirit, is the only one-two punch that can ever convince us of the need to confess and repent of any lies we believe so we can have a sound mind. We also need to have a sound mind if we want to love other people. *"Love one another fervently with a pure heart," (1 Peter 1:22).*

A purified soul will have a purified mind and heart that can love others sincerely. We cannot love others with a corrupt mind. Like a corrupt computer program, we are not going to process things correctly or function correctly to show God's unconditional love.

A transformed mind is also not an improved version of our old mind; it's a totally new mind. *"Having been born again, not of corruptible seed but incorruptible, through the word of God which lives and abides forever" (1 Peter 1:23).*

A new mind based on God's truth is incorruptible. It senses anything that is not true and rejects it, so the lie can't get into our minds to corrupt our thinking. A sound mind acts much like an anti-virus program that protects the computer program from anything that could corrupt the operating systems and software in the computer. When the sound mind senses something contrary to God's truth or ways, it doesn't allow it to enter. This is the role of the Holy Spirit and why it is so important to respond to the Holy Spirit's leading when He prompts us about any lies we hear.

God's Truth Protects

Just as a sound computer program has good anti-virus programs to protect against corruption, a sound mind is also a mind at peace, because it can't be corrupted as long as it's functioning only on the truth. When our minds are corrupt, they are not at peace, because a corrupt mind doesn't trust anything but itself and ends up with lots of anxiety and fear. Paul wrote,

> *"Be anxious for nothing, but in everything by prayer and supplication, with thanksgiving, let your requests be made known to God; and the peace of God, which surpasses all understanding, will guard your hearts and minds through Christ Jesus" (Philippians 4:6-7).*

A mind filled with nothing but the truth is not going to experience anxiety or fear or anything else that will steal its peace. The peace of God guards both our hearts and our minds.

Isaiah wrote, *"You will keep him in perfect peace, Whose mind is stayed on You, Because he trusts in You" (Isaiah 26:3).*

This verse appears to say if we trust God, then we will fix our minds on Him. And if we fix our minds on Him, then God will keep us in perfect peace. This is why it's so important for us to seek God so we can discover He is fully trustworthy. We will not trust anything we don't know. This is why we can't have a blind faith. But once we trust God, we must then do everything we can to keep that trust. This is probably the reason the writer of Proverbs wrote, *"Keep your heart with all diligence, for out of it springs the issues of life" (Proverbs 4:23).*

We guard our hearts by guarding our minds so no lies can enter. This is why we must not only seek God's truth, but why we must also ask God to show us the lies we still believe so we can confess, turn from, and replace them with God's truth.

Growing Our Mind

Based on the greatest commandment, Christians should be using 100% of their minds to love God. If that's true, then there may be a big gap we may not only need to close, but can close if Christ is living in us.

Peter wrote, *"You therefore, beloved, since you know this beforehand, beware lest you also fall from your own steadfastness, being led away with the error of the wicked; but grow in the grace and knowledge of our Lord and Savior Jesus Christ" (2 Peter 3:17-18).*

Peter wrote about the Day of the Lord in this chapter and included some warnings so verse *seventeen* would not become a reality. Then in verse *eighteen,* he said we need to grow.

It might be helpful at this point for us to think of our brain as a muscle. We know our muscles cannot grow stronger unless we exercise them and stretch them beyond their current capacity. It's a painful process physically, but there are great benefits if we faithfully exercise and stretch our muscles to make them stronger. The key is to continually stretch them beyond their current capacity.

The mind works in a similar way to muscles. Taking new information into our minds can stretch it, provided we believe it is worth remembering and can think about it long enough that we can do something with it. If you've ever heard of the expression, "It hurts my brain to think too much" or something similar, it's because we are stretching it like a muscle, and it does hurt in its own way. We need to understand this is a good thing and not a sign we need to think or meditate less. Because our human nature shies away from pain, our normal response will be not to stretch our mind. But not stretching our mind is the worst thing we could do, because our mind would then stop growing.

It may be the main reason most people don't use more than 15% of their brain's capacity.

We must also realize, just like feeding our physical bodies only makes us stronger when we exercise our bodies, feeding new information into our minds doesn't increase our mind's capacity until we actually use (exercise) it. Our physical bodies won't get stronger if we only eat food. They may get bigger, but they won't get stronger. We also have a limit on how much food we can take into our physical bodies because our stomach is only so big. Similarly, our brains can only take in so much information before we must do something with it. We must balance the feeding and exercising of our minds as well as our bodies.

Our brain also functions like a computer in that it has a temporary memory and permanent memory. Studies have shown we normally only retain 1-2% of what we hear or read each day. We forget the other 98-99%. One of the reasons this is so true in today's world is because we have access to so much information with all the different media sources trying to send information to us. All this information can become more of a curse than a blessing. This means we would probably do better by taking in less information and pondering it more so we could retain more of it. This is why we must develop the wisdom to be able to discern not only what information is worth reading or listening to, but how much of it to consume.

We would also retain more information if we were more eager to learn. In the Parable of the Sower in *Matthew 13:3-23, Mark 4:3-20, and Luke 8:4-15*, there were four kinds of ground the seed fell on, which represented four kinds of people. The first was the wayside (the path), the second was rocky soil, the third had thorns, and the fourth was the good soil. The following is the *Luke* version of the explanation of the parable.

> "Now the parable is this: The seed is the word of God. Those by the wayside are the ones who hear; then the devil

> *comes and takes away the word out of their hearts, lest they should believe and be saved. (Luke 8:11-12).*

This represents the hard-hearted person who believes they are fine the way they are and don't need to change. The word essentially bounces off them because they have very little desire to learn anything new.

> *"But the ones on the rock are those who, when they hear, receive the word with joy; and these have no root, who believe for a while and in time of temptation fall away" (Luke 8:13).*

A person such as this likes to hear God's Word, but they don't see a great need to apply it to their lives, so it doesn't go into their hearts. When temptations and tests come their way, they resort to their current way of thinking.

> *"Now the ones that fell among thorns are those who, when they have heard, go out and are choked with cares, riches, and pleasures of life, and bring no fruit to maturity" (Luke 8:14).*

The people in this group put greater value in the things of this world than they do in God's Word. They haven't made God's Word the center of their lives, but only one of many things.

> *"But the ones that fell on the good ground are those who, having heard the word with a noble and good heart, keep it and bear fruit with patience" (Luke 8:15).*

The fourth soil is the good soil and represents the person whose heart is soft and humble. They are hungry for God's truth, not only to read it, but to meditate on it and live by it increasingly more. They have developed an appetite for more, and it goes deep into their heart and becomes that person's character as they live by it. The truth has gone to a permanent place in their mind and heart because they've thought about it, meditated on it, decided it was true, and then applied it to their lives. It becomes a new habit.

Studies have shown it takes twenty-one days to develop a habit. This means we don't typically learn things quickly, but only over time with a sustained effort. Without the discipline to stay at it, we would not be able to develop new habits. This is why one of Satan's strategies is to distract us so we just keep doing the things we are currently doing and not learn new things that will change our thinking and actions. But when we persist in learning new truths and developing godly new habits, our mind's capacity will continue to increase, which in turn will enable us to continue learning new truths, develop even better new habits, and continue to expand our mind.

As we develop good new habits, we will also start using our time more effectively each day. This means we will end up replacing our bad habits with good habits increasingly more. We will not only be increasing our mind's capacity, we will be using it more efficiently. It would be like what a computer program does when it rearranges the memory more effectively instead of just putting it in the first available open spot.

We would probably be amazed at how much time we waste each day because we don't use our minds effectively. Some of this wasted time is from dwelling on the negative emotions being driven by not knowing or believing the truth about something. A significant amount of wasted time can come from viewing, reading, and listening to any information that isn't true or helpful to us. This is the equivalent of filling our minds with clutter that doesn't benefit us from an eternal perspective.

Scripture Memory Increases Faith and Mind

It's been said the most effective way to grow spiritually is to memorize Scripture. And from my experience, I would agree with that statement. When we memorize Scripture, we will increase the capacity of our minds with pure truth. This is why it's so important to develop the habit of memorizing Scripture. We don't really know a Scripture until we've memorized it. Have you ever tried to quote or live by a Scripture you didn't know? I know it was always frustrating for me to talk to somebody when a Scripture came to mind, but I didn't know it well enough to reference or use it properly in the conversation. That can be a missed opportunity to share with somebody a truth that could have been important to them. It can also be a missed opportunity for us to know a truth that could help us on an issue we are working through. For example, when we are anxious about things, then memorizing *Philippians 4:6-7* should help us. *"Be anxious for nothing, but in everything by prayer and supplication, with thanksgiving, let your requests be made known to God; and the peace of God, which surpasses all understanding, will guard your hearts and minds through Christ Jesus."*

Knowing and believing this verse is powerful. It is even more powerful if we learn to memorize and speak it out loud. God's Word is powerful and when God speaks, things happen. I've been amazed at the times when I've spoken *Philippians 4:6-7* out loud after I started to feel anxious and experienced the peace it brought to me within minutes.

The challenge with memorizing Scripture is it's going to take an investment of our time and a rearranging of our priorities. So, we must be convinced knowing God's Word will increase our mind's capacity and soundness, and help us live the best life possible. Many people say they can't memorize Scripture, but that really isn't true. Anybody can memorize Scripture, it's just a matter of developing the discipline to practice for a few minutes several times each day. Therefore, we must also realize we must start with tiny steps and give ourselves time to learn Scripture and increase our mind's capacity to memorize more Scripture.

No child learns to walk immediately. They take tiny steps and fall a lot, but they get back up and keep trying. Little children never give up trying to walk. Before we know it, they walk, and then go from walking to running, and we wonder how they did it so fast. In the same way, it may make more sense for a beginner to try to memorize one Scripture a week for a few months just to prove they can memorize some verses. This only takes a couple of minutes a day initially, and probably won't require more than ten minutes a day for the first few months. They could then increase to working on two verses a week for a few months. If a person stuck with this for one year, they could memorize fifty to one hundred scriptures. They might even know more scriptures than 99% of professing Christians in one year. If true, it would prove the intensity of the battle we are in with Satan, who will do everything he can to discourage us from even starting to memorize Scripture.

Another way to memorize Scripture is to use verses in our prayers. Much of my prayer time now is just praying God's Word and promises back to Him. There are many prayers in the Bible, so it's also a good way to make sure our prayers are consistent with God's Word, ways, and promises. John wrote,

> *"Now this is the confidence that we have in Him, that if we ask anything according to His will, He hears us. And if we know that He hears us, whatever we ask, we know that we have the petitions that we have asked of Him"* (1 John 5:14-15).

Many of the prophets and people in the Bible prayed for God to act in accordance with His Word and promises and for the sake of His name. We can be sure God will do anything in line with His Word or promises.

Now it doesn't seem we should need to remind God of His Word or promises, or even His attributes, but it's clear from the way God responded to the prayer of Moses (see *Numbers 14:11-23*) we indeed can influence God's decisions.

God said to Moses, *"I will strike them with the pestilence and disinherit them, and I will make of you a nation greater and mightier than they" (Numbers 14:12).*

God had declared a judgment. Yet, He relented on some of that judgment based on what Moses said to Him in *verses 13-19*. God is still making judgments about things, and our prayers can make a difference when we pray His Word and promises to Him.

David wrote, *"God is a just judge, And God is angry with the wicked every day. If he does not turn back, He will sharpen His sword; He bends His bow and makes it ready" (Psalm 7:11-12).*

This means anytime God makes a judgment, His judgment is right. In other words, He has given each person an adequate opportunity to believe and trust in Him. God also gives us a chance to turn back to Him. But eventually, there will be consequences if we don't turn back to God in His timetable.

It's also been my experience my prayers have no real power unless I can pray God's truth into them. This may be the best reason we need to learn God's Word. If we keep praying certain scriptures to God, we will eventually memorize them. This will, in turn, strengthen our prayer life, because we will be praying God's truth instead of our desires.

Praying God's Word each day is also a good way to know what we believe or what our real doctrine is. A brother in Christ asked me how I learned or practiced my gospel message to others. It dawned on me when he asked me that question, I pray the gospel message to God each day. It includes all the scriptures I've memorized that address the fundamentals of the gospel. If we learn to do this, it will help guide us on what scriptures we should focus on memorizing first.

As we learn to pray more verses, we'll discover we can memorize many more scriptures than we thought possible. This is because we'll be increasing our mind's capacity as we learn new scriptures. I've heard all Jewish children, during Old Testament days, memorized the first five books in the Old Testament by the time they were twelve years old. There are one-hundred eighty-seven chapters in these five books and about five thousand verses. This indicates, unless we were born with a mental deficiency, we should be able to memorize at least five thousand verses of Scripture in less than twelve years. This means we would need to memorize around five hundred verses a year on average. I said earlier we should start by trying to memorize one Scripture a week initially. At that rate, it would take us about one hundred years to memorize five thousand verses. So, we would need to work up to memorizing more than one Scripture a day fairly soon to get to five thousand verses in ten years.

I know this sounds overwhelming to most people, but until we've developed the habit of focusing on memorizing scriptures for ten to fifteen minutes a day, we won't realize what's possible. I can tell you from my experience, a person can memorize five thousand scriptures in ten years. Plus, once we've learned five thousand verses, we'll discover we want to learn another five thousand verses and will have an even greater desire to do so. We'll realize our relationship with God becomes richer and more intimate as we get to know Him through memorizing scriptures.

Most of you have heard of William Wilberforce. Because of his many years of perseverance, he was credited with bringing an end to slavery in England. It's hard for us to imagine the obstacles that had to be overcome to make this happen. In Eric Metaxas's book, *7 Men*[10], he said Wilberforce was known as a man of prayer and a man who read and memorized scriptures every day accordingly. Eric said he memorized Psalm 119, which has one hundred and seventy-six verses in it. To many people, this may seem impossible, but *"with God nothing will be impossible" (Luke 1:37)*.

I know it's possible, because I've also memorized it and pray all of

---

[10] 7 Men, Eric Metaxas, Nelson Books, Nashville TN, 2013, 2016

it over the course of a typical week. Eric said when Wilberforce sometimes walked the two-and-a-half miles from Parliament to his home, his walk would take him through Hyde Park, and Wilberforce had it timed so if he began reciting Psalm 119 when he entered the park, he would be finished by the time he got home. It took about twenty minutes for him to recite it. Wilberforce made his faith part of all his life, including his work, and what God did through him had a huge impact on the world. Each of us has this same opportunity to positively impact the people around us each day, but until God's Word takes residence in our hearts because we've memorized it, we will only be able to do a fraction of what's possible.

Narrow Road Leads to a Broad Mind

Jesus said something sobering.

> *"Enter by the narrow gate; for wide is the gate and broad is the way that leads to destruction, and there are many who go in by it. Because narrow is the gate and difficult is the way which leads to life, and there are few who find it"*
> *(Matthew 7:13-14).*

If we were on a hike, and we came to a place where we had to choose one of two paths to take, and one sign said the "Easy Way" and the other said the "Difficult Way," which would we choose? According to this verse, most of us would take the "Easy Way." Yet this verse says it will lead to destruction. But if we took the difficult road, it would lead to life.

Our natural mind also prefers to take the easy, comfortable, or most pleasurable road. It does not want to read, study, memorize, or meditate. It would rather watch television or other forms of entertainment, play games, or do anything else that would not require us to use or stretch our minds. Yet, no matter what we are doing, our minds are always working in some way. It's taking in whatever we are focusing on. We are feeding our minds with either truth, lies, or worthless information. Yet when we feed our minds with truth and then study, memorize, meditate on those truths, and live by them, it will cause our minds to grow in God's wisdom.

Jesus said,

> *"Do not lay up for yourselves treasures on earth, where moth and rust destroy and where thieves break in and steal; but lay up for yourselves treasures in heaven, where neither moth nor rust destroys and where thieves do not break in and steal. For where your treasure is, there your heart will be also" (Matthew 6:19-21).*

Jesus is telling us more in these verses than we may realize. It is talking about what we treasure in our minds and hearts. It's commonly believed if our heart is right, then our treasures will be right. But verse *twenty-one* says, *"For where your treasure is, there your heart will be also."* This means the treasure comes first, not the heart. Our hearts will go with what our minds treasure. What we think about the most is what guides us the most. If we focus on the truth of God, then our thinking will be guided by that truth. But if our thinking is more on the things of this world, then we are going to be guided by the things of this world which have no eternal value and will eventually lead us to destruction. The apostle Paul wrote, *"If then you were raised with Christ, seek those things which are above, where Christ is, sitting at the right hand of God. Set your mind on things above, not on things on the earth" (Colossians 3:1-2).*

When we set our minds on heavenly things, we reap heavenly rewards because our mind will be filled with heavenly thoughts. Our minds were designed by God to function on truth, and a mind that functions on truth will have an ever-increasing capacity.

Those who know, love, and trust God, which includes His ways, truths and promises, are going to spend time in His Word, because the Bible is the best place for us to learn about God. This is no different than spending time with a person so we can get to know him or her. When we truly know someone, we will also know how he or she would respond to any situation he or she might face. And when we know God intimately, we should either know what He would do in almost any situation or be so close to Him we could quickly connect with Him for direction.

King David wrote something profound. *"The secret of the Lord is with those who fear Him, and He will show His covenant to him"* (*Psalm 25:14*).

King Solomon wrote something similar. *"For the perverse person is an abomination to the Lord, but His secret counsel is with the upright"* (*Proverbs 3:32*).

It should be an advantage to anyone to hear God's voice in the many ways He can speak to us, but for God to make His secrets and secret counsel known to us is a level beyond that. One might wonder why God would share His secrets with those who fear the Lord. That may be because we may not understand what the 'fear of the Lord' really is. The Psalmist wrote *in Psalm 111:10, "The fear of the Lord is the beginning of wisdom; A good understanding have all those who do His commandments. His praise endures forever."* (See also *Proverbs 9:10*.)

One of the most amazing things about God is He chooses to do much of His work through imperfect humans. Yet His work is also so important He can't ask just anybody to do it. He can only give it to people He can trust because they trust and revere Him. This means we must first trust God, so He can trust us. And God must build that trust in us. It's a two-way road that is going to take some time. Plus, God is going to test us through different circumstances in our lives to show us what we believe in our heart.

God Tests the Heart and Mind

Only God can see into our hearts. Therefore, He knows how we are going to respond in given circumstances before they happen.

"You know my sitting down and my rising up; You understand my thought afar off. You comprehend my path and my lying down, and are acquainted with all my ways. For there is not a word on my tongue, but behold, O Lord, You know it altogether" (Psalm 139:2-4).

Yet, even though God knows what we are going to do in given circumstances, the scriptures still say God examines and tests our hearts and our minds. The following scriptures confirm this.

"For the righteous God tests the hearts and minds" (Psalm 7:9).

"Would not God search this out? For He knows the secrets of the heart" (Psalm 44:21).

"But, O Lord of hosts, You who judge righteously, testing the mind and the heart" (Jeremiah 11:20).

"I will kill her children with death, and all the churches shall know that I am He who searches the minds and hearts" (Revelation 2:23).

(See also *Psalm 17:3, Jeremiah 12:3, 17:10, 20:12, and Exodus 16:14.*)

There are also several specific situations in the Bible where God tested His people.

"Then the Lord said to Moses, 'Behold, I will rain bread from heaven for you. And the people shall go out and gather a certain quota every day, that I may test them, whether they will walk in My law or not.' (Exodus 16:4).

"And Moses said to the people, 'Do not fear; for God has come to test you, and that His fear may be before you, so that you may not sin.'" (Exodus 20:20).

(See also *Deuteronomy 8:2, 16, 13:3, Judges 2:20-22, 1 Chronicles 29:17, and 2 Chronicles 32:31.*)

Since there are several scriptures that talk about God testing the heart, it's clear He didn't want us to miss this point. You may be wondering why God tests us when He already knows what we believe in our mind and hearts at any given time. It's the same reason we take tests in school and in the workplace, to get a driver's license, or a number of other things. We don't know what we think we know until we get tested. It's easy to say we know or believe something. It's another thing to act on what we say we believe or know. Because of God's great love for us and because He is so patient, gracious, and merciful, He is going to do everything He can to show us what we believe.

The mind is a battlefield where the truth and ways of God and the lies of Satan and the world are constantly fighting for control of our heart. It is one of the primary ways Satan uses to try and draw us away from God, because our heart will always determine what we say or do in any situation. Satan knows if he can convince us there is no harm or danger in doing something that looks beneficial to us, we will usually do it. But if it turns out to be harmful or dangerous, then we will likely suffer the consequences, depending on God's mercy and grace.

Because there is such a critical battle for our souls, we should never take this lightly, and we should also be as proactive as we can to make sure our minds and hearts are being guided by the truth. For King David, it was so important he wrote the following in two of the Psalms.

"Examine me, O Lord, and [test me] prove me; try my mind and my heart. For Your lovingkindness is before my eyes, and I have walked in Your truth" (Psalm 26:2-3).

"Search me, O God, and know my heart; try me, and know my anxieties; and see if there is any wicked way in me, and lead me in the way everlasting" (Psalm 139:23-24).

If we understand the seriousness and intensity of this battle, it would be a good idea to make these four verses part of our daily prayers so we can do our part to be proactive in making sure our mind and heart are being led by God's truth. When we ask God for something that will ultimately glorify Him, He will give it to us, provided we've confessed and repented of any sin in our lives.

James wrote, *"If any of you lacks wisdom, let him ask of God, who gives to all liberally and without reproach, and it will be given to him" (James 1:5).*

This tells us God will give us all the wisdom we want, if we earnestly want it and are following Him. However, we must read the next three verses.

> *"But let him ask in faith, with no doubting, for he who doubts is like a wave of the sea driven and tossed by the wind. For let not that man suppose that he will receive anything from the Lord; he is a double-minded man, unstable in all his ways" (James 1:6-8).*

This is another reason it's so important to have a close relationship with God that enables us to know Him so well we'll not doubt who He is, what He can do, and what He expects of us. He is ready and willing to give us access to all the wisdom we want as well as a host of other resources available to those who love and trust Him with all their heart.

Final Thoughts on a Sound Mind

I'm sure most people have heard the expression, "The mind is a terrible thing to waste," or something similar. One of the reasons a person would waste their mind is because they are not aware of what I've talked about in these last two chapters. The mind is powerful and can take us down any road we allow it to take us. But there is only one good road, and it is marked with God's truth. If we underestimate the potential power our minds are capable of, we are going to also underestimate the power of God.

Mike Garst

Chapter 11
What or Who Am I Investing In?

During one of my mission trips to Germany a few years ago, I was talking with two young-adult friends, Tobias and Nicolai, who had come to see me at one of the homes where I was blessed to stay. As we were talking, I said something about investing in people, which resonated with them since they realized in that moment I was investing in them. Not many people consider relationships with people as an investment, but in the kingdom of God, that is the fundamental thing we are doing in our connections with other people. It's the only investment we can make that can have an eternal return on investment.

Before I go any further, let me clarify what I mean by investing in people. I believe we invest in people when we encourage and challenge them to use all their skills and talents to be all God created them to be so they can live a purposeful life in the eyes of God. It's a different kind of investment, because we get nothing in return in this life other than the fulfillment that comes from knowing we made the effort to help somebody move closer to reaching their full potential in Christ.

Mike Garst

Different Ways to Invest

If we are like many people, we typically think investing is placing our money into something where we will hopefully gain a good and timely return, such as in the stock market, real estate, mutual funds, etc. We do this in the hope of building a better life for ourselves, including our retirement years, and to fund our children's education, personal travel, and possibly to have more money to give to the church, mission organizations, or other charities.

We can also invest in our work career to increase our income or our influence and effectiveness at work. This could involve taking classes, getting an advanced degree, or just working longer hours. One thing financial investments and personal investments have in common is they require an investment of our time. Even if we delegate financial management to a professional, we still need to make the time to monitor how well they are managing our money.

Because time is such a precious resource, and since it seems to speed up as we get older, we need to use it wisely to invest in the things that will give us the best return. It's been said if we want to know a person's real priorities, we just need to look at how they spend their money. Looking at what we invest our time in is also another way we could determine what our priorities are. It appears to me most people spend their time with their families and friends, at work, doing hobbies, exercising, reading books or articles, or watching TV and other forms of media entertainment. The challenge for all of us is to determine what's most important, and to prioritize them properly so we are using our time wisely.

When we spend time with our families and friends, and even when we spend time with our coworkers, we ideally are also investing in them. We invest in them when we influence them in a positive way to help them become all God created them to be. One of the key questions all of us should ask ourselves is, am I influencing the people in my life so they can know the truth about themselves and God and reach their full potential? Another question might be, am I investing more in things for myself or in other people? These are important questions, because when we get to the end of our life, what we have invested in will either have an eternal value, or it will be burned up. In *1 Corinthians 3:9,* the apostle Paul wrote, *"For we are God's fellow workers; you are God's field, you are God's building."*

Paul used a farming analogy as he was talking to the church in Corinth and said he and those with him were God's fellow workers and the Corinthian church was like a field. Just like a farmer invests in his fields by sowing seed so he can have a crop to harvest, Paul was saying he would be sowing into them so there could be a fruitful harvest. He also uses an analogy of a building in the next verse.

> *"According to the grace of God which was given to me, as a wise master builder I have laid the foundation, and another builds on it. But let each one take heed how he builds on it. For no other foundation can anyone lay than that which is laid, which is Jesus Christ"*
> *(1 Corinthians 3:10-11).*

In this analogy, he started with what's most important in a building, which was the foundation. The church's foundation is Jesus Christ, and Paul was saying he had laid that foundation with the Corinthians, and they were to be careful to build only on it. Then he said the fruit of whatever they built would be revealed some day, good or bad.

> *"Now if anyone builds on this foundation with gold, silver, precious stones, wood, hay, straw, each one's work will become clear; for the day will declare it, because it will be revealed by fire; and the fire will test each one's work, of what sort it is. (1 Corinthians 3:12-13).*

Fire can either burn something up (like wood, hay, or straw) or heat up materials like metal (gold, or silver), and precious stones to the point where it can drive out the impurities. A precious metal has no impurities in it, and in the case of gold becomes like a mirror. Paul's investment in the church was to make everyone a precious metal so they could reap an eternal reward someday. *"If anyone's work which he has built on it endures, he will receive a reward. If anyone's work is burned, he will suffer loss; but he himself will be saved, yet so as through fire"* (1 Corinthians 3:14-15).

Paul said whatever we build on Christ's foundation will receive a reward if it endures. If it doesn't endure, it will be burned up. Verse *fifteen* says if someone's efforts have earnestly been built on the foundation of Christ, they would still be saved even if their work burned up.

These are very intense and important verses, and I'm not an authority on everything they are saying. But it appears to me if a person is investing in other people using Christ as the foundation, and they are being built into Christ's likeness, which includes living by His truth and ways, then they are going to receive eternal rewards. Whereas, investing in anything other than this may have no value and be destroyed in the end.

If this is true, the only way to finish strong is to be a person who is an investor in people using Christ as the foundation and not in things for themselves while in this life. If we use our years of experience wisely to build a Christ-centered solid foundation, we should be in position to be spiritual fathers, spiritual mentors, and spiritual friends to a great number of people, especially younger people. This may be the greatest need in the church and in our world today, because it seems very few people in this world have any spiritual mentors, fathers, or friends who are investing in them to any extent. I can think of no better legacy than to be known as a godly man or woman who invested deeply in the lives of others, using Christ as the foundation, and to have those people be the ones who testify how positively we impacted their lives by pointing them to Christ and encouraging and challenging them to grow into Christ's likeness.

It would be especially impactful if older people were mentoring and investing in younger people to bridge the generation gap. Sadly, some younger people aren't interested in learning from more mature adults. This may be true when a young person's experiences with older adults have been negative. But as a grandfather, father, and a man who has spent some significant time with many younger people in the last twenty-plus years, I've learned young people want older people to take an interest in them. And because many younger and middle-aged adults still focus more on themselves, it's very difficult for young people to find other young or middle-aged people who will take a genuine interest in them. For this reason, older people have a great opportunity to invest in younger people's lives, not only because they should have so much wisdom and experience to share, but because they shouldn't be living the busy, self-centered lives many younger and middle-aged people appear to be living.

Apostle Paul—Primarily an Investor in People

The apostle Paul is known for writing over half of the New Testament books, for planting a lot of churches, and for going through a lot of hardships to share and show the love of Christ. But what can get overlooked about Paul is he was primarily an investor in people. If we carefully read through all the books he wrote in the New Testament, we will see he mentions a lot of names of people with whom he ministered. *Romans 16* is an especially revealing chapter when it comes to the names of Paul's acolytes, and how dear they were to him. I encourage you to read *Romans 16:1-15*.

Paul named twenty-seven people in those verses, plus two more unnamed people, two households, one house church, and several unnamed brothers and sisters of these people. And these are only a few of the people Paul named in his epistles. If we read further, we will see eight more names in *Romans 16:21-23*.

Investing in People Through Prayer

Paul also prayed for a lot of people in all the churches he planted. These were intense prayers, indicating Paul wanted all of them to grow to maturity in Christ, and he would not be content with anything less. Paul was a spiritual father who would not let his spiritual children grow up into anything less than mature disciples of Christ who in turn would raise up other mature disciples. He expressed it in this way. *"And the things that you have heard from me among many witnesses, commit these to faithful men who will be able to teach others also" (2 Timothy 2:2).*

Paul was mentoring Timothy, and he wanted Timothy to teach what he learned from Paul to faithful men, who, in turn, were to teach others. There are four spiritual generations in this verse: Paul, Timothy, the faithful men Timothy taught, and the people the faithful men would teach. I'm sure Paul intended this to keep going beyond these four spiritual generations.

Let's look at some of Paul's prayers for the people he was investing in so we can see the depth of what he prayed for them. These are model prayers we can use to pray for the people we are investing in. This may be one of the most effective ways we can invest in people because we are asking and trusting God to do the things we can't do. Plus, it would demonstrate we believe our prayers will be heard by God, and He will do something with them, even if the Holy Spirit needs to intercede for us with the right words (see Romans 8:26-27). *"Therefore I also, after I heard of your faith in the Lord Jesus and your love for all the saints, do not cease to give thanks for you, making mention of you in my prayers: (Ephesians 1:15-16).*

Paul is first thankful for everyone who has faith in Christ and how they love one another. Plus, he says he mentions them in his prayers. This implies he mentions them by name. Then he prays *"that the God of our Lord Jesus Christ, the Father of glory, may give to you the spirit of wisdom and revelation in the knowledge of Him," (Ephesians 1:17).*

This is a prayer for others to know Jesus more deeply, which would mean they would know God better as well. Next, Paul prays *"the eyes of your [heart] understanding being enlightened; that you may know what is the hope of His calling, what are the riches of the glory of His inheritance in the saints" (Ephesians 1:18).*

Paul is not only praying others would know Jesus and His Father intimately; he wanted them to know their ultimate hope and how rich and glorious their inheritance would be. Paul not only wanted other believers to know about the blessings of this life, he wanted them to know what the eternal blessings were. The reason this is important is that our lives on earth are infinitely shorter than eternal life, and our focus should be on eternity instead of this life. Then Paul prays, *"and what is the exceeding greatness of His power toward us who believe, according to the working of His mighty power" (Ephesians 1:19).*

Paul also wants believers to know God can do immensely powerful things in and through us that have no earthly explanation, so people can notice something is remarkably different about the people in the church.

When we consider everything Paul said in this prayer, it should challenge us to examine whether this is the way we are praying for our fellow believers. We don't know how many of the people Paul knew by name, but based on what he wrote in *Romans 16*, we can be confident he knew many of them personally. Therefore, he wasn't just praying for a faceless group of people. He was praying for individuals he knew as well as the church. This is a reminder God is deeply interested in each of us as well as the church as a body, because we need each other. God not only wants to be in relationship with each of us, He wants us to be in an intimate relationship with each other, so we can experience the depth of peace and joy possible in this life and in the life to come.

Ephesians 3 has another of Paul's very powerful prayers. He starts this prayer by saying,

> *"For this reason I bow my knees to the Father of our Lord Jesus Christ, from whom the whole family in heaven and earth is named, that He would grant you, according to the riches of His glory, to be strengthened with might through His Spirit in the inner man," (Ephesians 3:14-16).*

Like *Ephesians 1:19*, Paul starts by praying for his fellow believers to be strengthened with power. In a world that has so much hate, corruption, greed, selfishness, and many other ungodly behaviors, it's important for the world to witness a power that can only be explained by belief in God. After this, he prays, *"that Christ may dwell in your hearts through faith; that you, being rooted and grounded in love, may be able to comprehend with all the saints what is the width and length and depth and height—" (Ephesians 3:17-18).*

Paul wanted all believers to have a saving faith that had Christ living in their hearts and a faith built on a foundation of God's multi-dimensional and unconditional love. In a world that relies so heavily on conditional love, the church must be a body of people who both show and share the unconditional love of Christ in every part of their lives. Paul wanted all believers to understand this as much as possible because people are not going to be drawn to a group of people that act the same as the rest of the world. Then Paul prays more about this love. *"To know the love of Christ which passes knowledge; that you may be filled with all the fullness of God" (Ephesians 3:19).*

Paul believed the love of Christ was more important than knowledge and prayed for his fellow believers to be so full of the love of God they would become increasingly more like Him.

Colossians 1:9-12 is another prayer that shows the depth of what Paul wanted all believers to become. *"For this reason, we also, since the day we heard it, do not cease to pray for you, and to ask that you may be filled with the knowledge of His will in all wisdom and spiritual understanding;" (Colossians 1:9).*

Like some of Paul's other prayers, he began praying for the believers at Colosse as soon as he heard about their faith. Also, as in the previous prayer, *Ephesians 3:16-19*, Paul didn't pray for believers to just have some knowledge, wisdom or understanding; he instead wanted them to be *filled* with it. This is a consistent theme in Paul's prayers. His understanding of faith was everyone needed to grow to maturity, which meant to become like Christ as much as possible. His prayer goes on to describe what maturity looks like in seven ways in the next two verses.

> *"That you may walk worthy of the Lord, fully pleasing Him, being fruitful in every good work and increasing in the knowledge of God; "Strengthened with all might, according to His glorious power, for all patience and longsuffering with joy;" (Colossians 1:10-11).*

Paul ended this prayer by thanking God, since He is the One who has enabled us to share in the inheritance of all faithful believers. *"Giving thanks to the Father who has qualified us to be partakers of the inheritance of the saints in the light" (Colossians 1:12).*

Philippians 1:3-6 is another of Paul's prayers that starts off thanking God when he thinks of the believers in Philippi. But it's also an encouraging prayer, because Paul talks about how joyful and sure he is in God's ability to finish what He started. This is especially important for anybody who thinks there is no way God could transform them into Christ's likeness.

> *"I thank my God upon every remembrance of you, always in every prayer of mine making request for you all with joy, for your fellowship in the gospel from the first day until now, being confident of this very thing, that He who has begun a good work in you will complete it until the day of Jesus Christ;" (Philippians 1:3-6).*

Some of Paul's other prayers I encourage you to read, so you can see how consistent he was in what he prayed, include *Philippians 1:9-11, Romans 1:8-12, 1 Thessalonians 1:2-4, 1 Thessalonians 3:9-13, 2 Thessalonians 1:11-12, 2 Corinthians 13:7-9, and Philemon 1:4-6.*

As you can see, these are not just ordinary prayers. They are powerful prayers, indicating Paul wanted the people he knew to have a deep, strong, and mature faith that would get them through anything and enable God to work through them to reach more and more people with the gospel. As we read these prayers and the others I referenced, plus others in all the epistles, we will see Paul, Peter, John, James, and Jude all had a deep affection for the people they were investing in. Paul cared deeply for them. He wasn't just interested in sharing the gospel; he earnestly enjoyed his time with them. He longed to see them and their progress in the faith so he could experience the joy that comes from that kind of relationship. It's similar to the kind of joy a parent has when they see their child growing up into a godly young man or woman who is making wise and godly choices in their life. It's the joy we will also experience as we invest in people and see their good progress.

The apostle John wrote,

> *"Beloved, I pray that you may prosper in all things and be in health, just as your soul prospers. For I rejoiced greatly when brethren came and testified of the truth that is in you, just as you walk in the truth. I have no greater joy than to hear that my children walk in truth" (3 John 1:2-4).*

I'm convinced we, as disciples of Christ, can have no greater joy than to know all the people we are investing in are walking in the truth. No amount of money or possessions in this world can even come close to matching that kind of joy. I know, because I continue to experience it increasingly more.

Being a Godly Model

The apostle Paul was not ashamed to urge the people in the churches he was working with to imitate him.

> "Therefore, I urge you, imitate me. For this reason I have sent Timothy to you, who is my beloved and faithful son in the Lord, who will remind you of my ways in Christ, as I teach everywhere in every church" (1 Corinthians 4:16).

> "Imitate me, just as I also imitate Christ"
> (1 Corinthians 11:1).

This means we must be confident we are setting a godly example to follow, because we won't be able to mentor people effectively if we are not modeling what we are trying to teach them. People are more likely to model what they see, not what they hear. Paul was so bold he even sent Timothy to the Corinthians to remind them of his ways in Christ he taught to every church.

Paul also urged the Galatians and Philippians to become like him and to follow his example.

> "Brethren, I urge you to become like me, for I became like you. You have not injured me at all" (Galatians 4:12).

> "Brethren, join in following my example, and note those who so walk, as you have us for a pattern" (Philippians 3:17).

He even said they should take note of those who were following Paul's example. This was a strong message to the early Christians that their lives needed to be a testimony of what they believed, and they needed to know if their fellow believers were truly modeling Christlikeness. Paul wasn't urging Christians to imitate him just so they could model him; he wanted them to experience the peace that comes with following Christ. Paul wouldn't have encouraged anybody to follow him if he didn't believe it was going to lead to godly peace. *"The things which you learned and received and heard and saw in me, these do, and the God of peace will be with you" (Philippians 4:9).*

Paul's example included every area of life, including his work, as the following verses say.

> *"For you yourselves know how you ought to follow us, for we were not disorderly among you; nor did we eat anyone's bread free of charge, but worked with labor and toil night and day, that we might not be a burden to any of you, not because we do not have authority, but to make ourselves an example of how you should follow us"*
> *(2 Thessalonians 3:7-9).*

Even though Paul knew those who serve full-time in the body of Christ deserve to be compensated for their work, he didn't exercise that right. Instead, he worked for a living just like everybody else, so he wouldn't be a burden to anybody. He also set an example of someone who didn't need to be paid to help people grow in their faith. This is the reality for most Christians, because everyone who follows Christ is in fulltime ministry, whether they are at work, at home, or any place else.

Investing in People Takes Time

As you are reading this, you may be thinking, "This is going to take a lot of time!"

It does, and the only way you can do this is by first stopping any activities that don't have an eternal value. It's hard to effectively add anything to an already full list of things-to-do. We must first decide to stop doing whatever has no eternal value and then replace it with something that has everlasting value. It's making the decision to invest in people instead of things or selfish pleasures. And we will never be able to do this until we belong to Christ and He has become the true center of our life, so He can change our thinking to be like His thoughts and ways.

You may also be thinking there are some people who may need a large investment of our time. This is where wisdom is required, because the people with the messiest lives need the greatest amount of help. Jesus was not afraid to get involved in messy lives. But He showed us a different way to do it than what we typically do today. When Jesus met the unnamed Samaritan women at the well in *John 4*, He met a woman who was clearly living a messy life, especially when you consider the culture at that time. She had been married five times and was then living with a man who was not her husband. Divorce wasn't common in those days, so for her to have been divorced five times was very unusual. Plus, living with a man who was not your husband was not the norm in that culture. She had to be the talk of the town, which is probably why she was alone drawing water in the middle of the day. Yet Jesus taught us something important about how to deal with messy lives. He didn't ask what He could do for her. He asked her to do something for Him! He said to her, *"Give Me a drink" (John 4:7).*

In those days, Jews wouldn't have even talked to a Samaritan, much less asked them for a drink of water. But Jesus' goal was to get her into a conversation, which is what He did.

The first mistake we typically make when we get involved in messy lives is asking what we can do for them. As a result, that opens the gate for us to do many more things for them. But since Jesus was God's Son and had an intimate relationship with His Father, He knew her background, and He knew she needed to know the truth more than anything. She responded by saying, *"How is it that You, being a Jew, ask a drink from me, a Samaritan woman?" (John 4:9).*

Jesus wasted no time bringing God into the conversation when He responded, *"If you knew the gift of God, and who it is who says to you, 'Give Me a drink,' you would have asked Him, and He would have given you living water" (John 4:10).*

Jesus did want to give her something, and that, of course, was Himself as her ultimate Savior, Redeemer, Deliverer, and Lord. This woman ended up bringing the whole village to Jesus. This was a very rapid and radical change in her life!

When we try to change a messy life by doing things for them, we can end up sacrificing countless hours and not make any real progress with them. But if we ask them to do something for us, with the intent of engaging them in conversation about God so we can connect them to the ultimate source they really need, it will require much less of our time and limited resources.

Jesus also got involved in the messy life of a man named Legion. If we thought the Samaritan woman had a messy life, look at this one.

> *"And when He had come out of the boat, immediately there met Him out of the tombs a man with an unclean spirit, who had his dwelling among the tombs; and no one could bind him, not even with chains, because he had often been bound with shackles and chains. And the chains had been pulled apart by him, and the shackles broken in pieces; neither could anyone tame him. And always, night and day, he was in the mountains and in the tombs, crying out and cutting himself with stones" (Mark 5:2-5)*

I don't think many of us would volunteer to get involved in a messy life like this, especially since there was also the possibility he could hurt us physically. Jesus had to first drive out the unclean spirit in him to get him into his right mind. His mind had gone totally corrupt, and only Jesus can give anyone a new mind. And that, of course, is the key to every messy life we will ever get involved in. Their thinking has become corrupt, and the only way we can really help them is to replace their corrupt thoughts with God's truth and grace, so they can come back to their senses and live the powerful life grace and truth make possible. Jesus also showed us another important thing about how to deal with messy people once they start living by God's truth in *Mark 5:18-20*.

> *"And when He got into the boat, he who had been demon-possessed begged Him that he might be with Him. However, Jesus did not permit him, but said to him, 'Go home to your friends, and tell them what great things the Lord has done for you, and how He has had compassion on you.' And he departed and began to proclaim in Decapolis all that Jesus had done for him; and all marveled."*

When you impact a messy life, they will likely want to stay with you. And while that might be appropriate at times, if they need to be mentored and you're in position to do that, there are times when they need to pay forward what they've received. This is especially true when they have a powerful testimony of what happened to them they need to share with others.

Final Thoughts on Investing in People

I hope this chapter has given you some things to think about in terms of what and who you are investing in, as well as some ways you can do that. I also hope you learned praying for people is one of the most effective ways we can invest in people, since we are asking God, who has way more resources than we do, to join us in this investment. I'll continue to talk about why we should invest in people and how we should feel about them in the next chapter.

Mike Garst

Chapter 12

Why Should We Invest in People?

In the previous chapter, I talked about different things we can invest in and that investing in people may give us the best return on our investment from an eternal perspective. In this chapter, I want to talk more about why we should invest in people, how we should feel about the people we are investing in, and why it's worth it.

Paying It Forward

There was a novel released in 1999 by Catherine Ryan Hyde entitled *Pay It Forward*. It was also adapted a couple of years later into the motion picture *Pay It Forward*. The book is about a young boy who decided to start doing unexpected good deeds for other people and the impact it had on them. One of the challenges most people have is they feel obligated to pay people back for what they have done for them. Many professing Christians have the same challenge, because they sometimes feel they need to pay God back for what He's done for them. In the case of people, it's possible we might be able to pay them back more than what they gave us or did for us. But with God, there's no way we could ever pay Him back for what He has given us through His Son, Jesus Christ. Plus, that's not what He wants from us. What He wants is for us to love Him, believe Him, trust Him, and obey His commands going forward.

God is concerned only about now and the future. His gift of salvation means He doesn't remember our sin or count it again us when we turn to Him and put our faith in Him. The Old Testament prophets and King David told us over and over God's plan was to forgive us and not remember our sins. These are some of the verses that tell us this great news.

> *"For I will forgive their iniquity, and their sin I will remember no more" (Jeremiah 31:34 – See also Heb 8:12 and 10:17).*

> *"As far as the east is from the west, so far has He removed our transgressions from us" (Psalm 103:12).*

> *"I, even I, am He who blots out your transgressions for My own sake; And I will not remember your sins" (Isaiah 43:25).*

> *"He will again have compassion on us, and will subdue our iniquities. You will cast all our sins Into the depths of the sea" (Micah 7:19).*

> *"Indeed it was for my own peace that I had great bitterness; but You have lovingly delivered my soul from the pit of corruption, for You have cast all my sins behind Your back" (Isaiah 38:17).*

> *(See also Jeremiah 33:8, 50:20, Isaiah 6:7, 27:9, 40:2, 44:22, 55:7, 65:16-17, Ezekiel 18:21-22, 33:18.)*

These verses confirm that from the beginning God wanted us take the gift He was planning to give us all along and then use it to bless and invest in others. This is the foundation of the second commandment.

> *"You shall not take vengeance, nor bear any grudge*

against the children of your people, but you shall love your neighbor as yourself: I am the Lord" (Leviticus 19:18).

See also *Matthew 22:39, Mark 12:33,* and *Luke 10:27.*

Therefore, we not only don't need to be concerned about our past sins, we also don't need to be concerned about those who have sinned against us. This is why God has commanded us not only to love and trust Him, but to love all the other people in our lives in the same way we want to be loved. This means, as believers in Christ, we have no excuse not to invest in and bless other people, including encouraging them to be reconciled with God and doing our part to reconcile with others whom we may have sinned against in some way. *"That is, that God was in Christ reconciling the world to Himself, not imputing their trespasses to them, and has committed to us the word of reconciliation" (2 Corinthians 5:19).*

If we are believers in Christ, we should be very concerned about the eternal destiny of the people we know and the people we will have the opportunity to know. Jesus set an example for us when He prayed,

> *"I do not pray for these alone, but also for those who will believe in Me through their word; that they all may be one, as You, Father, are in Me, and I in You; that they also may be one in Us, that the world may believe that You sent Me"*
> *(John 17:20-21).*

When we believe in Christ, we are united with Christ. The church is called the body of Christ. We are called to be united with one another and to share and show the good news of the gospel of Christ to all those around us each day, since our eternal future and the eternal future of those around us will be dependent on the choices each of us makes in this life. We only have one lifetime, regardless of how long that life is, to point people to Christ. A compassionate believer should have no other desire than to lay down his or her life fully, so all the people in their lives can have a chance to know the truth about eternity.

God's purposes and plans all involve trying to save the people He created from eternal destruction. *"For God did not send His Son into the world to condemn the world, but that the world through Him might be saved" (John 3:17).*

When we belong to Christ, our plans and purposes will be the same as His. This means we will use our unique gifts and talents, along with our relationships with the people God has uniquely connected us with, so they can know the truth about God, His Son, the Holy Spirit, and eternity.

How Should We Feel About the People We Are Investing In?

The interesting thing about investing in people is the depth of love God will build into our hearts for these people. Paul again demonstrated this in the epistles he wrote to the churches. I'm going to walk through some of these verses so you can get a sense of the love he had for these people. First, we see Paul wanted to spend time with them and not have just a quick visit. *"For I do not wish to see you now on the way; but I hope to stay a while with you, if the Lord permits" (1 Corinthians 16:7).*

We can tell a lot about people based on how much quality time they are willing to spend with us to talk about important things and not superficial things that don't connect us with our heart. The kinds of conversations we have with people we are investing in should get them thinking about their life more seriously. Chances are good they won't have many conversations like the ones they have with us. When we invest in people, we can also connect them with other people we have relationships with. This enables us not just to share greetings with other people, but a "hearty" greeting in the Lord. *"The churches of Asia greet you. Aquila and Priscilla greet you heartily in the Lord, with the church that is in their house. All the brethren greet you. Greet one another with a holy kiss" (1 Corinthians 16:19-20).*

You get the sense much hugging and holy kissing was going on in the early church! When we have deep and meaningful relationships with people, they become very important and very dear to us. This will not only bring us great peace and joy; it can also bring pain when we need to confront them about anything going on in their lives that needs a rebuke or correction of some kind to get them on track, because we care about them so much.

> "For out of much affliction and anguish of heart I wrote to you, with many tears, not that you should be grieved, but that you might know the love which I have so abundantly for you" (2 Corinthians 2:4).

We can have such a deep relationship with someone we are investing in we won't be able to rest and stay somewhere if we don't find that person there.

> "Furthermore, when I came to Troas to preach Christ's gospel, and a door was opened to me by the Lord, I had no rest in my spirit, because I did not find Titus my brother; but taking my leave of them, I departed for Macedonia" (2 Corinthians 2:12-13).

Paul's commitment to people was so intense he wanted those following Christ to be so much like Jesus, others could read the gospel by just being with them, so they could sense God's presence in their presence.

> "You are our epistle written in our hearts, known and read by all men; clearly you are an epistle of Christ, ministered by us, written not with ink but by the Spirit of the living God, not on tablets of stone but on tablets of flesh, that is, of the heart" (2 Corinthians 3:2-3).

Since God is looking at our hearts, it is always a good idea to open our hearts up not only to God but also to all those around us who trust in God. Paul urged the Corinthians to open their hearts, because Paul and those with him were opening their hearts wide to them.

> "O Corinthians! [Our mouth is open] We have spoken openly to you, our heart is wide open. You are not restricted by us, but you are restricted by your own affections. Now in return for the same (I speak as to children), you also be open" (2 Corinthians 6:11-13).

When we are investing in someone, we are essentially showing our hearts to them and urging them to do the same thing with us. The best relationships we will ever have in this life happen when both parties are striving for transparency. When we have nothing to hide, then we will never need to waste time trying to cover anything up. True freedom happens when truth, honesty, and openness reach a point where there's nothing left to hide. One of the reasons we model this kind of relationship with people we are investing in is so they can learn how to do this with other people.

It's also important to communicate regularly with the people we care about, so we both can know what is going on in our lives as much as possible. This will comfort their hearts, especially when we are doing something that may appear risky to them. Paul sent Tychicus to the Ephesians and Colossians for the express purpose of telling them how he was doing.

> "Tychicus, a beloved brother, faithful minister, and fellow servant in the Lord, will tell you all the news about me. I am sending him to you for this very purpose, that he may know your circumstances and comfort your hearts, with Onesimus, a faithful and beloved brother, who is one of you. They will make known to you all things which are happening here" (Colossians 4:7-9 – See also Ephesians 6:21-22).

When Paul wrote to the Thessalonians, he not only described himself as a mother cherishing her children, but told them why he was sharing with them what was going on his life and the lives of those with him.

> *"But we were gentle among you, just as a nursing mother cherishes her own children. So, affectionately longing for you, we were well pleased to impart to you not only the gospel of God, but also our own lives, because you had become dear to us"* (1 Thessalonians 2:7-8).

Paul also put on his "father hat" when he said,

> *"You are witnesses, and God also, how devoutly and justly and blamelessly we behaved ourselves among you who believe; as you know how we exhorted, and comforted, and charged every one of you, as a father does his own children, that you would walk worthy of God who calls you into His own kingdom and glory"*
> *(1 Thessalonians 2:10-12).*

All these verses show the depth of Paul's love for all the people he ministered to and with, and shows us investing in people is the only way we will ever experience the depth of love possible in this life, not only for God but also for all the people He connects us with.

It's Worth Investing in People

Although ministry and investing in people will have its hardships, what Paul wrote in *2 Corinthians 4:17-18* summarizes why it's worth it.

> *"For our light affliction, which is but for a moment, is working for us a far more exceeding and eternal weight of glory, while we do not look at the things which are seen, but at the things which are not seen. For the things which are seen are temporary, but the things which are not seen are eternal."*

Investing in people gives us eternal meaning and purpose that will keep us moving forward to a strong finish. Since everything else will be burned up anyhow, we really have nothing to lose by investing in people.

But we will not be able to do this if we don't first trust that God will take care of us. People in general worry a lot about the things in the world, but Jesus told us not to worry. Instead, He said, *"But seek first the kingdom of God and His righteousness, and all these things shall be added to you" (Matthew 6:33).*

When we are confident God will take care of our needs, it will be much easier for us to focus our time on other people. It's a win-win situation since we not only get to help and encourage others, we will also find it to be the most rewarding thing we can do in this life.

My Journey in Learning to Invest in Others

When I look back over my life, it is very clear I was investing only in myself before I surrendered my life to Christ as my Lord and Savior at forty-six years old. Any investment I may have made in my family, friends, and even co-workers before then was at best done for the wrong reasons. But then, I was clueless before I surrendered my heart and life to Jesus. But that has dramatically changed since then, and it took some serious work in my mind and heart by God before that transformation could even start.

Although God has been working on me since I was born, I was about thirty-six years old when I finally started to seek Him, which is when I read the Bible for the first time in my life and started going to church services again after growing up going to them regularly. I decided at that time I was going to read the whole Bible, and did it in one year, reading a King James Bible my grandparents had given me when I was ten years old, but had hardly opened in twenty-six years. About a year and a half later, my wife Susie and I joined the church. Shortly after that, I helped teach a Sunday school kindergarten class, but I hadn't given my whole heart to the Lord at that point. I also didn't have much of a clue about how to pray and rarely prayed for anyone. The best investment I was making, and it wasn't much, was helping to teach the Sunday school kindergarten class.

I continued this for the next nine years, but not much else changed in my life. The one thing I started to hear during these years was Christians were supposed to share the gospel with others, which was something I didn't know how to do, mainly because I didn't know the gospel very well. The church I was part of at that time also started going on mission trips to Costa Rica in the mid-nineties. During that time, I sensed God was stirring my heart to go on a mission trip, which I finally did in 1997 with a group of ten people led by our youth pastor, Bud Miller, who was becoming a dear brother and friend in Christ.

It wasn't an easy decision to make, because I had heard testimonies about some of the difficulties that some of the first groups experienced. Plus, I had never traveled outside of North America. But it was one of the best decisions I ever made, because it got me outside my comfort zone and gave me a chance to experience focusing on God for a solid week, which may be the most important thing about going on a mission trip. I came back with the desire to live my life each day more like I experienced it on that mission trip. Unfortunately, even though I met some new people in Costa Rica, I still wasn't at the point where I regularly prayed for them or anybody else.

The main desire I had then was to learn how to share my faith, and I had a chance to do that through an evangelism class at my church within the next year, after I had gone back to Costa Rica a second time. It was during that evangelism class I realized I didn't trust God completely yet and knew I needed to do it. I still look back on this epiphany as a pivotal point in my faith. It was as if I had been in a plane going down the runway for a long time and finally got off the ground.

I ended up going back to Costa Rica for another three years, including two trips in two of those years. I even had thoughts that maybe

I should be a missionary some day in Costa Rica. During that time, I got to know a few people there and am still connected to some of them. But I still had not developed the habit of praying for them or staying connected, which was much more difficult then because email and cell phones were just starting to be used.

After seven trips to Costa Rica, I had the opportunity in 2001 to go to Germany on a mission trip with a small group from my church and another church in Deer Park, Texas, leading a Baseball Camp. We used the game of baseball to draw youth to a camp where we could also talk with them about God, share testimonies, preach sermons, and sing praise songs.

Before my trip to Germany, I thought the trips to Costa Rica were great, but God was just preparing me for the primary group of people it appears He wanted me to invest in. This mission trip took me to a new level, because I sensed a deeper love for the German people than I had felt for anybody prior to then. And when I came back from that trip, I had a list of names of the people I met during the camp, and for the first time in my life, I started to pray over that list every day. Since email was in place at that time, I was even able to stay connected to several of the Germans I connected with. Looking back, I realized it was the first time I had invested in other people to any degree. I was also getting to know them and their stories. We don't really know a person until we know his or her story. I returned to Germany the next year to continue building on those relationships and expand my prayer list.

I had planned to go back to Costa Rica for the sixth year in a row, but didn't get to go because the travel agency we used never bought my ticket or a number of other tickets for the people in our group. But God wasn't done with the mission effort in Costa Rica, even though the way we were doing those trips shut down after the next year. The good news is it started up again a couple of years later through Bud Miller with a much different approach, which was to build relationships and make disciples. However, God had engraved Germany on my heart, and when the decision was made after the second camp for it only to be held every two years, I felt God was encouraging me to take a small team back the following year and do what we called a "Discipleship Camp," which was done in a smaller and simpler way. God showed me another level of investment in people when Bud Miller said he wanted to go to teach me how to lead a mission trip, since I had never led one before. He sacrificed a week of his time to invest in me, which left a huge impact on me. It was also very important, because Bud confirmed what I felt God was leading me to do. We need that kind of encouragement when we are still new to the faith and stepping outside our comfort zone. I had hoped the format of the camp for the next year would be more of a discipleship camp when it would be led again by the original camp leaders. And although it was modified to have more Bible teaching and study time that year, it went back to the original format the next time the camp was held, and the camp was only held every other year.

By then God had put it in my heart to start another baseball camp somewhere, and by 2008 God worked through me and a German couple, Roberto and Iris, who are my lifetime friends, to start a camp in Aurich, Germany, where we have held camps every year, except for 2020 when the Coronavirus was in its early stages. In 2015, God connected me with another church in Vechta, Germany, where we also started a Baseball Camp that has also continued every year except 2020. God also started a Baseball Camp in 2022 in Osterholz-Scharmbeck through me and a young German man who was at the first Baseball Camp in Aurich when he was eleven years old and participated in it for nine straight years. The investment in the birthday letters and cards I have continued to send him every year since 2008 may be the main reason that Baseball Camp started.

I'm sharing this information with you, so you have a better idea of the process I went through to learn how to invest in people. The evidence God was building a desire in my heart for investing in people was the ever-growing size of my prayer list. It didn't take long to figure out if I was praying for people in Germany, I should also be praying for my family, my friends, my fellow brothers and sisters in Christ in my local church and in Costa Rica, my coworkers, and other people I had some regular interaction with. I also developed a list of people I wanted to send birthday cards or greetings to after the first couple of Baseball Camps in Germany, which also includes people I'm connected to in the USA and Costa Rica. I've continued to do that and send birthday cards or letters to everybody I can get an address for who participates in a camp.

One of the benefits of praying for others is many of them will also be praying for you, which is what all believers are called to do for each other. It's always a blessing to know people are praying for us, especially since we all need prayer, and we all need the Holy Spirit interceding and turning those prayers into requests within God's will, which will ultimately cause the Holy Spirit to prompt us to do things others are praying for us to do. The prayers of the saints never get lost. The apostle John wrote about the prayers of the saints in *Revelation*.

> *"Now when He had taken the scroll, the four living creatures and the twenty-four elders fell down before the Lamb, each having a harp, and golden bowls full of incense, which are the prayers of the saints"*
> *(Revelation 5:8).*

> *"Then another angel, having a golden censer, came and stood at the altar. He was given much incense, that he should offer it with the prayers of all the saints upon the golden altar which was before the throne. And the smoke of the incense, with the prayers of the saints, ascended before God from the angel's hand" (Revelation 8:3-4).*

All believers in Christ are saints, so each of the prayers we've prayed in faith will never get lost. They will always be an eternal investment.

May all of you become investors in people so you can have your own testimony about how that impacted your life so positively and gave you a greater purpose for this life; one that will keep you going strong all the way to the end of your earthly life.

Mike Garst

Chapter 13

What Does an Intentional Life Look Like?

People do not drift toward holiness. Apart from grace-driven effort, people do not gravitate toward holiness, prayer, obedience to Scripture, faith, and delight in the Lord. We drift toward compromise and call it tolerance; we drift toward disobedience and call it freedom; we drift towards superstition and call it faith. We cherish the indiscipline of lost self-control and call it relaxation: we slouch toward prayerlessness and delude ourselves into thinking we have escaped legalism; we slide toward godlessness and convince ourselves we have been liberated. - D.A. Carson

The quote above is something I believe all Christians should take to heart. A friend of mine told me the motto in one of the Caribbean islands was "Let the day come to you." That sounds good on the surface, especially for anybody who is overwhelmed with life, but it will put you at the mercy of the world and make you a slave to what the world wants you to do. And that is not how a believer in Christ should live. Instead, we should *"And let us consider one another in order to stir up love and good works, not forsaking the assembling of ourselves together, as is the manner of some, but exhorting one another, and so much the more as you see the Day approaching" (Hebrews 10:24-25).*

Intentional Living

The question for all of us who profess faith in Christ is are we living our life intentionally, so we can use our God-given talents, strengths, and abilities to honor and glorify God increasingly more each day? When we exhort one another spiritually, we speak the truth in love to encourage or challenge each other to keep growing in our faith and love. In this process, the Holy Spirit can convince us to change the things in our life that don't glorify and honor God. When we do this, it will bring us freedom and blessings beyond our comprehension.

Many of us have either struggled to make the changes we need to implement in our lives in a timely manner, or we've not made them at all up to this point in our life. One of the key reasons most people struggle with creating new habits and killing old ones is because they underestimate how difficult it is for even professing Christians to make radical alterations in their lives. It's difficult because creating new habits takes sustained time and effort. It means we must stop our old ways of doing things, which can be as hard as establishing new ways. It means we may have to create not only a new to-do list but also a to-stop list. Sometimes, that to-stop list includes people and places taking us away from the life God has called us to and to set new boundaries in our life.

Jesus addressed this in the following verses.

> *"When an unclean spirit goes out of a man, he goes through dry places, seeking rest, and finds none. Then he says, 'I will return to my house from which I came.' And when he comes, he finds it empty, swept, and put in order. Then he goes and takes with him seven other spirits more wicked than himself, and they enter and dwell there; and the last state of that man is worse than the first. So shall it also be with this wicked generation" (Matthew 12:43-45).*

These verses tell us if we get rid of something bad in our life, we must replace it with something good, or we will end up developing another habit much worse than the old one we expunged. Knowing this may make it even more difficult to attempt making a change, since we understand the consequences of not replacing it with something good.

Replace the Old with New

Most of us find structure in our lives at work or in school, but when we get home, we don't have the same level of discipline (understandably if we have families and personal demands), so it's important for us to build habits into our home life that help define who we are becoming. One of the reasons this is so hard is because most people look forward to going home in the evenings and being home on weekends, so they don't have to live with as much structure in their lives and can be free to do what they want to do. This may sound like a good thing, but it can cause us to live an undisciplined life at home most of the time.

I said in chapter five, "How Can I Become Like Jesus," it will take the same kind of effort to become a disciple of Christ as it does to become a great doctor or athlete. Establishing any new habit takes a similar effort. Jesus said,

> *"No one puts a piece of unshrunk cloth on an old garment; for the patch pulls away from the garment, and the tear is made worse. Nor do they put new wine into old wineskins, or else the wineskins break, the wine is spilled, and the wineskins are ruined. But they put new wine into new wineskins, and both are preserved"* (Matthew 9:16-17).

Intentional living requires that we focus on getting rid of the old and developing something entirely new. Plus, we must know what our part in this process is and what God's part is. We must build good solid disciplines into our life that help us eliminate the ineffective and wasteful things we do, and create the new habits that help us do only what honors and glorifies God. This is why we can't allow our time at home in the evenings or on the weekends to be wasted doing things that are not a part of the kingdom of God. We need to ask ourselves, "What is it I have to stop doing and what do I have to start doing in its place?" Once we decide what those things are, we must then build the discipline and structure in our life to do those things.

Building the disciplines into our personal lives that help us put to death anything that doesn't glorify God and helps us to better know God and what honors and pleases Him could be called the fundamentals. It's about becoming brilliant at the basics.

We can learn a lot from sports in terms of fundamentals, practice, and building skills. When a team looks at game films after they lose a game, many times the real reason for the loss was not executing on the fundamentals. In football, it can be blocking and tackling, catching, or holding the ball properly, or being in the right position on the field. In basketball, it can be rebounding, passing, setting screens, playing defense, and being in the right position on the court. Any team that doesn't develop and keep the fundamentals sharp will eventually falter in their performance during games.

The same thing can happen in our spiritual lives. When we don't have the fundamentals in our spiritual life in place, we end up wasting our time on other things that eventually hurt us one way or the other.

When it comes to waste, we should remember what Jesus said after feeding five thousand men plus their families. *"So when they were filled, He said to His disciples, 'Gather up the fragments that remain, so that nothing is lost.'" (John 6:12).*

Some translations use the word "wasted" instead of "lost." If Jesus was concerned about not losing or wasting any of the food God provided for the thousands of people out of the five loaves of bread and two fish, then it would be a good idea for us not to waste any of the resources God gives us. We don't have much time on this earth, and it will go by faster than we could ever imagine. King David wrote,

> "Lord, make me to know my end, and what is the measure of my days, That I may know how frail I am. Indeed, You have made my days as handbreadths, and my age is as nothing before You; certainly every man at his best state is but vapor" (Psalm 39:4-5).

We must recognize our natural body does not like change or discipline. It wants what's comfortable, painless, pleasurable, or safe, and it wants it now. When we build discipline into our lives, it will help us keep our natural bodies from determining what we should do.

Imagine trying to lose weight and not ignoring your natural desire to eat when hungry. To effectively lose weight, we must say no to our natural desires and do only what will keep us on track to lose weight and keep it off.

There's an important lesson we can learn from what it takes to effectively lose weight and keep it off. The reason most people end up putting back on the weight they lost, and this includes people who lose hundreds of pounds, is because they go on a program to lose the weight, but after they lose it, they go back to their old way of life. When we live disciplined lives, we are living life intentionally all the time. There's no taking a day or week or month to go back to doing what we did before. People who effectively lose weight and keep it off are people who have permanently changed the way they eat and exercise. If we don't effectively develop new habits, we will always fall back on our old bad habits, which will be unhealthy for us physically and spiritually. It's our responsibility to use our time wisely to do things that strengthen our faith and bodies, and not destroy them. If we do our part, God will always do His part to make our faith and love grow. The only thing that can keep us from becoming great men and women of God is not building the discipline into our lives required to become men and women after God's own heart.

Write Down Your Purpose and Objectives

Most organizations today take the time and effort to develop a mission statement to clarify why they exist. Sometimes this also includes a vision, which is what they want to become at some point in the future. Once they establish these things, they typically develop a strategic plan for how they will accomplish their mission and vision. This also includes specific goals, which are the activities and tasks that make the mission and vision a reality. Good organizations put this in writing and take the time to communicate it to everyone in their organization. They also monitor how they are doing and communicate the results to everyone in their organization. Plus, an effective organization typically updates their strategic plan and goals yearly. Yet if we asked most people what their mission is, we would probably not find more than 1-2% who have anything written down. If a person has not put a mission in writing, he or she is probably going to have a difficult time trying to verbalize it to anybody who asks what it is, much less live it.

Without a written-down mission, people are also not going to have a vision or a strategic plan or goals. God told the prophet Habakkuk to,

> *"Write the vision and make it plain on tablets, that he may run who reads it. For the vision is yet for an appointed time; but at the end it will speak, and it will not lie. Though it tarries, wait for it; because it will surely come, it will not tarry" (Habakkuk 2:2-3).*

These verses tell us why it's important to write down God's vision for our life. First, he says *"That he may run who reads it."* It's hard to go in the right direction if we don't know where we are going. As it's been said, if we don't have a destination in mind, any road will get us there.

Jesus also told us to,

> *"Enter by the narrow gate; for wide is the gate and broad is the way that leads to destruction, and there are many who go in by it. [How] Because narrow is the gate and [confined] difficult is the way which leads to life, and there are few who find it"* (Matthew 7:13-14).

The wide gate and broad road in this verse can be the "any road" when we don't have a specific destination in mind. The broad road may seem like the wisest choice so we can have multiple options depending on how things go, but if none of those options line up with God's plans for us, it's not going to get us where God wants us to go. And ultimately, God's destination for us is His kingdom.

The first part of *Habakkuk 2:3* says, *"For the vision is yet for an appointed time; but at the end it will speak, and it will not lie."* Once we have a destination, we then need to determine what it is going to take to get us there. If it's a God-given vision, and we're earnestly seeking it, we will get there, but the timeframe may not be clear. Our part is to do the things we must do to get there and leave the timetable in God's hands, because God must first build His character into us before we can reach our destiny.

In the game of *Monopoly*, we must get to the "pass go" block on the board to get $200, which is one way to get the money we need to win the game. Like the game of *Monopoly*, where you keep going around the board and try to avoid losing money on your turn, so you gain money, we typically must go through a number of stages and tests before God's character will be formed in us. His plan is to transform us into Christ's likeness so He can carry out His purposes through us. Therefore, it will take as long as needed for us to become enough like Christ so God can work through us.

The last part of *Habakkuk 2:3* says, *"Though it tarries, wait for it;*

Because it will surely come, It will not tarry." Most of us think we are ready before we are truly God-ready, so it may seem like it's taking much longer than it should to get where we think we are supposed to go and do what we think God wants to do through us. This means we must be patient and let God continue to do in us what's needed for us to be ready for Him to do what He wants to do through us.

If we look at the Israelite's crossing of the desert to get to the Promised Land, we know it took forty years. When you look at the actual distance they had to travel, that trip could have been done in ten to twenty days. That means it took them roughly a thousand times longer to get to the Promised Land than needed! But God wasn't going to let them go into the Promised Land if they weren't ready to do their part in fighting for it and living in a right way before God so they could defend it and keep it. During that forty years, God had to destroy an entire generation, except for Caleb and Joshua, before He let their children go into the Promised Land. We need to take this to heart and realize we aren't going to get to the kingdom of God if we are not living in a way that enables God to form His character in us, so He can carry out His purposes through us.

> *In Matthew 11:12, Jesus said this about the kingdom of God. "And from the days of John the Baptist until now the kingdom of heaven suffers violence, and the violent take it by force" (Matthew 11:12 – See also Luke 16:16).*

To take something by force or to press into it requires effort on our part. God isn't going to drop the kingdom of God in our laps and say, "Here it is, it's yours." He's offered us the gift of salvation, and His Son Jesus Christ did His part to make it possible and tell us the cost. This is why we must live intentionally, because part of the cost will involve overcoming obstacles in our life. Many of those obstacles will not appear to be a problem if we don't recognize how they affect our thinking and thus how we should live. We can end up feeling comfortable and secure in our lives, but have no clue about our true condition. Jesus said to the church in Laodicea,

> *"Because you say, 'I am rich, have become wealthy, and have need of nothing'—and do not know that you are wretched, miserable, poor, blind, and naked—I counsel you to buy from Me gold refined in the fire, that you may be rich; and white garments, that you may be clothed, that the shame of your nakedness may not be revealed; and anoint your eyes with eye salve, that you may see"* (Revelation 3:17-18).

According to this verse, professing Christians can believe they are rich and wealthy, and they don't need anything. And even though most believers in Christ know in their head the riches of this world won't do them any good in the end, they can still pursue them more than they pursue God, which is what will end up making them lukewarm. An intentional plan can help us be proactive in every area of our life so we can recognize if we are lukewarm or not. It will help us know what our mission and goals truly are, and enable us to examine how we are doing in pursuit of them.

The American Dream or God's Plan?

The first thing we must determine is whether the mission and goals for our life are something we've adopted from our culture, or if it's truly God's purpose and plans for our lives. Chances are good if we don't have a written plan for our life, it may indicate other people or things are really in control of our life, or we've just adopted the American dream as we understand it. When other people or things take control of our life, it's a good indicator we are either more interested in pleasing people or just doing what we want to do. The apostle Paul said, *"For do I now persuade men, or God? Or do I seek to please men? For if I still pleased men, I would not be a bondservant of Christ"* (Galatians 1:10).

When we are not able to say "no" to the expectations of others, or we are just more interested in making other people happy, we are going to have a difficult time not only determining what God's purpose is for our lives but also carrying out whatever goals we have set for ourselves. Allowing other people to be in control of our lives may be the biggest reason people struggle with writing a mission statement and having goals and objectives to carry it out, because they will always do first what other people want and not what they need to do in order to achieve their goals.

If we have just adopted the typical American dream as the mission for our life, then we are going to do what most Americans appear to be doing with their lives. It seems to me the American dream looks something like this; retire as soon as possible and have a nice paid-for house, good and reliable cars, adequate financial resources, great vacations, enjoyable hobbies, plenty of entertainment, and a family that can also experience this American dream. In other words, it includes lots of pleasure, comfort, and security.

Now if this is what most people want, then some of them may be able to accomplish some of these things. But that dream may make it difficult for them to finish their life in a way that glorifies and honors God. If this isn't your dream, and you really want to finish strong in a God-honoring way, then you must take control of your life as much as possible, and become much more intentional about what you do and whom you spend your time with. This means you must have a God-given mission and vision, some well-defined goals, and a strategic plan for achieving those goals. You need a mission that puts God in control of your life, in which you identify your God-inspired priorities and make sure your daily plans enable you to live by those priorities. It will also require you to regularly examine your life closely, so you can see if you are living according to the plan and making the progress you need to make. As you do this, you will also need to regularly adjust your plans to either get back on course or better align your plans with God's purpose for you.

No matter what mission we may write down and pursue, we must realize if it's not God's mission for us, then we are going to be functioning on only our own strength and resources to accomplish it. When we are on God's plan, we are going to regularly experience His provision, guidance, grace, patience, forgiveness, mercy, compassion, help, encouragement, and all the other ways He loves and blesses us.

One of the ways to determine if we are on God's plan versus our plan is to examine the fruit of the Spirit (see *Galatians 5:22-23*) in our lives. If we are on God's plan, we are going to experience peace, joy, and the other fruits of the Spirit increasingly more. We will also become more and more excited about where God is leading us. On the other hand, if our plan is wearing us out, it's a good indication we are not on God's plan. One of the things I've noticed about many middle-aged people I know, especially those who are advancing in the companies they work for, is many are suffering "burnout." This drives them to work even harder to build up financial resources so they can retire from their jobs as soon as possible and live a more relaxing life away from the pressures of work. This is an example of being on a plan that is not God's plan. God didn't design us or the world to be in the so-called "rat race," where one rat is always trying to get ahead of or outdo the other rat, and constantly wearing ourselves out. God wants us to enjoy our work and daily be refreshed and look forward to going to work, because we were designed to work and in a way that honors God.

> *"Here is what I have seen: It is good and fitting for one to eat and drink, and to enjoy the good of all his labor in which he toils under the sun all the days of his life which God gives him; for it is his [portion] heritage"*
> *(Ecclesiastes 5:18 – See Ecclesiastes 2:24 also).*

At the end of *Psalm 78*, which is a sobering Psalm about the Israelites journey through the desert but also encouraging because of God's faithfulness, it says,

> *"He also chose David His servant, and took him from the sheepfolds; from following the ewes that had young He brought him, to shepherd Jacob His people, and Israel His inheritance. So he shepherded them according to the integrity of his heart, and guided them by the skillfulness of his hands" (Psalm 78:70-72).*

Verse *seventy-two* tells us the two most important things about work. First, we must do our work with integrity of heart. This is another way of saying we must do things following God's ways and truth and not succumb to following the competitive and evil ways of the world. Second, we must have skillful hands. In other words, we must discover and develop the gifts and talents God gives us so we can do something worthy with our hands. This includes creating, designing, and building whatever is needed to enable us to live in healthy community with one another. This also means we must have people in all the different kinds of vocations needed for a society to function properly. God in His sovereignty and wisdom creates the right mix of people with the unique talents needed to make this happen. When we have all the different vocational skills working together in a healthy way, people are going to enjoy what they are doing.

Knowing and Living by God's Truth

God's Word is the only truth, and when we are living intentionally, we are essentially trying to identify what truths we don't believe or understand yet so we can confess the lies we've believed, accept the truth, and adjust our lives to that truth. When we turn to the truth, we must not rely on what the pastor is preaching or the Sunday school leader is teaching, or what any other recognized Christian authority says or writes.

We need to be like the Bereans Paul wrote about in *Acts 17*. Even though Paul was a student of the well-known Gamaliel and was taught directly by the resurrected Jesus, the Bereans still did their homework. *"These were more [noble] fair-minded than those in Thessalonica, in that they received the word with all readiness, and searched the scriptures daily to find out whether these things were so" (Acts 17:11).*

We should never leave it up to what other people believe God's Word is saying, no matter how much of an authority they appear to be. Even Jesus, who only spoke the truth, was thoroughly tested by the Pharisees, Sadducees, and the Teachers of the Law. We also need to look deeply at what our true priorities are by examining what we are doing with our time and resources. We can talk about what we think we believe, but true belief will always lead to some form of action that shows what we really believe. I'm pretty sure God orchestrates our lives to give us a chance to see how we will respond to different circumstances we encounter. God didn't spare Abraham what we might think was the toughest test ever when He told him to offer his son as a sacrifice (see *Genesis 22*). Both God and Abraham had to know if there was anything Abraham might worship more than God because of what God promised He would do through Abraham. When Abraham passed that test, he secured his place as the father of faith for all of us.

We Have a Desire and Capacity Deficiency

Another important reason we must live intentionally is because our spiritual bodies have a desire and a capacity deficiency for God that can only be strengthened when we take the necessary steps to increase our love for God. If we don't do this, we will have difficulty developing a more intimate relationship with Him. None of us naturally want to spend time with God just like nobody naturally wants to start going to the gym to improve their physical fitness. But what happens when a person makes a commitment to go to the gym, works out five or six days a week, and ends up doing it for a while? That person grows stronger, loses weight, increases his or her endurance, feels more energetic, and becomes healthier. As a result, the desire to go to the gym increases, and he or she ends up looking forward to going to the gym, because he or she experiences all the benefits and realizes it's a good thing to do.

The same thing happens to people who run. Their natural body doesn't want to run initially, but after a while, they actually look forward to running. It's even been said runners can get a little "high" from running, or they can become addicted to running.

When we increase our endurance through workouts at the gym or by running, we are increasing our capacity. We can lift heavier weights, we can do exercises longer before we get tired, and we can run faster and longer. Nobody who runs a marathon starts out running a marathon. In some cases, people can barely run one hundred yards the first time they try to run, because they are so out of shape. But if a person starts running daily, that distance will steadily increase, and they will eventually be able to run a marathon. A person like this would develop a capacity four-hundred-fifty times more than when he or she started initially, only being able to run one hundred yards.

Our spiritual bodies are like our physical bodies in this respect. Nobody has a natural desire to spend time with God in His Word or in prayer. We can only develop and increase our desire to do this by committing to doing it daily long enough to make it a habit. When we faithfully do this, we will also increase our spiritual capacity, especially if we continuously increase the length of time we spend with God in His Word and in prayer. That is why mature Christians who have spent years developing an ever-increasing daily quiet time with God can spend hours with Him in His Word and prayer and look forward to it each day. If we want to measure the maturity of our faith, we can always look at the frequency and length of time we want to spend with God each day as an indicator. Spending time in God's Word each day is one of the key spiritual disciplines we must build into our lives if we want to become strong and finish strong. Discipline only comes about when the effort we've invested in doing something becomes an enjoyable habit.

Intentional Love

In chapter one, I included a quote from Granny Brand's son Paul[11], "This is how to grow old. Allow everything else to fall away until those around you see only love."

I'm convinced this is only going to happen if we become intentional about getting rid of anything in our lives that isn't love and making sure we are doing the things that show God's love. Love and truth go together, along with many of God's other attributes. Although we can talk about what's different in each of God's attributes, all of them are a different expression of His love toward us. Anything in our lives that doesn't reflect God's love is going to be an obstacle that can keep us from becoming strong or finishing strong. For example, if we are short on patience, we are going to rush into doing things that could bring a lot of unnecessary problems into our lives because we were either not ready, or we hurriedly made a bad choice with serious negative consequences.

Think about the young couple that rushes into marriage but doesn't understand what true commitment is, how to be a godly spouse, or haven't talked about what either of them wants out of life or their marriage, including basic things like if they want to have a family. If there is one thing that has significantly changed in the last fifty years, it's the percentage of divorces not only in the USA, but in many other countries. Marriage is not easy for anybody, so we must be patient not only to find

---

[11] Granny Brand Her Story, Dorothy Wilson Clarke Paul Brand Publishing Seattle WA, 1976, Page 206

the right person, but more importantly to become the right person for someone to marry.

When we are short on giving grace and showing mercy, we are going to find it difficult to have relationships with people, whether it's our spouse, our friends, or the people we work with, who God may have placed in our lives specifically to help us carry out His plans and purposes for and through us. When we need more knowledge and don't have enough godly advisers in our lives, then we are going to make bad decisions because we didn't get God's full perspective. Any bad decisions we make are going to take us off course and could require a lot of time to get us back on course.

Bottom line, any attribute of God's love that hasn't been developed fully in us is going to be a liability that can take us off course from God's plan for us. This is why we must be intentional about what we are doing each day. Love doesn't grow naturally without any effort on our part. Love also doesn't grow only on our efforts. We sow the seeds and water when needed, but God makes our love grow (see *1 Corinthians 3:6-7*). Because God is faithful, we can be assured He will always do His part. But we must also do our part regardless of the circumstances in our life. A disciplined life will not allow the dysfunctional lives around it to take it off course.

Chapter 14

What Are the Dangers of Not Living Intentionally?

"And because lawlessness will abound, the love of many will grow cold. (Matthew 24:12).

Jesus told the verse above to His disciples when they asked Him about the end times. But it's a verse all professing Christians should take to heart since it says *"the love of <u>many</u> [my emphasis] will grow cold."* One of the most important reasons we must live intentionally is to make sure our love is growing stronger and not colder.

Is My Love Growing Cold or Hot?

Jesus made it clear at the beginning of *Matthew 24:12* how our love could grow cold. *"Because lawlessness will abound."* It's very easy for some Christians to assume this doesn't apply to them since they may not understand what lawlessness is. Lawlessness isn't just what hardened criminals do, it's anything opposed to God's truth, ways, and promises. Most of us don't like to think of ourselves as lawless just because we have some bad habits in our lives. But all bad habits have sin at the root of them, including the things we do and don't do. The book of *James* gives us a very simple description of sin. *"Therefore, to him who knows to do good and does not do it, to him it is sin" (James 4:17).*

This means as we come to know God's truth, ways, and promises, we must then act and live according to those truths. And when we don't live by those truths, we will be resisting the leading of the Holy Spirit and putting ourselves in danger as the following verses tell us.

> *"Therefore, as the Holy Spirit says: 'Today, if you will hear His voice, do not harden your hearts as in the rebellion, in the day of trial in the wilderness, where your fathers tested Me, tried Me, and saw My works forty years. Therefore I was angry with that generation, and said, "They always go astray in their heart, and they have not known My ways.'" So I swore in My wrath, 'They shall not enter My rest.'" (Hebrews 3:7-11).*

This means professing Christians must intentionally and continually put sin to death in their lives, so they can be blameless before the Lord all the time, and so they can be transformed more and more into Christ's likeness daily. When they do this, their love for God and for people will grow. When they don't, their love for God and people will grow cold as the second part of *Matthew 24:12* says.

One of the reasons we can struggle with putting sin to death in our lives is because we can have doubts about God, which will cause us to resist obeying Him. This is why we must overcome our doubts about God, or we will be double-minded. James wrote,

> *"But let him ask in faith, with no doubting, for he who doubts is like a wave of the sea driven and tossed by the wind. For let not that man suppose that he will receive anything from the Lord; he is a double-minded man, unstable in all his ways" (James 1:6-8).*

Since Christians have Christ living in them via the Holy Spirit, there isn't any legitimate reason they should let any sin or doubt continue to live in their minds or hearts. Christ not only gives power to believers, He also can sympathize with them because He's walked in their shoes. *"For we do not have a High Priest who cannot sympathize with our weaknesses, but was in all points tempted as we are, yet without sin"* (Hebrews 4:15).

Sin is also deceptive (see *Hebrews 3:13*), and it will harden us if we don't respond to the Holy Spirit's prompting to confess and turn from sin. Plus, once we know about sin in our life, it can eventually separate us from Christ if we refuse to acknowledge it and do our part to put it to death. If we fail to agree with God, or do what He commands us to do, we become His enemy because our actions will be showing we don't believe or trust God. This is why living intentionally will help us stay close to God and quickly acknowledge the sin the Holy Spirit reveals to us, so we won't develop a hard heart and fail to confess and repent. One way we can be intentional is by proactively asking God to show us any sin in our lives. This is what King David did when he wrote, *"Search me, O God, and know my heart; try me, and know my anxieties; and see if there is any wicked way in me, and lead me in the way everlasting"* (Psalm 139:23-24).

This is a great verse to include in our daily prayers, since it would show how serious we are about purging sin out of our heart so we can endure to the end. *Matthew 24:13* says why this is so important. *"But he who endures to the end shall be saved."*

When our love is growing, we will be standing firm and being saved. But we must do our part to make sure our love is growing. This is why we need to have a plan on how we are going to keep our love growing. Our natural inclinations and the devil are going to do everything they can to keep us from growing in our love. The apostle Paul wrote these words in *2 Timothy 3:1-5*.

> *"But know this, that in the last days perilous times will come: for men will be lovers of themselves, lovers of money, boasters, proud, blasphemers, disobedient to parents, unthankful, unholy, unloving, unforgiving, slanderers, without self-control, brutal, despisers of good, traitors, headstrong, haughty, lovers of pleasure rather than lovers of God, having a form of godliness but denying its power. And from such people turn away!"*

If we are honest about the culture in the USA, the words in the verses above would describe many people, including many who profess to be Christians. We don't have to watch much television or spend much time on social media to see almost all the bad behaviors in the verses above are being promoted to some extent. That is why Satan is called a "deceiver." We don't fall easily into a lifestyle that has very little, if any purpose. Instead, we are slowly led into it, because we aren't seeing or hearing the truth with God's eyes or ears, or we aren't putting it into practice. This is why we must regularly examine if our love for God and for people is growing hotter or colder.

Comfort Zone Dangers

Another reason we must live intentionally is so we can prevent ourselves from being trapped in our own comfort zones. All of us have comfort zones that can keep us from doing things beneficial to us. Plus, Satan can appear to us as an angel of light (see *2 Corinthians 11:14*) when he tries to lead us to think about our comfort zone when confronted with a new opportunity to serve God.

Comfort zones from a spiritual perspective can keep us from doing anything that has what we might think are unnecessary risks in it. In other words, if we believe there could be some negative outcomes we don't want to experience, we may decide it's not a good thing for us to do. It is good to look to God to comfort us when we need to be comforted in difficult situations, but a comfort zone is quite different from being comforted by God when we are in danger or hurting. Plus, comfort zones don't have to be necessarily healthy situations. They can be anything we've grown accustomed to. For example, when the Israelites faced situations in the desert they didn't like, it didn't take them very long to want to go back to their life of slavery in Egypt.

> *"And all the children of Israel complained against Moses and Aaron, and the whole congregation said to them, 'If only we had died in the land of Egypt! Or if only we had died in this wilderness! Why has the Lord brought us to this land to fall by the sword, that our wives and children should become victims? Would it not be better for us to return to Egypt?'" (Numbers 14:2-3).*

A situation they didn't like at one time looked very comforting to them when they thought they weren't going to have enough food or water in the desert.

We must become aware of our comfort zones and be proactive in doing new things that will keep us from settling into a given way of life that may cause our love to grow cold. It will require us to continually learn and try new things that will help us grow in our faith. And since we are called to love and serve others, there are countless things we can do that will help us experience God's love in new ways, and thus strengthen our faith and increase our love. Jesus didn't just teach His disciples by reading and sharing insight on God's Word. He sent them out to minister to people who needed to experience and hear about God's love.

> *"After these things the Lord appointed seventy others also, and sent them two by two before His face into every city and place where He Himself was about to go. Then He said to them, 'The harvest truly is great, but the laborers are few; therefore pray the Lord of the harvest to send out laborers into His harvest. Go your way; behold, I send you out as lambs among wolves. Carry neither money bag, knapsack, nor sandals; and greet no one along the road'"*
> *(Luke 10:1-4).*

This will require we take risks, because people will not always be receptive to what we may be offering them. As you can see in the above verses, Jesus told them He was sending them *"out as lambs among wolves,"* which would put them way outside their comfort zones, especially when Jesus also told them not to take anything with them in verse *four*. They were not only going to face opposition, they were going to need to depend on people they didn't know to house and feed them. Rejection alone is hard for all of us, because we are natural people-pleasers. Because of this, our natural mind will always try to keep from doing anything that might result in rejection. Our comfort zones typically have no room for people who are not pleased with us.

Security Dangers

Comfort and security can be closely related, because we feel much more secure in our comfort zones. Wanting security in this life will lead us to spend time and resources on things that make us feel secure in the short term. As disciples of Christ, our security must be in knowing God will cover all our needs in this life if we love and trust Him. Jesus told His disciples,

> *"Therefore do not worry, saying, 'What shall we eat?' or 'What shall we drink?' or 'What shall we wear?' For after all these things the Gentiles seek. For your heavenly Father knows that you need all these things. But seek first the kingdom of God and His righteousness, and all these things shall be added to you" (Matthew 6:31-33).*

Jesus was telling His disciples if they set their minds to learning and doing what pleases God, He would take care of all their needs. They didn't need an insurance policy. They just needed to trust God completely. Our call as disciples of Christ in today's world is no different. Since God has never failed to deliver on His Word or His promises, we can be assured He is going to take care of us if we focus on learning and doing what is right in God's eyes.

When we use our resources and time to increase our security for things in this life, then we likely are going to make serving and helping others a lower priority than those things. For example, instead of spending our money and time to go on a short-term mission trip, we may invest that money in a way to increase our retirement income. We can also fail to give to worthy causes for God for the same reason. This can lead to a lifestyle of "Never Enough." When I lived in Maryland, I drove on a road where there was a sign at the driveway entrance to a home that said "Never Enough." That, unfortunately, appears to be the mentality of many people in today's world; especially in the USA.

I've also noticed as we get older, we take fewer risks in every area of our life. We may travel less and not do activities that may cause injuries to our bodies, doing what we think are safer things. This is the opposite of the way God wants us to live. As I talked about in chapter one, Granny Brand set an incredible example for all of us. If she had decided to seek more security and more comfort, she would have left India after her husband Jesse died. But not only did she continue working as a missionary in the undeveloped mountains of India until she was ninety-five, she persevered through several serious injuries, including a broken hip, broken rips, and falling headfirst off a horse.

Neither comfort nor security were serious factors for Granny Brand when she made decisions. Yes, she suffered some serious injuries that didn't all completely heal, but it didn't keep her from carrying out the mission she believed God called her to do. And even though it may take longer to heal as we get older, God doesn't stop healing us as much as necessary for us to keep doing His work.

When we live intentionally, we need to take steps to make sure we aren't investing too much of our time or resources to be more secure in this life.

Not Effectively Implementing and Evaluating Our Goals

It's been said a poor plan violently executed is much better than a great plan poorly implemented. This is why it may be easier for people to develop a mission with goals for their life than it is to carry them out. This is why the implementation and evaluation of our goals may be a more important part of the process and why it's important to work harder on this part.

If we look at most good organizations, we see they have some way of measuring how they are doing. For example, if we sent our kids to schools, and they didn't take tests or do any other kind of assignments or tasks that showed what they had learned, we'd have no idea if they were making good progress or not. Can you imagine a professional sports team not keeping statistics on how each of their players were doing, or how the team was doing? Statistics are being gathered increasingly more for just about everything we do. This is why technology is being used increasingly more to measure different processes so they can be controlled better.

In the manufacturing business, good companies always have a control plan for each of the manufacturing processes they use to build their products. Most times it includes what is called "Statistical Process Control," which is a process where you define specifications for a component with an upper and a lower limit, and then regularly measure those parts to see if they are within those limits. But the purpose of statistical process control is not to let you know when you are outside the upper and lower limits, it's monitoring the trend so you can see when it's drifting toward one of those limits, so you can make adjustments before you start manufacturing parts outside the specification. When you wait to make changes after you get outside the specification, you may need not only to throw away defective parts, you may also need to rework any existing products that may have been built with defective parts. And depending on how fast your product gets to the market, or how long it took you to recognize the defect, you may have to replace products the customer already has. In other words, it can be very expensive for companies to let their plans or processes get out of control.

We use process control in manufacturing companies, but very few people do anything like this with their personal or spiritual lives, except possibly to control their weight. Scales make it easy for anybody to check weight as often as he or she wants, to keep weight under control. And just like manufacturing companies want to keep their processes from getting out of control, those who want to keep their weight under control will make changes in their eating or exercise habits, so they can get their weight back to where they want it before it gets out of control. It's much easier to lose five pounds than to lose ten or twenty pounds.

The apostle Paul wrote about examining ourselves in *1 Corinthians 13:5*. *"Examine yourselves as to whether you are in the faith. Test yourselves. Do you not know yourselves, that Jesus Christ is in you? — unless indeed you [you do not stand the test] are disqualified."*

In the epistles Paul wrote, he was constantly telling others to imitate him. Because of this, he needed to evaluate constantly his spiritual health so he wouldn't be a hypocrite. He wanted to be a genuine godly example for them to follow and especially wanted to honor and glorify God in all his actions and words.

Paul also talked about examining yourself before taking communion.

> *"But let a man examine himself, and so let him eat of the bread and drink of the cup. For he who eats and drinks in an unworthy manner eats and drinks judgment to himself, not discerning the Lord's body. For this reason many are weak and sick among you, and many [are dead] sleep. For if we would judge ourselves, we would not be judged. But when we are judged, we are chastened by the Lord, that we may not be condemned with the world"*
> *(1 Corinthians 11:28-32).*

These verses seem to be saying (and I encourage each of you reading this to discern what you believe God is saying) God gives each of us an opportunity to proactively enable the Holy Spirit to convict us of any sin in our lives that needs to be confessed and turned from, especially before we take communion. If we do this, God will not need to discipline us. But if we fail to examine our lives, and we have unconfessed sin still living in us the Holy Spirit has clearly shown us before we take communion with our fellow believers, then God is going to discipline us. And this discipline can result in weakness, sickness, and even death, as *verse thirty* above says.

Now, if we are in Christ and Christ is in us, then coming under God's discipline will keep us from being condemned with the world as *verse 32* says. But if there are rewards in heaven, as the scriptures talk about often (*see Ruth 2:12, 2 Samuel 2:22:21, Psalm 19:11, 58:11, 62:12, Proverbs 11:18, 13:13, 25:22, Isaiah 40:10, 49:4, 62:11, Jeremiah 32:19, Matthew 5:12, 6:1, 4, 6, 18, 10:41-42, 16:27, Luke 6:35, Romans 2:6, 1 Corinthians 3:8, Colossians 3:24, Hebrews 10:35, 11:6, 11:26, 2 John 1:8, and Revelation 11:18, 22:12*), then it would be a good idea to make sure we don't exit this world any sooner than necessary; especially if God has plans to do something in and through us. Again, each of us needs to go to God for a better understanding of what these verses are saying, but the need to proactively examine ourselves is clear, especially if we combine it with *2 Corinthians 13:5*.

Living Intentionally Each Day

One of the key reasons people struggle with implementing any goals they set for themselves is because they fail to plan it into their daily lives. Whatever goals we have, we must get them onto our calendar and prioritize them as much as possible. For example, if we are going to develop a more intimate relationship with God, and a relationship with

Him is our highest priority, then it needs to be the first thing we plan into our daily schedule. The apostle Mark wrote, *"Now in the morning, having risen a long while before daylight, He went out and departed to a [deserted] solitary place; and there He prayed" (Mark 1:35).*

If Jesus made it a priority to get up early in the morning and find a quiet place to go and spend time with His Father, it would be foolish for us not to do the same thing. I believe it is the most important discipline I've built into my life. And as I have talked to more and more people about how solid their relationship with the Lord is, I've concluded those who fail to establish this discipline into their lives seem to have the most difficult time staying close to the Lord consistently. Because of how important this is, I recommend this be possibly your only goal initially if you are just starting to establish your mission and goals, so you can focus on getting this firmly established in your life. The success of every other goal you set going forward will be dependent on how well you develop this habit.

Every additional objective we set must be approached the same way. We must establish which day or days we are going to do it and what part of the day we will commit to doing it. At this point in my life, I've concluded the main reason I don't do something I hoped to do is because I didn't put it onto my calendar. In the business world, nothing gets done if it doesn't get built into the schedule. So why would we think we can operate any differently with things we want to do in our personal lives? Because this is so critical, I recommend you don't write any goal without committing to the day, days, and/or time of day you are going to do it. Otherwise, you are going to be disappointed and discouraged when you realize you have not worked on a goal you intended to do. One of the main reasons people stop setting goals for themselves is because they do so poorly at accomplishing them. And it's simply because they didn't seriously build them into their schedule.

One of the other reasons people find it difficult to meet the goals they set out to do is because they failed to first stop doing something else. Because most people already have a full schedule, there really isn't any way they can do something new without removing something from their existing schedule. This is why when we are deciding to do something new, one of the first things we need to do is determine what we are going to stop doing going forward. Most people with full plates have things they are doing that aren't helping them grow in their love for God or people. For example, if we are spending several hours a day watching television, or surfing the net, or playing games on our computer, we have an opportunity to use that time instead to prepare our heart and mind for eternity. It's just a matter of making good decisions about what is important in this life and what is not important. We can only finish strong if we stop doing unimportant things.

We Must Be Intentional About Our Relationships

Many of the goals we develop over time involve other people if we are loving our neighbor as ourself and investing in other people. And like all other goals, we need to determine what that goal should be in a measurable way as much as possible. If we say we are going to work on having a better relationship, and that is the goal we write down, it's going to be very difficult to evaluate that goal. For that reason, I recommend you focus on spending time with people, so you get to know them, and they can see you care enough to spend time with them. That will go a long way in our busy world. Just meeting people regularly over some kind of drink, or for breakfast, lunch, or dinner is a very good way to intentionally work on building a relationship with a person. The key is we must build this into our schedule. Whatever relationships we include in our goals, we need to make sure we make time to spend with those people, and then build that time into our weekly or monthly schedule. Whether it's weekly, bi-weekly, monthly, or quarterly, we need to ensure we schedule time on our calendar, so we can always get it set up in advance at a time that works for both people.

When it's difficult to see people face-to-face because of distance, we also need to consider all the technologies that can be used in place of face-to-face conversations. Telephone calls, Skype sessions, Zoom, Facetime, letters, texting, email, or any other media that enables us to have conversations with a person can be used. This enables us to have long-distance relationships around the world, which often develop when we go on short-term overseas mission trips and connect with people in the host countries during our trip. Many of my relationships are long-distance relationships now because technology made that possible. But I still need to plan those conversations into my schedule, or they won't happen.

Refining Our Goals Over Time

As I talked about earlier in this chapter, it's important to establish a process that enables us to know as soon as possible if we are off track. Because of this, if we write some goals but don't examine them until a year later, chances are very high we will not have accomplished what we hoped. This is why we must examine how we are doing toward our goals on a weekly, monthly, quarterly, and yearly basis if we want to make progress. This may appear to require a lot of time, but it is much less time-consuming than we might think if we build it into our daily, weekly, and monthly schedules. Initially, all we need to do is determine if we are working on the objective by crossing it off as done on a daily and weekly basis. We'll know we're making progress simply by knowing if we are working on our goals as planned. It will be like going grocery shopping and crossing everything we buy off the list. By examining whether we are working on our goals we know if we need to make any adjustments. If we are too often not crossing off as done something on our list, that's the first clue we need to examine if we are trying to do too much, or if there are some things we've not stopped doing, we need to first put aside.

Another thing we will discover in this process of setting and examining goals is our goals may not be specific enough to measure well. Anytime it's hard for us to determine how well we have done on any given goal, then chances are good it wasn't as specific as it should have been. For example, if our goal was to read the Bible every day, then all we would have needed to do to meet that goal was read one verse a day, which probably wasn't what we had in mind. This is why we either must have a goal to read it for a given number of minutes or to read a certain number of chapters a day. We can even say which books in the Bible we are going to read over a given time. If we are working on a relationship, and we haven't said specifically what we are going to do with that person, then we may need to establish when we are going to meet, how often, and what method(s) of communication we are going to use when we meet.

Is It Helping You to Become Strong and Finish Strong?

It's sometimes easy to lose sight of the forest because of the trees. The main purpose in living life more intentionally is to help us grow in our love for God and our love for our neighbors. This is why we need to have a mission with goals that help us evaluate this realistically. It's also why we must ask for feedback from those who know us best. The best friends we can ever have in this life are those who speak the truth in love to us. The sad reality for many people is they don't have people in their lives who do this. This happens because they either don't want it, or they've not tried to find people who are willing and able to do this. Many people are clueless on why this is important, and one of Satan's strategies is to make us clueless about what is important in life. On the other hand, God is doing everything He can to show us what's important. We really have no excuse.

If our efforts to determine our mission, vision, plans, and goals are not increasing our faith and love, then we either need to revise them or find another way to increase our faith and love. One way or the other, each of us must be willing to take an honest look at our lives and eliminate anything that doesn't glorify God and build in things that do glorify Him. Otherwise, we are going to waste away one of the most precious resources we have, which is time.

Our time on earth is our time to prepare for eternal life, and we should be looking forward to it because of all God's promises and rewards. This means each of us must determine our real priorities. We are the ones who need to determine what we must do differently with our lives if we want to glorify and honor God in our life here on earth. If we've not built the time into our schedule to do something we said was important, then it wasn't important to us, or we've let something else that's not important continue using up our time. These are the eternal decisions we must make if we want to make progress toward becoming the man or woman of God who becomes strong and finishes strong in this life. If we don't stop doing the things with no heavenly value, so we can start doing the things important in the kingdom of God, it will keep us from becoming the man or woman of God He is calling us to be.

There's one other reason a person may not be willing to put in the effort to intentionally make changes in his or her life. It's possible people don't believe God can change them, even if they do their part in the process. If this is the case, then it reveals much more about what they believe about God than what they believe about themselves. Or it means they don't really want to be changed. If you don't believe God is capable of doing His part, now is the time to seek God's heart with all your heart so you can know and trust Him. He's promised you'll find Him if you seek Him.

And those who know Your name will put their trust in You;

for You, Lord, have not "forsaken those who seek You"
(Psalm 9:10).

"And you will seek Me and find Me, when you search for Me with all your heart" (Jeremiah 29:13).

Based on what I've experienced, it is worth whatever time and effort we put into it!

Chapter 15
Am I Listening to God's Warnings?

"See that you do not refuse Him who speaks. For if they did not escape who refused Him who spoke on earth, much more shall we not escape if we turn away from Him who speaks from heaven, whose voice then shook the earth; but now He has promised, saying, 'Yet once more I shake not only the earth, but also heaven.'" (Hebrews 12:25-26).

I've heard people say the Bible is God's love letter to us. If a parent writes a love letter to a son or daughter in college, the parent suspects is going down some wrong paths, it will not only include words of affirmation and encouragement, but it will likely include words of warning, so the child can know it's a serious letter intended for the child's good. The Bible is much the same way. God's wants us not only to know how much He loves us, His promises, commands and ways, and what His Son has done for us, He also wants us to be aware of all the dangers we can face. Everything God does is for our good and His glory. His goal is for us to live the best life possible during our time on earth. Yet this life on earth is only a glimpse of what the unimaginable eternal life with God will be like for those who know and trust Him to be in control of our life now.

God doesn't sugarcoat anything in the Bible and doesn't leave us guessing about anything. He tells it like it is. He has given us both unconditional and conditional promises. It's important for us to know the difference between the two and do our part to ensure we can experience all His promises. I heard one time there were about three thousand promises in the Bible. Therefore, it would take multiple books to even come close to talking about them all. Instead, I'm going to focus mostly on what can keep us from experiencing God's promises and keep us from finishing our life on earth in a God-glorifying way.

When we learn to drive a car, we not only learn how to start it, stop it, turn it, slow it down, and maintain it, we also learn all the warning signs on roads so we can adjust our driving when needed to avoid accidents and death. In the same way, careless living can lead to serious health problems and premature death that will keep us from finishing strong. In this chapter, I'm going to talk about some of the ways God warns us so we can be alert to the dangers around us at all times.

Warnings From What Happened to the Israelites

The apostle Paul used *1 Corinthians 10* to share what happened to the Israelites in the wilderness because of disobedience, so we could learn from their mistakes.

> *"Moreover, brethren, I do not want you to be unaware that all our fathers were under the cloud, all passed through the sea, all were baptized into Moses in the cloud and in the sea, all ate the same spiritual food, and all drank the same spiritual drink. For they drank of that spiritual Rock that followed them, and that Rock was Christ.*
> *(1 Corinthians 10:1-4).*

Paul tells us the Israelites had been rescued out of Egypt, their sins had been forgiven, and they had been nourished with the same spiritual food Christ gives us today. This means they experienced God as

Protector, Deliverer, Provider, Healer, Helper, and Leader. If you think about the oppression the Israelites endured under Pharoah's rule before God brought them out of Egypt, it was hopeless without God. But once God sent Moses and Aaron to confront Pharaoh and ask him to let the Israelites go, the Israelites saw firsthand the incredible miracles that eventually led to their deliverance from the Egyptians. It was a great story that should have given the Israelites great confidence in God so they could live the way God intended His people to live. But the next verse tells us the sad reality. *"But with most of them God was not well pleased, for their bodies were scattered in the wilderness" (1 Corinthians 10:5).*

Paul then tells us why this happened, and they serve as examples so God will not be displeased with us. *"Now these things became our examples, to the intent that we should not lust after evil things as they also lusted" (1 Corinthians 10:6).*

The Israelites that died were still desiring ungodly things, even after all God did for them. For us today, this means we must not only know what is right and what is evil in God's eyes, but we must recognize quickly when we are doing anything displeasing to God, so we can confess and turn from it. We must also not plead ignorance when we don't know the truth only because we didn't seek it earnestly. God will give all of us adequate time to get to know His truth, ways and promises. Nobody will have an excuse not to know what is right in God's eyes and what is evil in His eyes.

The next verse is another example of what we shouldn't become. *"And do not become idolaters as were some of them. As it is written, 'The people sat down to eat and drink, and rose up to play.'" (1 Corinthians 10:7).*

Idolatry includes anything we worship more than God. This can be money, position, possessions, power, reputation, outward appearance, material things or anything else in the world that is more important to us than God. When Moses warned the Israelites about idolatry, he first said,

> *"Take careful heed to yourselves, for you saw no form when the Lord spoke to you at Horeb out of the midst of the fire, lest you act corruptly and make for yourselves a carved image in the form of any figure: the likeness of male or female,"* (Deuteronomy 4:15-16).

It may seem irrelevant to us today to think anybody could worship a statue. Yet sports stars, sports teams, entertainment stars, political figures, and many other high-profile people become idols anytime we spend more time watching them or reading about them than we do God. But the real test to determine if there is anything more important to us than God is when we must choose between God and something else at a given moment. We will always choose what's more important to us. Even family and friends can become idols when pleasing them is more important to us than choosing God's will in any situation.

Moses went on to include statues of animals, birds, and sea-creatures as potential idols.

> *"The likeness of any animal that is on the earth or the likeness of any winged bird that flies in the air, the likeness of anything that creeps on the ground or the likeness of any fish that is in the water beneath the earth"* (Deuteronomy 4:17-18).

Again, it may seem strange for people to think any animals, birds, and sea-creatures could become idols. But think about how important dogs, cats, and other kinds of pets are to some people. When they become more important than God, they become idols.

Finally, Moses talked about the sun, moon, stars, and everything in the heavens.

> *"And take heed, lest you lift your eyes to heaven, and when you see the sun, the moon, and the stars, all the host of heaven, you feel driven to worship them and serve them,*

> *which the Lord your God has given to all the peoples under the whole heaven as a heritage. But the Lord has taken you and brought you out of the iron furnace, out of Egypt, to be His people, an inheritance, as you are this day"* (Deuteronomy 4:19-20).

Because most of us have heard about people who worship the sun and stars, and are aware of people who put their faith in the horoscope, it's not as hard to see these as idols in a person's life. As I said before, anytime any of these things become more important than God, they will be directing our lives and not God.

An intimate relationship with God is the best defense we have against idolatry, because He will lead and counsel us to live according to His Word, ways, and promises. As a result, we will be able to quickly see the truth when we are tempted to do anything that would not honor or glorify God, which is what we are called to do as believers and followers of Christ.

The next thing we are warned about is *"Nor let us commit sexual immorality, as some of them did, and in one day twenty-three thousand fell; (1 Corinthians 10:8).*

Sexual immorality may have been as big a problem during the Israelites' journey through the wilderness as it is in today's world. And as much as the world would have us believe God's ways and truth about sexual relationships between a man and woman are outdated, God knew what He was doing when He established the boundaries about sexual relationships in the Bible. Like everything else, God's commands were established to protect us. If you think about all the terrible sexually related diseases in the world today, it's obvious the sexual freedom the world desires was not what God had in mind, especially when we read twenty-three thousand died in one day because of it.

In the next verse, we are also warned about testing God. *"Nor let us tempt Christ, as some of them also tempted, and were destroyed by serpents; (1 Corinthians 10:9)*.

When we do evil things out of ignorance or immaturity, God will always give us a chance to confess and repent. He may even be merciful because that is one of His attributes of love, and He knows the intentions of our heart. We tempt and test God when we know what we are doing is not pleasing to Him, and we take His grace and forgiveness for granted. This is called willful disobedience, and God warned us about the consequences. *"For if we sin willfully after we have received the knowledge of the truth, there no longer remains a sacrifice for sins, but a certain fearful expectation of judgment, and fiery indignation which will devour the adversaries" (Hebrews 10:26-27)*.

In *1 Corinthians 10:9*, it says they were destroyed by serpents. In *1 Hebrews 10:27*, the consequences sound like Hell. What should get our attention is complaining has the same consequences. *"Nor complain, as some of them also complained, and were destroyed by the destroyer. (1 Corinthians 10:10)*.

In the book of *James*, we are told grumbling can lead to condemnation. *"Do not grumble against one another, brethren, lest you be condemned. Behold, the Judge is standing at the door!" (James 5:9)*.

We like to think complaining and grumbling are not that bad an offense against God. But in the book of *Jude*, grumblers were identified in the group of people who live to satisfy their natural desires. *"These are grumblers, complainers, walking according to their own lusts; and they mouth great swelling words, flattering people to gain advantage" (Jude 1:16)*.

As you can see from this verse, we grumble and complain when we don't get what we want. This doesn't mean we shouldn't provide constructive feedback to people or organizations when the service they provide is not up to the standards they set. But constructive feedback is spoken or written in love to make people aware of any poor service provided so they can make improvements in the future. We do this because we don't want other people to experience the poor service we received. But when we complain because people or organizations, or even God, are not living up to our expectations, we are implying God's ways are not as good as ours, and He should be sensitive to what our selfish nature wants. This means we are exalting ourselves above God, which is the same as saying God should worship us. And all of us know that's never going to happen.

Everything talked about in the first ten verses of *1 Corinthians 10* was written for our benefit, so we won't fall into the same trap Satan tries to lure all believers into. *"Now all these things happened to them as examples, and they were written for our admonition, upon whom the ends of the ages have come" (1 Corinthians 10:11).*

Yet the good news is no matter what sin or temptation we are dealing with, God will always give us a way out so we can become overcomers. This is why He always warns us first, so we can't say we didn't know.

> *"Therefore, let him who thinks he stands take heed lest he fall. No temptation has overtaken you except such as is common to man; but God is faithful, who will not allow you to be tempted beyond what you are able, but with the temptation will also make the way of escape, that you may be able to bear it" (1 Corinthians 10:12-13).*

Are We Guarding What God Has Entrusted to Our Care?

The apostle Paul wrote in his first letter to Timothy, *"O Timothy! Guard what was committed to your trust, avoiding the profane and idle babblings and contradictions of what is falsely called knowledge—by professing it some have strayed concerning the faith. (1 Timothy 6:20-21).*

What was committed to Timothy's trust? In verse *twenty-one*, it appears some of the believers were straying from the faith by following some false knowledge. Therefore, it seems Timothy was being warned to guard his faith. This means we must also guard our faith, especially since it is a gift from God.

> *"For by grace you have been saved through faith, and that not of yourselves; it is the gift of God, not of works, lest anyone should boast" (Ephesians 2:8-9).*

> *"For the wages of sin is death, but the gift of God is eternal life in Christ Jesus our Lord" (Romans 6:23).*

This is the reason every believer needs to grow and become strong in his or her faith, and to do it by focusing on God's Word and doing what it says. Our faith, like every living thing in this world, must be fed and nurtured so it can grow. No living thing can survive if it is stagnant. As we know, stagnant water will eventually smell bad. And if our faith becomes stagnant, it will also turn into what Paul called *"profane and idle babblings and contradictions of what is falsely called knowledge"* in *1 Timothy 6:20*. The only way water can stay fresh is to keep it flowing. The same principle applies to our faith. It cannot stand still.

Solomon wrote, *"Keep your heart with all diligence, for out of it spring the issues of life" (Proverbs 4:23).*

Both "guard" and "keep" are used in different translations of the Bible. When we guard something, we are trying to protect it from all harm. When we are keeping it, we not only protect it, we also nurture it so it can grow. I believe "keeping" is a better translation, since it means we must do everything we can to protect and help it to grow stronger and be more fruitful. If we read through the Bible, we find the word "heart" used close to a thousand times. It is probably the most used word in the Bible besides the names of God and Jesus Christ. It may be because of what Solomon wrote in the second part of the verse above about life springing from it. All our actions and words flow from our heart, which is to say all actions and words flow from what we believe. *"A good man out of the good treasure of his heart brings forth good; and an evil man out of the evil treasure of his heart brings forth evil. For out of the abundance of the heart his mouth speaks" (Luke 6:45).*

When our heart is right, our actions and words will be right in God's eyes. We must stay focused on God's truth if we want our heart to be in line with God's heart. When we desire to have a fruitful garden, we must keep the weeds out or they will use up the nutrients and water in the soil and produce nothing fruitful with it. The weeds in our heart are the lies we believe instead of God's truth. And they will lead us to do things that don't honor or glorify God. It's why lies, like weeds, must be pulled up by the roots, so only the truth of God remains.

Solomon also wrote,

> *"The highway of the upright is to depart from evil; He who keeps his way preserves his soul" (Proverbs 16:17).*

> *"He who keeps the commandment keeps his soul, but he who is careless of his ways will die." Proverbs 19:16.*

Upright people have hearts that purge the evil out as quickly as possible. They are not careless about what they do with their time each day. Instead, they protect and nurture the ways of God, so they do what is right in God's eyes and preserve their souls.

Unfortunately, it's not going to be possible for anyone to keep his or her heart if he or she doesn't have God living in it. The apostle Paul told Timothy, *"That good thing which was committed to you, keep by the Holy Spirit who dwells in us" (2 Timothy 1:14).*

The Holy Spirit is the Spirit of God living in us when we trust Jesus as our Lord and Savior. It's the little voice that speaks truth, so we know the truth in every situation we face daily. Anything not consistent with God's truth is a lie and will encourage us to wander from our faith.

Mike Garst

Are We Being Watchful?

Guarding and watching have very similar meanings, but I want to focus on the verses in the Bible that talk about watching in this part of this chapter. The apostles Paul and Peter wrote often about the end of the spiritual journey we are all on. Based on what they wrote, they may even have sensed Christ might return during their lifetime.

"But the end of all things is at hand; therefore, be serious and watchful in your prayers" (1 Peter 4:7).

"Therefore, let us not sleep, as others do, but let us watch and be [self-controlled] sober" (1 Thessalonians 5:6).

We are to be watchful, serious, and self-controlled all the time, not just some of the time. It has only been in the last five hundred years or so that cities or kingdoms didn't have night watches all the time to guard against the attacks of their enemies, who were looking for a time when the city "let down its guard." Our enemy, Satan, is always looking for an open door or window he can enter so he can lead us astray. We leave those doors and windows open when we are taking our faith for granted, as if it's an inanimate object we own and not a living faith that requires us to feed, exercise, and protect it.

Self-control is an important part of being watchful too, since we must make choices throughout each day that show we are either following the truth or following a lie. This includes every word that comes out of our mouth. *"He who guards his mouth preserves his life, but he who opens wide his lips shall have destruction" (Proverbs 13:3).*

Our actions and words are both important. We should use words all the time that not only honor and glorify God, but build people up and not tear them down. Jesus warned us we will have to give an account for every word that comes out of our mouth. *"But I say to you that for every idle word men may speak, they will give account of it in the day of judgment.*

For by your words you will be justified, and by your words you will be condemned" (Matthew 12:36-37).

We are going to sin with our words many times throughout our life, both before and after we put our faith in Christ. But the frequency will decrease as we grow in our faith. The good news is all the sin from our words will be forgiven and forgotten when we continue to confess and repent after we put our trust in Christ. But we can't assume we will be forgiven if we ignore the guidance of the Holy Spirit and don't confess and turn from sin. This is why we must realize God is watching all the time, and our sin is always against God. Joseph was a good example of how to view sin when his master's wife tried to seduce him. *"There is no one greater in this house than I, nor has he kept back anything from me but you, because you are his wife. How then can I do this great wickedness, and sin against God?" (Genesis 39:9).*

When we know the right thing to do and don't do it, we are sinning against God, not necessarily against other people. Yet we can also sin against other people at the same time. Plus, we can sin with other people. In this case, Joseph would have been sinning not only against God, but against his master. He would not have been sinning against his master's wife, but with her. It's never acceptable to sin against God or other people even for a moment.

It can be tempting at times to think it's okay to enjoy some of the pleasures of the world, especially when it is something that doesn't look bad on the surface. But God is always looking at our motives, not necessarily the activity we are doing. *"Therefore, judge nothing before the time, until the Lord comes, who will both bring to light the hidden things of darkness and reveal the counsels of the hearts. Then each one's praise will come from God" (1 Corinthians 4:5).*

For one person, an activity they are doing would glorify God, because the motive for doing it is good. For example, if the primary reason someone does an activity is to build relationships with other people and have the opportunity to show and share the love of Christ with them, then the motive would be good. If it's a physical activity, a person could also be doing it for the exercise and fellowship. But if it's a sports activity, and the primary reason the person competes is for personal glory, then the motivation would be driven by pride. That is not to say winning a sports competition is always a sin, but rather if all we care about is winning, then God will likely not be honored or glorified, especially should we happen to lose.

God is a good Father who expects His children to be obedient all the time and doesn't approve of anything not in line with His will. He is Lord all the time and not Lord some of the time. A child of God should have the same mindset Moses had.

> *"By faith Moses, when he became of age, refused to be called the son of Pharaoh's daughter, choosing rather to suffer affliction with the people of God than to enjoy the passing pleasures of sin, esteeming the reproach of Christ greater riches than the treasures in Egypt; for he looked to the reward"* (Hebrews 11:24-26).

We should not think sin is not pleasurable. The question is how long is it pleasurable. Our natural bodies like pleasure. And God has given us pleasurable things in this life to enjoy, but we must do them in moderation and not overindulge in them. Overindulgence is sin. But many pleasurable things are not right in God's eyes and will lead to our death and destruction if we don't place our faith in Christ and confess and turn from our sin before the end of our earthly life.

Are We Watching and Guarding with Prayer?

In the sixth chapter of *Ephesians,* the Apostle Paul talked about putting on the full armor of God, starting in verse thirteen. This included *"having girded your waist with truth"* and putting on the *"breastplate of* righteousness," having *"shod your feet with the preparation of the gospel of peace," taking the "shield of faith"* and the *"helmet of salvation, and the sword of the Spirit, which is the Word of God."* In the next verse, he then said, *"Praying always with all prayer and supplication in the Spirit, being watchful to this end with all perseverance and supplication for all the saints—"* (Ephesians 6:18).

Prayer is a vital part of the life of a believer in Christ as he or she grows in faith. Prayer must be continuous, meaning we must be in communication with God as needed throughout the day. It must also be proactive and reactive, meaning we should start every day praising and thanking God for what He's done, who He is, what He has promised, and what He is going to do. This includes acknowledging and recognizing all of His attributes and asking God to do what is necessary to strengthen our faith and transform us into Christ's likeness increasingly more, so everybody we encounter each day can sense God's presence in our presence, and we can persevere through every test and trial we face. We pray reactively when things come up as we are watching what is going on around us and need God's guidance and help with anything that happens during the day. And we pray in the same way we prayed proactively.

Paul also wrote to the believers in Colosse to *"Continue earnestly in prayer, being vigilant in it with thanksgiving"* (Colossians 4:2).

In addition to being thankful in every situation, our prayers must also be earnest and persistent. The prayer of the widow (see *Luke 18:1-8*) reminds of us why persistence is so important. In the last two verses, Jesus told His disciples,

> *"And shall God not avenge His own elect who cry out day and night to Him, though He bears long with them? I tell you that He will avenge them speedily. Nevertheless, when the Son of Man comes, will He really find faith on the earth?" (Luke 18:7-8).*

When we ask for God's justice to be done, and we are persistent at it, He will answer. But we must trust in His timing and continue to do our part to strengthen and grow in our faith.

Will I Be Ready When Jesus Comes?

Jesus wrote to the church in Sardis,

> *"Be watchful, and strengthen the things which remain, that are ready to die, for I have not found your works perfect before God. Remember therefore how you have received and heard; hold fast and repent. Therefore, if you will not watch, I will come upon you as a thief, and you will not know what hour I will come upon you" (Revelation 3:2-3).*

I've talked already in the previous section of this chapter about the need to be watchful and strengthen our faith. But Jesus went on to say some things were about to die. and the works of the church at Sardis were not perfect before God. This sounds like Jesus was saying some areas of their faith had become stagnant. In verse three, Jesus told them to "hold fast" and "repent," which confirms some areas of their faith were strong, but some areas required a change of heart. Jesus finishes verse three by telling the church at Sardis why they must keep watch. Nobody knows when Jesus is coming back, so we can never let down our guard. This is why we can never let our faith stagnate or shrink. The apostle Paul also told Timothy, *"Take heed to yourself and to the doctrine. Continue in them, for in doing this you will save both yourself and those who hear you" (1 Timothy 4:16).*

Paul said it was not only important for Timothy to continue in the truth (doctrine), so he could save himself, but so those who heard him could be saved. This is why all believers must be strong to the finish. We will not be able to coast across the finish line into God's arms based on the things we've done in the past. We must keep watch always and exercise our faith all the way to our last breath on earth.

The apostle Peter finished his second book with the following. *"You therefore, beloved, since you know this beforehand, beware lest you also fall from your own steadfastness, being led away with the error of the wicked; but grow in the grace and knowledge of our Lord and Savior Jesus Christ"* (2 Peter 3:17-18).

Peter was warning his readers of the same dangers Paul and Jesus wrote about, and he told us the solution was to grow in the grace and knowledge of our Lord and Savior Jesus Christ. Having an attitude that says "I must never stop learning or growing in my faith" is the only way we can finish strong.

None of us knows when Jesus is coming or what is going to happen on any given day, including when the end of our life will be. Jesus made that clear.

> *"Watch therefore, for you do not know what hour your Lord is coming. But know this, that if the master of the house had known what hour the thief would come, he would have watched and not allowed his house to be broken into. Therefore you also be ready, for the Son of Man is coming at an hour you do not expect"* (Matthew 24:42-44).

We must always be ready, which is why developing an intimate relationship with God that enables us to see what is going on around us throughout each day and know what the next right thing for us to do is the best way for us not to let our guard down. Jesus told us to watch and pray and the reason why. *"Watch and pray, lest you enter into temptation. The spirit indeed is willing, but the flesh is weak"* (Matthew 26:41).

Temptations are not going to disappear during our lifetime on earth. They will come not only from Satan, but from anything in this world trying to draw us away from God. The apostle Paul also said we should never stop praying. *"Pray without ceasing,"* (1 Thessalonians 5:17).

A life of prayer happens when we continuously sense God's

presence and are ready to praise Him for anything we see Him do or call on Him at any moment of the day for whatever we need. A person who does this will be ready when Jesus comes.

Chapter 16
Am I Being Faithful?

In this chapter on faithfulness, we will explore God's faithfulness to us and our call to be faithful to Him. It's important for us to know what God is responsible for and what we are responsible for in this life. Figuring this out as early as possible helps us avoid wasting time either expecting God to do something He will not do or by trying to do what only God can do. For example, if we think God is going to drop a big blessing into our laps while we lounge in our recliner, we are probably going to be disappointed, unless we are resting because we just expended a lot of energy doing something that glorified and honored God. But if we are in our recliner taking life easy, we need to consider what the apostle Paul wrote. *"Do not be deceived, God is not mocked; for whatever a man sows, that he will also reap" (Galatians 6:7).*

And if we think we don't need to carry a spare tire and car jack in case we get a flat tire because we think God will always show up to help us, we are likely going to be disappointed when our tire goes flat.

The Serenity Prayer summarizes this kind of thinking very well. It is a prayer written by American theologian Reinhold Niebuhr, and it is commonly quoted, *"God, grant me the serenity to accept the things I cannot change, courage to change the things I can, and wisdom to know the difference."*

Life on this earth is way too short for us to attempt things destined to fail because it's a responsibility God has given Himself. At the same time, the things we can change will not change if we don't have either the wisdom or the courage to do it.

God's Faithfulness

God is and will be faithful to do what He is responsible for. All God's attributes are important, but it seems some may be more important than others. God's faithfulness is one of His attributes talked about in over forty Bible verses in the New King James Version (NKJV). In *Psalm 89*, the psalmist wrote about God's faithfulness six times in the NKJV (*verses 1, 2, 5, 8, 24 and 33*) and eight times in the New International Version (*verses 1, 2, 5, 8, 14, 24, 33 and 49*).

Why is this attribute of God possibly one of His most important, if not most important, attributes? Simply because He has never failed, nor will He ever fail to deliver on a promise. If God speaks, we can be sure it's going to happen, because He is the perfect Promise Keeper. From the time He spoke the world into being until this moment, and forever more, whatever He says will happen. His Word is a promise. He can never be anything but a holy, righteous, just, good, unconditionally loving, merciful, compassionate, saving, comforting, helpful, forgiving, gracious, gentle, and kind God, just to name a few of His attributes. Plus, He could not call us to be faithful if He was not faithful Himself.

The definition of Faithful and Faithfulness in Webster's Dictionary includes:

1) Steady in allegiance or affection; loyal.
2) Firm in adherence to promises.

3) Given with strong assurance; binding promise
4) True to the facts, to a standard
5) An unswerving adherence to a person or thing or to the oath or promise by which a tie was contracted.

In summary, God's faithfulness is an unswerving adherence to His truth, ways, and promises. In other words, we can rely on God to be who He is and to do what He says all the time.

What are some of the ways God shows His faithfulness? *Psalm 119:75 says, "I know, O Lord, that Your judgments are [righteous] right, and that in faithfulness You have afflicted me.*

This tells us God is a good Father who will discipline His children if that is what it takes to get our attention or to correct us when we are living outside His truth and ways. If God was not faithful to do this, then we would not learn to follow His ways and truth, and we would not learn to delight in them. *"Unless Your law had been my delight, I would then have perished in my affliction" (Psalm 119:92).*

Reluctant obedience to God's commands is not what pleases Him. He wants us not only to obey His commands, but to love them, because we trust they are the best thing for us. That is why He will not only discipline us; He will patiently teach and train us. He is also faithful to answer our prayers. *"Hear my prayer, O Lord, give ear to my supplications! In Your faithfulness answer me, and in Your righteousness" (Psalm 143:1).*

Now we might not initially like the timing or answer to our prayers, but God does answer our prayers. Yet He first wants us to develop an intimate relationship with Him so we will not only trust Him completely, but also hear His voice and do what He is leading or teaching us to do as quickly as possible. This means His answers, and the timing of the answers will always be aligned with His goal for us to know His heart.

Because of this, He won't give us an answer too soon or an answer that would not deepen our trust in Him.

Garth Brooks wrote a song a few years ago called "Thank God for Unanswered Prayers." The song is a story about a guy who attends a high school football game at his alma mater with his wife and kids and runs into the high school sweetheart who broke his heart years before. Although he at one time prayed she would take him back, he now realizes his life is much better with the girl he eventually married, and so he is grateful his prayer was not answered.

God is also faithful to us as a provider. King David wrote, *"Trust in the Lord, and do good; Dwell in the land, and feed on His faithfulness" (Psalm 37:3).*

We never have to be concerned about not having our basic needs met if we trust God, because He has promised He will bless those who trust Him.

> *"Blessed is that man who makes the Lord his trust" (Psalm 40:4).*
>
> *"O Lord of hosts, Blessed is the man who trusts in You!" (Psalm 84:12).*
>
> *"Blessed is the man who trusts in the Lord, and whose hope is the Lord" (Jeremiah 17:7).*

God is also faithful to give us a way out when we are tempted.

> *"No temptation has overtaken you except such as is common to man; but God is faithful, who will not allow you to be tempted beyond what you are able, but with the temptation will also make the way of escape, that you may be able to bear it" (1 Corinthians 10:13).*

This means faithful followers of Christ should sin less and less as they grow to maturity in Christ. The apostle Paul also tells us God will be faithful to help us grow to maturity and be blameless at the coming of our Lord Jesus Christ.

> *"Now may the God of peace Himself sanctify [set you apart] you completely; and may your whole spirit, soul, and body be preserved blameless at the coming of our Lord Jesus Christ. He who calls you is faithful, who also will do it" (1 Thessalonians 5:23-24).*

God is also faithful not only to help us grow to maturity in our faith, He is also faithful to be our Protector to guard us from Satan. *"But the Lord is faithful, who will establish you and guard you from the evil one" (2 Thessalonians 3:3).*

This gives us assurance Satan doesn't have free access to do whatever he wants and hurt us any time or any way he wants, unless we give it to him through willful disobedience. God has put a spiritual protective hedge around those who trust in Him. We may think this is not true when we read the beginning two chapters in the book of Job. But we must remember God told Satan he couldn't take Job's life. We may still not want God to allow Satan to afflict us in the way Job was afflicted, but we must remember Job came to know God much better after his ordeal, and God blessed him double what he had before he was afflicted by Satan.

We are also thankful God sent His own Son, Jesus, who was *a "faithful High Priest"* and *"the faithful witness"* to pay the penalty for all our sins.

> *"Therefore, in all things He had to be made like His brethren, that He might be a merciful and faithful High Priest in things pertaining to God, to make propitiation for the sins of the people" (Hebrews 2:17).*

> *"And from Jesus Christ, the faithful witness, the firstborn from the dead, and the ruler over the kings of the earth. To*

Him who loved us and washed us from our sins in His own blood" (Revelation 1:5).

Without God's and Jesus' faithfulness to do this, we would have no hope for an eternal future in paradise with God as is promised to those who love and trust Him completely. Plus, *"If we confess our sins, He is faithful and just to forgive us our sins and to cleanse us from all unrighteousness" (1 John 1:9).*

The continual forgiving and cleansing of our sin by God as we confess and repent is what makes us blameless before Him and gives us the grace to continue growing into Christ's likeness. This is needed, so disciples of Christ can grow to maturity and make other disciples of Christ, who, in turn, will grow to maturity in their faith. It's what keeps the kingdom of God growing and advancing throughout all generations.

We can also trust God is faithful to do the impossible, as Sarah experienced. *"By faith Sarah herself also received strength to conceive seed, and she bore a child when she was past the age, because she judged Him faithful who had promised" (Hebrews 11:11).*

God is also our faithful Creator, not only because He created the whole universe and everything in it for our benefit, but also because He continues to do so every day. *Therefore, let those who suffer according to the will of God commit their souls to Him in doing good, as to a faithful Creator. (1 Peter 4:19).*

From *Psalm 139:13-16*, we know God creates each one of us.

> *"For You formed my inward parts; You [wove] covered me in my mother's womb. I will praise You, for [You are fearfully wonderful] I am fearfully and wonderfully made; Marvelous are Your works, and that my soul knows very well. My [bones] frame was not hidden from You, When I was made in secret, and skillfully wrought in the lowest parts of the earth. Your eyes saw my substance, being yet unformed. And in Your book, they all were written, the*

days fashioned for me, when as yet there were none of them."

We also know God judges in righteousness and fights evil for us through His Faithful Son, Jesus Christ. *"Now I saw heaven opened, and behold, a white horse. And He who sat on him was called Faithful and True, and in righteousness He judges and makes war" (Revelation 19:11).*

God is also faithfully going to make everything new when Jesus comes back to gather all His saints together to live in God's heavenly paradise with Him. *"Then He who sat on the throne said, 'Behold, I make all things new.' And He said to me, 'Write, for these words are true and faithful.'" (Revelation 21:5).*

This means the saints (everyone destined for eternal life with God) won't have to be concerned about any of the bad things that happened to them in this life, because they won't remember them. Plus, we will all be brothers and sisters in Christ with a pure love for each other and no remembrance of any conflicts we may have had, even within the church, during our earthly life. This may be one of God's greatest gifts to us as part of His salvation.

God is also faithful to give us a glimpse of the future so we can not only know what lies ahead, but so we can have adequate opportunity to place our trust in Him before it happens. *"Then he said to me, 'These words are faithful and true.' And the Lord God of the holy prophets sent His angel to show His servants the things which must shortly take place" (Revelation 22:6).*

Thus, we know everything is going to be made right someday. Because of this, we also will have no excuse if we fail to heed any warnings and surrender our lives to God.

God's faithfulness also doesn't depend on our faithfulness, as the apostle Paul wrote,

> *"If we are faithless, He remains faithful; He cannot deny Himself" (2 Timothy 2:13).*
>
> *"For what if some did not believe? Will their unbelief make the faithfulness of God without effect?" (Romans 3:3).*

If we reject God by not believing His Word, ways, or promises, that is our choice. But it will never be because God wasn't faithful to us. We have only one lifetime to trust in God. And although the length of our days vary, we will never have an excuse not to trust God. *"For since the creation of the world His invisible attributes are clearly seen, being understood by the things that are made, even His eternal power and [divine nature, deity] Godhead, so that they are without excuse" (Romans 1:20).*

Call to Faithfulness

Chapter *three* in *Hebrews* in the NKJV is titled *"Be Faithful"* and describes the process God designed to transfer His attribute of faithfulness to us through Jesus Christ. The first two verses say, *"Therefore, holy brethren, partakers of the heavenly calling, consider the Apostle and High Priest of our confession, Christ Jesus, who was faithful to Him who appointed Him, as Moses also was faithful in all His house. (Hebrews 3:1-2).*

It's important for believers to know they share in the heavenly calling and to know Jesus was faithful to God who appointed Him. They also need to know these other things about Jesus.

> *"God, who [in many portions] at various times and in various ways spoke in time past to the fathers by the prophets, has in these last days spoken to us by His Son, whom He has appointed heir of all things, through whom also He made the [ages] worlds; who being the brightness of His glory and the express image of His person, and*

> *upholding all things by the word of His power, when He had by Himself purged our sins, sat down at the right hand of the Majesty on high," (Hebrews 1:1-3).*

One of the reasons God sent His Son Jesus to the earth was so people could interact with God face-to-face to know Him better. It was therefore important Jesus be an exact representation of God, which is what the writer of Hebrews is telling us in these first three verses. After this, it says,

> *"And Moses indeed was faithful in all His house as a servant, for a testimony of those things which would be spoken afterward, but Christ as a Son over His own house, whose house we are if we hold fast the confidence and the rejoicing of the hope firm to the end" (Hebrews 3:5-6).*

Verse 6 is our call to be faithful to Jesus to the end of our earthly lives. Faithfulness requires we stay the course, regardless of the obstacles in our way. And there will be obstacles, because we live in a physical body that doesn't want to be uncomfortable, and we have Satan working against us throughout our journey. Plus, God is going to test our faith so we can know if it's genuine or not.

God gives us access to Himself through the Holy Spirit, which includes His thoughts, plans, purposes, promises, ways, and resources. Because of this, He doesn't randomly give His Holy Spirit to everybody, but only to those who trust Him, at least to some degree. I say 'to some degree' because the more we come to know God, the more we will trust Him. Yet *Hebrews 3:7-8* tells us something else that is important for all of us to know. *"Therefore, as the Holy Spirit says, "Today, if you will hear His voice, do not harden your hearts as in the rebellion" (Hebrews 3:7-8).*

God never makes us do anything, even after we have been given the Holy Spirit. He gives us a choice. This is why we must not harden our hearts when we hear God's voice. He could be leading us to do something by reminding us of one of His commands or revealing something new to us. It's sacred information that gives us an opportunity to prove how much we love and trust God. When we act on it, we are taking it to heart, which enables our faith in God to grow. Being faithful will always cause our faith to grow stronger.

On the other hand, if we ignore or refuse to act on what God is saying to us, then our heart will become harder and more resistant to God's voice. We become rebellious and show we don't believe in our hearts God is fully trustworthy. This is how we test and try God. Then God will need to discipline us, so we can know we don't fully trust Him and have the opportunity to confess and repent. If we don't, then it will be increasingly more difficult to hear God's voice.

All parents can relate to this, because they deal with this scenario all the time while raising their children. This is why good parents discipline and punish their children as needed so they can ultimately make their hearts softer and more receptive to God's voice. This is why grace is so important in the salvation process. When we humble ourselves before God, and acknowledge our sin or rebellion, He will give us grace, which gives us an opportunity to repent. *"But He gives more grace. Therefore, He says: 'God resists the proud, but gives grace to the humble.'" (James 4:6* – See also *1 Peter 5:5, and Proverbs 3:34).*

The faithful understand this and know they must do their part to keep their hearts soft and receptive to hearing God's voice and obeying what they hear. They are aware of the possible consequences of disobedience and take to heart the warnings throughout Scripture. *Hebrews 3:12-15* is one of those strong warnings.

> *"Beware, brethren, lest there be in any of you an evil heart*
> *of unbelief in departing from the living God; but*
> *[encourage] exhort one another daily, while it is called*
> *'today' lest any of you be hardened through the*

> *deceitfulness of sin. For we have become partakers of Christ if we hold the beginning of our confidence steadfast to the end, while it is said: 'Today, if you will hear His voice, do not harden your hearts as in the rebellion.'"*

Sin is deceitful, just like Satan. It's why we must keep seeking to know God's heart and mind with all our hearts and minds. The last part of *Hebrews 3:12* says, *"in departing from the living God."* This is saying we can be in a relationship with God, yet leave Him if we allow our hearts to become too calloused. It's why, as *verse 13* says, we must encourage or exhort each other daily. That is what the church, which is the body of Christ, is called to do. It's also the reason we must continually keep watch over each other and hold each other accountable to be faithful. Jesus told us in *Matthew 24:42-44, "Watch therefore, for you do not know what hour your Lord is coming. Therefore you also be ready, for the Son of Man is coming at an hour you do not expect."*

As believers in the Lord Jesus Christ, we can never let our guard down. But then, why would we want to ever let our guard down? Wouldn't we show we don't need or want God for those times in our lives? Or should we instead be like Moses who implores God in *Exodus 33* to always be with the people of Israel?

> *"And He said, 'My Presence will go with you, and I will give you rest.' Then he (Moses) said to Him, 'If Your Presence does not go with us, do not bring us up from here. For how then will it be known that Your people and I have found grace in Your sight, except You go with us?'"*
> *(Exodus 33:14-16).*

Shouldn't we, like Moses, desire God's presence all the time? Shouldn't we want Him to go with us everywhere we go throughout each day? Shouldn't we want to experience His grace immediately whenever we need it? After Jesus told us to keep watch in *Matthew 25:42-44*, He then said.

> *"Who then is a faithful and wise servant, whom his master made ruler over his household, to give them food in due season? Blessed is that servant whom his master, when he comes, will find so doing.*
>
> *47 Assuredly, I say to you that he will make him ruler over all his goods. (Matthew 24:45-47).*

Blessings will flow to us when we are faithful to live in God's presence throughout each day and do the things He called and prepared us to do. Who doesn't want blessings from God? The only question is whether we are willing to do our part to receive those blessings by being faithful.

What Causes Unfaithfulness?

Just like learning to drive a car requires us to know all the warning signs, being faithful will require us to be aware of the things that can lead to unfaithfulness. Jesus said,

> *"But if that evil servant says in his heart, 'My master is delaying his coming,' and begins to beat his fellow servants, and to eat and drink with the drunkards, the master of that servant will come on a day when he is not looking for him and at an hour that he is not aware of, and will cut him in two and appoint him his portion with the hypocrites. There shall be weeping and gnashing of teeth" (Matthew 24:48-51).*

Any time we take our eyes off Jesus and start living outside His presence, we open the door to Satan's temptations and to the desires of our own physical body and the world around us. This in turn will entice us to start doing things either not pleasing or detestable in God's sight. As a result, this servant wasn't ready when his master returned, and the consequences were devastating since he was appointed to Hell. The consequences of not being faithful are severe and eternal.

The last part of *Hebrews 3* points to the root of why people were not faithful and unable to enter in God's rest. *"So we see that they could not enter in because of unbelief" (Hebrews 3:19).*

They didn't know or trust God. Before God did any of the miracles to get Pharaoh to let His people go, He told Moses to tell the Israelites the following.

> *"I will take you as My people, and I will be your God. Then you shall know that I am the Lord your God who brings you out from under the burdens of the Egyptians. And I will bring you into the land which I swore to give to Abraham, Isaac, and Jacob; and I will give it to you as a heritage: I am the Lord" (Exodus 6:7-8).*

We would think this would have caused them to rejoice and celebrate over such a promise. Instead, this is how they responded to Moses. *"But they did not heed Moses, because of anguish [shortness] of spirit and cruel bondage" (Exodus 6.9).*

If the Israelites had trusted God, His words would have given them hope and encouragement. Instead, their response showed they not only didn't believe God could do what He said; they didn't fear Him either. When we have no reverent fear of God, we are not going to take Him at His Word, because we won't believe He is trustworthy. True faith must precede obedience. Unbelief or not trusting God will lead us to disobedience.

Knowing the condition of their hearts, it's not surprising God had to destroy a whole generation of Israelites in the journey through the wilderness, other than Caleb and Joshua, so He could prepare a new generation that would trust in Him and be obedient to His commands, and they could take possession of the Promised Land. Every one of us must learn to trust and obey God so we can not only hear His voice, but obey it throughout our lives. Eugene Peterson wrote a book titled *A Long*

Obedience in the Same Direction[12], a title that aptly describes what faithfulness is. We don't get to obey God only when it's convenient or not costly, or when we see some benefit. We are called to trust and obey God regardless of the cost or benefit to us. God wants us to trust Him with our whole heart, mind, soul, and strength. It's the reason we must go on a spiritual journey with Him, so He can teach and train us until we can trust Him with every part of our lives. The bottom line is faithfulness is not an option for true believers in the Lord Jesus Christ. The consequences of not being faithful are talked about in the following verses.

> *"When they go with their flocks and herds to seek the Lord, they will not find Him; He has withdrawn Himself from them. They are unfaithful to the Lord" (Hosea 5:6-7).*

> *"For indeed, those who are far from You shall perish; You have destroyed all those who [are unfaithful to You] desert You for harlotry" (Psalm 73:27).*

God will withdraw Himself from us and ultimately destroy those who are unfaithful to Him. This is why we must understand why we need to be faithful.

Jesus told the apostle John to write this to the church in Ephesus. *"Be faithful until death, and I will give you the crown of life" (Revelation 2:10).*

We can only receive the crown of life if we are faithful until our death on earth.

---

[12] A Long Obedience In the Same Direction, Eugene Peterson,

Chapter 17
Am I an Overcomer?

Without faithfulness, which I talked about in the previous chapter, we could never become an overcomer, which is what all believers in the Lord Jesus Christ are called to do. We must overcome all the challenges in our lives if we want to experience everything God has promised to those who believe and trust in Him, His Son Jesus Christ, and what Jesus not only has done for us, but what He's made possible for us. Jesus came not only to pay the price for our sins, but He came to deliver us from our sins and transform us into His likeness increasingly more until God brings us to our heavenly home. Deliverance and transformation are just as important as redemption in the gospel. We must not try to separate them. An overcomer will be continually forgiven and become increasingly more like Jesus. *"Beloved, now we are children of God; and it has not yet been revealed what we shall be, but we know that when He is revealed, we shall be like Him, for we shall see Him as He is"* (1 John 3:2).

Let's look at the verses in the Bible that talk about overcoming to see what we can learn from them.

Mike Garst

Take Hold of and Hold Fast to God's Promises

The first place in Scripture that uses the word "overcome" is *"Then Caleb quieted the people before Moses, and said, 'Let us go up at once and take possession, for we are well able to overcome it.'" (Numbers 13:30).*

Caleb trusted God and believed He wanted Israel to take possession of the Promised Land shortly after they crossed the Red Sea. He also believed God was going to be with them and fighting for them. Caleb and Joshua were the only two of the twelve spies Moses sent to scout out the Promised Land who believed it could be done. Unfortunately, it was another forty years before they were able to start the conquest of the Promised Land because, other than Moses, the rest of their generation didn't believe they could do it, even with God's help. And God wasn't going to lead the Israelites into the Promised Land if they didn't trust Him to do His part or weren't willing to do their part. But after forty years in the desert, God raised up another generation willing to go into the Promised Land and take possession of it.

Overcomers take possession of God's promises. The prophet Isaiah said, *"And there is no one who calls on Your name, who stirs himself up to take hold of You; for You have hidden Your face from us and have consumed us because of our iniquities" (Isaiah 64:7).*

This verse tells us when we don't call on God or lay hold of Him, He will give us over to our sins, which is a sure way not to overcome and, thus, miss out on experiencing His promises. It may be helpful to visualize what King David wrote in the next verse. *"Nevertheless, I am continually with You; You hold me by my right hand" (Psalm 73:23).*

When two people hold hands, their hands are clasped together. It's much easier for us to help someone get up if they hold tight to our hand while we are holding tight to theirs. In the same way, we must take hold of God's hand so we can have a mutually firm grip on each other. The apostle Paul wrote about this as well. *"Not that I have already attained, or am already perfected; but I press on, that I may lay hold of that for which Christ Jesus has also laid hold of me" (Philippians 3:12)*

This is another a way saying we must claim the promise of salvation by taking hold of it and not letting go. It also reminds us Christ took hold of us first, and the promise of salvation is a work in process in this life we can't fully claim until we finish the race. An overcomer must cross the finish line. The apostle Paul also emphasized this a couple of times in his first letter to Timothy.

> *"Fight the good fight of faith, lay hold on eternal life, to which you were also called and have confessed the good confession in the presence of many witnesses" (1 Timothy 6:12).*

> *"Let them do good, that they be rich in good works, ready to give, willing to share, storing up for themselves a good foundation for the time to come, that they may lay hold on eternal life" (1 Timothy 6:18-19).*

In *1 Timothy 6:12,* Paul also tells us, *"Fight the good fight of faith."* This is a reminder following Jesus is going to require us to be like well-trained soldiers in His army, who can take possession of everything they are fighting for. It's not going to be like a stroll in the park; it's going to be a battle. That is why we must "take hold of" or "hold fast" to God and His promises if we want to overcome.

The next two scriptures tell us to "hold fast" to God and are worded as commands.

> *"You shall fear the Lord your God; you shall serve Him, and to Him you shall <u>hold fast</u>, [my emphasis.] and take oaths in His name" (Deuteronomy 10:20).*

> *"You shall walk after the Lord your God and fear Him, and keep His commandments and obey His voice; you*

> *shall serve Him and <u>hold fast</u> [my emphasis] to Him"*
> *(Deuteronomy 13:4).*

(Also see *Joshua 22:5, 23:8, 2 Timothy 1:13, Hebrews 4:14,* and *Philippians 4:1.*)

To "hold fast" to God has never been an option either in the Old Testament or the New Testament. The apostle Paul said, *"By this gospel you are saved, if you <u>hold firmly</u> [my emphasis.] to the word I preached to you. Otherwise, you have believed in vain" (1 Corinthians 15:1-2).*

This means holding fast or holding firmly to God or to His Word is required for salvation. Otherwise, we could believe "in vain." This is why we must think of our faith journey as a battle we must win if we want to claim our heavenly rewards. Nobody has ever been able to claim victory in any kind of race if they didn't cross the finish line.

The next two verses tell us to "hold fast the confession of our hope" and to "hold fast our confession."

> *"Let us <u>hold fast</u> [my emphasis.] the confession of our hope without wavering, for He who promised is faithful"*
> *(Hebrews 10:23).*

> *"Seeing then that we have a great High Priest who has passed through the heavens, Jesus the Son of God, let us <u>hold fast</u> [my emphasis.] our confession" (Hebrews 4:14).*

When we place our faith in Christ, we must confess our faith in the presence of other witnesses so Jesus will acknowledge our confession before the angels of God. *"Also I say to you, whoever confesses Me before men, him the Son of Man also will confess before the angels of God" (Luke 12:8).*

But if we deny Jesus before men, He will also deny us. *"But he who denies Me before men will be denied before the angels of God" (Luke 12:9).*

As I talked about in the chapter on faithfulness, God will always be faithful, and because of that, He expects us to be faithful to Him. This means there is no reason to waver in our faith. When Jesus commended the church at Smyrna, He said, *"And you <u>hold fast</u> [my emphasis] to My name, and did not deny My faith even in the days in which Antipas was My faithful martyr, who was killed among you, where Satan dwells" (Revelation 2:13).*

When we hold fast to God, we are also holding fast to His name. God has many names, so we don't just hold fast to some of them; we hold fast to all of them. This is another way of saying we must hold fast to all of God's attributes of love, which cover everything we will ever need.

God Is Greater

It's sometimes easy for us to forget all of God's names and how powerful He is. He created the universe and everything that's in it, and the world we live in is only a tiny part of it. Because of this, the apostle John reminded us, *"You are of God, little children, and have overcome them, because He who is in you is greater than he who is in the world" (1 John 4:4).*

When Jesus is our Lord and Savior, we have the power of the God that created the universe living in us, so we can overcome all the evil forces coming against us in this life. This is also why we must lay hold of God, so His power can always be available to us. When we lay hold of God, we are staying connected to Him, which is what enables His power to flow to and through us, so we can overcome whatever problem we are facing.

This same principle applies to electricity. When the cord of a lamp is plugged into an electrical outlet, the electricity flows through to the light bulb, causing it to shine. The electricity flowing through the lamp originates at the power plant that generates the electrical power. In the same way, God's power, which starts with Him, is what flows to and through us to cause us to shine.

All of us are going to have challenges and problems in this life we will need to overcome. Jesus made this clear. *"These things I have spoken to you, that in Me you may have peace. In the world you will have tribulation; but be of good cheer, I have overcome the world" (John 16:33)*.

I don't know very many people who are happy about the trouble they face. Yet Jesus told us to *"be of good cheer,"* because He has already secured the victory for us. It will be like the sports event we didn't see when the game was played, but we know the outcome and recorded it so we could watch it later. If you have ever done this for your favorite team, you'll know it's still enjoyable to watch, because you won't get upset about any negative things that happen to your team, since you already know they won, regardless of any setbacks that happen while you are watching the replay. It becomes even more enjoyable when they are behind late in the game and need to do something unusual to pull out the victory. This is how believers should live each day, since they know God is going to get them through every challenge they will ever face if they hold fast to His promises, His Word, and His name.

The next verse tells us more specifically what we are holding onto when we are lay hold of God. *"I have written to you, young men, because you are strong, and the word of God abides in you, and you have overcome the wicked one. (1 John 2:14)*.

When God is abiding in us, His Word is living in us. Because God is invisible, we need to have something that can help us see Him by what we know about Him. The Bible tells us about all the attributes of God so we can recognize Him in the things happening around us and at least know, in general, how He's going to respond in different situations. When we know His character, His truth, His promises, and His ways, we can be confident, regardless of our circumstances, He's going to be walking through every challenge with us and leading us to an ultimate victory, even if we lose a battle here and there because we weren't using God's weapons and resources.

Overcome Evil with Good

> *"Do not be overcome by evil, but overcome evil with good" (Romans 12:21).*

The verse above tells us to overcome our enemies, we must do good to them, instead of taking revenge. This is certainly counterintuitive, but we shouldn't be surprised, since the way God thinks is much different from our thought process. *"For My thoughts are not your thoughts, nor are your ways My ways," says the Lord. "For as the heavens are higher than the earth, so are My ways higher than your ways, and My thoughts than your thoughts" (Isaiah 55:8-9).*

We will see things much differently when we see them through God's eyes. And this will enable us to take an approach that will utilize God's power and resources when we face new challenges.

In *Romans 12*, the apostle Paul shares several counterintuitive ways to do good and overcome evil. For example, *"Bless those who persecute you; bless and do not curse" (Romans 12:14).*

Our natural selves could never bless someone who persecuted us. That's why Jesus must first take up residence in us so we can have the desire, wisdom, and strength to do this. Jesus living in us is what empowers us to do what is pleasing to God and not what is pleasing to our flesh. We will resist the "bless-our-enemies" approach as much as possible until our spiritual body is stronger and we are more confident God's thoughts and ways are indeed higher and better than ours. The longer we go on the journey with God in this life, the quicker we will be able to think the way He thinks. Then we will *"Repay no one evil for evil. Have regard for good things in the sight of all men" (Romans 12:17).*

In every situation, we will only do what is right in the eyes of God, because we will know it is never acceptable to do evil in return for the evil done to us. Christians know and believe all vengeance belongs to God, since He alone can deal with evil in a just way. *"Beloved, do not avenge yourselves, but rather give place to wrath; for it is written, 'Vengeance is Mine, I will repay,' says the Lord" (Romans 12:19).*

Instead of vengeance, our enemies will experience God's patience and kindness. *"Therefore if your enemy is hungry, feed him; If he is thirsty, give him a drink; For in so doing you will heap coals of fire on his head" (Romans 12:20).*

All of us respond better to goodness and patience than we do to judgment. *"Or do you despise the riches of His goodness, forbearance, and longsuffering, not knowing that the goodness of God leads you to repentance?" (Romans 2:4).*

If we want to overcome evil, God will also need to develop in us the character traits of goodness (kindness), forbearance (tolerance), and longsuffering (patience), so our enemies can be led to repentance.

Rewards for Overcomers

Incentives can be an effective way to inspire and encourage us to pursue things. And God has told us about some of the rewards of overcoming to inspire and encourage us. In chapter five, "How Can I Become Like Christ," I talked about the rewards of discipline, and included the seven verses from chapters *two* and *three* in Revelation that talk about the rewards given to those who overcame. The apostle John had rebuked five of the seven churches and told them they needed to repent. Even the two churches who weren't rebuked were still told they needed to overcome to receive a reward. This confirms "overcoming" is not an option, but a command. This also implies saving faith will lead a person to be an overcomer. Let's look at these verses again to see the rewards of overcoming. To the church in Ephesus Jesus said, *"To him who overcomes I will give to eat from the tree of life, which is in the midst of the Paradise of God" (Revelation 2:7).*

We know from reading the first book in the Bible the tree of life was in the garden of Eden. *"And out of the ground the Lord God made every tree grow that is pleasant to the sight and good for food. The tree of life was also in the midst of the garden, and the tree of the knowledge of good and evil" (Genesis 2:9).*

We also know God commanded Adam, *"Of every tree of the garden you may freely eat; but of the tree of the knowledge of good and evil you shall not eat, for in the day that you eat of it you shall surely die" (Genesis 2:16-17).*

This means we are finally going to be able to eat from the tree of life and not die, although we will no longer be in our earthly physical body, but in our heavenly body that will never die. This is confirmed in the letter to the church in Smyrna. *"He who overcomes shall not be hurt by the second death" (Revelation 2:11).*

There are two deaths we must face. The first is the death of our physical body, which everybody will experience. The second death, which is optional, is the death of our spiritual body. Therefore, overcomers will not experience the second death, but will live forever. Jesus told the church in Pergamum,

> *"To him who overcomes I will give some of the hidden manna to eat. And I will give him a white stone, and on the stone a new name written which no one knows except him who receives it" (Revelation 2:17).*

Our heavenly bodies are going to be fed in God's paradise, but it will be a different kind of food. We know that the Israelites ate the manna God gave them in the desert, which was also called the "bread of heaven:" *"Had rained down manna on them to eat, and given them of the bread of heaven" (Psalm 78:24* – See also *Nehemiah 9:15* and *Psalm 105:40*).

We're not told what *"hidden manna"* is, but Jesus told us, *"I am the living bread which came down from heaven. If anyone eats of this bread, he will live forever; and the bread that I shall give is My flesh, which I shall give for the life of the world" (John 6:51)*.

We also know Jesus *"Was clothed with a robe dipped in blood, and His name is called The Word of God" (Revelation 19:13)*.

It makes sense our spiritual bodies will always need to be nourished by *"The Word of God."* But there's a lot we won't know about what's going to be in heaven until we get there, including what the "white stone" with a "new name written" on it is going to look like exactly. We just know only those who receive it will know. We learn about the next thing overcomers will get in the letter to the church in Thyatira.

> *"And he who overcomes, and keeps My works until the end, to him I will give power over the nations—He shall rule them with a rod of iron; they shall be dashed to pieces like the potter's vessels'—as I also have received from My Father; and I will give him the morning star. (Revelation 2:26-28).*

The first thing we notice in *verse 26* is an overcomer must keep Christ's works until the end. This is confirmation we can't be an overcomer if we don't finish the race and keep the faith. We also see overcomers will have *"power over the nations"* and *"rule them with a rod of iron."* This seems to imply there are going to be nations of people in heaven, and there will be rulers with authority over them. Again, there is a lot of mystery about what heaven is going to be like and what it will include. But we know *"Nevertheless we, according to His promise, look for new heavens and a new earth in which righteousness dwells" (2 Peter 3:13)*.

We are also told in this chapter the current earth will be destroyed. This at a minimum will be the destruction of all evil so only righteousness will be left. The new heaven and earth will only have good and righteous things in it, something hard to imagine after living on the earth for any length of time.

In the letter to the church in Sardis we are told, *"He who overcomes shall be clothed in white garments, and I will not blot out his name from the Book of Life; but I will confess his name before My Father and before His angels"* (Revelation 3:5).

Being clothed in white garments probably indicates we will be pure and blameless since white is the color for purity. Since our sinful nature will be destroyed, we will only be capable of doing what is right. The next part of this verse seems to be saying every person's name is listed in the Book of Life, but some may subsequently be "blotted out" if they do not overcome. Put differently, it may be all of us start out with our name in the Book of Life, and our name will only be removed from the Book if we refuse to trust in Christ. That is, the only reason we would be removed from the roster of the righteous is we rejected Christ. Otherwise, why would this verse be worded this way? If this is the correct understanding of the verse, it could turn a lot of doctrines upside down. To explore this further would require another book, so I'll leave it as something for you to ponder.

The church in Philadelphia was told,

> *"He who overcomes, I will make him a pillar in the temple of My God, and he shall go out no more. I will write on him the name of My God and the name of the city of My God, the New Jerusalem, which comes down out of heaven from My God. And I will write on him My new name"*
> *(Revelation 3:12).*

A pillar is a permanent part of a building, which may be further evidence that once we are in the paradise of God, we will be there forever. We also see God's name, the name of the New Jerusalem, and Jesus' new name will also be written someplace on our spiritual bodies, which is another confirmation it's permanent.

The final letter, which was written to Laodicea, has what I think is the most incredible reward for overcomers. *"To him who overcomes I will grant to sit with Me on My throne, as I also overcame and sat down with My Father on His throne" (Revelation 3:21).*

We will get to sit with Jesus on His throne just like Jesus sat on His Father's throne. It's easy not to take this verse seriously, as it is with many of the verses I've just talked about. I sense many people want to get to heaven and be content in their little corner. But that is a pauper's mentality and not how a child of God should be thinking. God doesn't promise small things, so we should expect an inheritance beyond our imagination, which is what God has promised. *"But as it is written: 'Eye has not seen, nor ear heard, nor have entered into the heart of man the things which God has prepared for those who love Him.'" (1 Corinthians 2:9).*

Final Thoughts on Overcoming

I said earlier in this chapter overcoming is not optional based on the scriptures I referenced. The apostles Paul, Peter, Jude, and John all included warnings in their epistles about the need to be overcomers that finish and win the prize at the end of our spiritual journey here on earth. And as much as we might want this to be automatic and believe we can't resist God's will, I've included scriptures throughout this book that indicate we have part of the responsibility to make this happen. Paul warned us about people leaving the faith in his first letter to Timothy. *"Now the Spirit [explicitly] expressly says that in latter times some will depart from the faith, giving heed to deceiving spirits and doctrines of demons," (1 Timothy 4:1).*

Note Paul said it was the "Spirit" that said this and said it *"expressly or explicitly."* If God said it, then we know it will happen. Paul wanted to make sure his readers took this seriously. At the end of that same chapter, he said,

> "Meditate on these things; give yourself entirely to them, that your progress may be evident to all. Take heed to yourself and to the doctrine. Continue in them, for in doing this you will save both yourself and those who hear you" (1 Timothy 4:15-16).

Paul wanted Timothy to make spiritual progress that could be seen by others so he could save himself and those who heard him. This implies Timothy's salvation was dependent on him doing the things Paul wrote about. Paul also wrote, *"For we through the Spirit eagerly wait for the hope of righteousness by faith" (Galatians 5:5).*

Based on this verse, everybody's righteousness in Christ requires them to be overcomers that win the race because they live by faith all the way to the end of their life. The apostle Paul also said, *"For we walk by faith, not by sight" (2 Corinthians 5:7).*

(See also *Habakkuk 2:4, Romans 1:17, Galatians 2:20, Galatians 3:11 and Hebrews 10:38.*)

Living and walking by faith is our true calling. We should think of faith as a verb and not a noun, because faith is "continually trusting in God" or "continually believing in God," and showing that by what we do. Paul also wrote,

> *"for by faith you stand" (2 Corinthians 1:24).*

We must cross the finish line standing as overcomers who live by faith.

The apostle Peter also wrote, *"Therefore, brethren, be even more diligent to make your call and election sure, for if you do these things, you will never stumble; for so an entrance will be supplied to you abundantly into the everlasting kingdom of our Lord and Savior Jesus Christ" (2 Peter 1:10-11).*

The things Peter was talking about were the godly qualities he said we need to add to our faith (virtue, knowledge, self-control, perseverance, godliness, brotherly kindness, and love). We must be diligent to build on our faith to make it stronger and more effective in every part of our life, so we can keep ourselves from stumbling. A person with this kind of faith knows they can never take their faith for granted, but they must continue to exercise it and build up their spiritual stamina. This will give them the endurance needed to finish the race, much like a marathon runner must build the strength and stamina into his body, especially his legs, so he can finish the race and gain the prize. We won't be overcomers if we don't continually live by faith so we can increase our faith. The apostle Paul said in *Philippians 2:12, "Work out your own salvation with fear and trembling."*

We must think of our faith as a continual workout in which we exercise our spiritual souls so they can not only stay strong but also increase in strength as we stretch our faith beyond where it currently is. And even though we are responsible for feeding and exercising our spiritual bodies, only God can make it grow. God wants us to grow in our faith so He can do what *Philippians 2:13* tells us. *"For it is God who works in you both to will and to do for His good pleasure."*

God's purpose is to work in and through us to show His love and share it with the world around us. When God is working effectively in and through us, we will be energized to keep going, not on our strength, but on His strength and His power. And God's *"power that works in us"* will *"do exceedingly abundantly above all that we ask or think,"* as Paul wrote. *"Now to Him who is able to do exceedingly abundantly above all that we ask or think, according to the power that works in us, to Him be glory in the church by Christ Jesus to all generations, forever and ever. Amen" (Ephesians 3:20-21).*

When we are fully functioning on God's strength in all areas of our life, we will be overcomers who enter in the kingdom of heaven and receive our inheritance.

Mike Garst

Chapter 18
Am I Persevering?

I'm going to use this chapter to talk about another of the godly character traits we must have to finish strong. The words the Bible uses to describe this character trait include perseverance, endurance, patience, and standing firm. James wrote, *"Blessed is the man who endures temptation; for when he has been approved, he will receive the crown of life which the Lord has promised to those who love Him" (James 1:12).*

This verse not only says we will be blessed when we endure temptation, but persevering through temptation is what qualifies us for the promised crown of life given to those who love God.

Perseverance Produces Maturity and Character

Based on what James said, we need to learn to be thankful and happy about the tests and trials we go through because of what they produce. *"My brethren, count it all joy when you fall into various trials, knowing that the testing of your faith produces [perseverance or endurance] patience. But let patience have its perfect work, that you may be [mature] perfect and complete, lacking nothing" (James 1:2-4).*

The testing of our faith not only produces perseverance (patience or endurance), it helps us grow to maturity in our faith. Paul also wrote,

> *"And not only that, but we also glory in tribulations, knowing that tribulation produces [endurance] perseverance; and perseverance, [approved character] character; and character, hope" (Romans 5:3-4).*

Note that perseverance comes after suffering and before character. Without suffering, there would be nothing to persevere. And without perseverance, Christ's character could not be built into us. When Christ is being formed in us, it's His character being formed in us. At the beginning of this process, no matter what our age is, we have no godly character in us until Christ takes up residence in our hearts. This will be hard even for some Christians to believe if they don't fully understand how naturally sinful each of us is. No matter how many "good" things I thought I did before I trusted God and His Son Jesus Christ as my Lord and Savior, once I started to understand what true righteousness is, I realized the best I ever did before I trusted in Christ was do the right thing with the wrong motive. And if my motive wasn't right, then it really wasn't good in God's eyes.

We are on a Spiritual Journey

It's helpful for us to think of faith as a journey with God. The Psalmist wrote,

> *"Blessed is the man whose strength is in You, whose heart is set on pilgrimage. As they pass through the Valley of [weeping] Baca, they make it a spring; the rain also covers it with [blessings] pools. They go from strength to strength; [The God of gods shall be seen] each one appears before God in Zion" (Psalm 84:5-7).*

One of the reasons perseverance, or spiritual stamina, is so important is because God designed our life to be a journey that would take us through valleys of weeping and pools of blessings until we appear before

God. And we go from strength to strength by passing each test and trial we experience, so we can appear before God. The writer of Hebrews (some biblical scholars think it was Paul) believed this was so important he wrote,

> *"And we desire that each one of you show the same diligence to the full assurance of hope until the end, that you do not become [lazy] sluggish, but imitate those who through faith and patience inherit the promises"* (Hebrews 6:11-12).

We must persevere, or we could become lazy and not inherit God's promises. Our natural body is lazy and will do everything it can, with the help of Satan, to get us to let up and not continue with the diligence needed to finish well. This may be one of the main reasons we need to become like Jesus, since becoming like Christ is what will give us the spiritual strength and stamina to resist our unhealthy natural desires and the devil.

Suffering Produces Obedience

Jesus also had to overcome temptations by the devil and His earthly body to fulfill His purpose. He had to be obedient to do what His Father purposed Him to do so all of us could not only be forgiven, but to be delivered from our sin nature and be transformed into Christ's likeness. As we are changed into Christ's likeness, God can then carry out His purposes through us so we can inherit all His promises. It's easy to forget or under-appreciate the journey Christ had to go on before He was able to fulfill His purpose. Not only did He have to be crucified and suffer for our sins, He had to do it in the same physical body each of us have, so we could know we can also resist sin with Christ's help. *"For in that He Himself has suffered, being [tested] tempted, He is able to aid those who are tempted"* (Hebrews 2:18).

Jesus can help us when we are being tested and tempted, because He has walked in our shoes. Jesus also had to complete His journey for additional reasons.

> *"As He also says in another place: 'You are a priest forever According to the order of Melchizedek;' who, in the days of His flesh, when He had offered up prayers and supplications, with vehement cries and tears to Him who was able to save Him from death, and was heard because of His godly fear, though He was a Son, <u>yet He learned obedience by the things which He suffered. And having been perfected, He became the author of eternal salvation to all who obey Him.</u>" [emphasis added] (Hebrews 5:6-9).*

If Jesus never sinned, what does it mean He *"learned obedience by the things which He suffered?"* Possibly, it means the cost of obedience can increase the further we journey and suffer with the Lord. So even though Jesus didn't sin, the suffering caused by His obedience increased all the way to the cross, with physical death and three days of separation from His Father being the final suffering.

Jesus had to suffer and obey His Father all the way to the end of His earthly life to be *"the author of eternal salvation to all who obey Him."* We also need to obey Jesus all the way to the end if we want to live in the kingdom of heaven forever and receive our rewards. As a result, our suffering will likely also increase as we continue the journey with Christ because *"For everyone to whom much is given, from him much will be required; and to whom much has been committed, of him they will ask the more" (Luke 12:48).*

Maturity Takes Time

As children grow up, parents typically expect more of them and give them additional responsibility when they show they can handle it. Our Father in heaven expects more from us as we mature in our faith, so the assignments will become more challenging, and the tests and trials will get harder. His desire is to increase our spiritual strength so we will trust Him in all things and not trust in ourselves or in anything else in this world.

> *"For we do not want you to be ignorant, brethren, of our trouble which came to us in Asia: that we were burdened beyond measure, above strength, so that we despaired even of life. Yes, we had the sentence of death in ourselves, that we should not trust in ourselves but in God who raises the dead," (2 Corinthians 1:8-9).*

One of the likely reasons most Christians struggle with being transformed into Christ's likeness is because it doesn't happen quickly. It will take a lifetime, and each of us must be patient throughout the process, because the flesh is weak. We must make a sincere effort to persevere, so we won't get lazy or too comfortable. The apostle Paul knew how important it was for believers to do this, and when they didn't, it was painful for him. *"My little children, for whom I labor in birth again until Christ is formed in you, I would like to be present with you now and to change my tone; for I have doubts about you" (Galatians 4:18-20).*

Only a woman knows what labor pains are like, but Paul said his pain was similar as he watched the believers in Galatia struggle to become like Christ. So, we should not be surprised when today's believers also struggle in their faith. Rather, we should be like Paul and labor in pain because of our concern for them.

We live in a culture that wants things fast, so it's no surprise new Christians want the process of being transformed into Christ's likeness to happen much quicker than it does. It's why we must be patient and persevere, and why we must also be intentional in the way we live each day. Paul wrote,

> *"Meditate on these things; give yourself entirely to them, that your progress may be evident to all. Take heed to*

> *yourself and to the doctrine. Continue in them, for in doing this you will save both yourself and those who hear you"*
> *(1 Timothy 4:15-16).*

These two verses imply it's going to take some serious effort to be transformed into Christ's likeness, which is why becoming like Christ will not happen unless a believer can endure every test they face. Perseverance isn't an option for a Christian; it's a must to obtain salvation, to reign with Jesus, and to receive the crown of life.

> *"Therefore, I endure all things for the sake of the elect, that they also may obtain the salvation which is in Christ Jesus with eternal glory" (2 Timothy 2:10).*

> *"If we endure, we shall also reign with Him" (2 Timothy 2:12).*

> *"For you have need of endurance, so that after you have done the will of God, you may receive the promise: For yet a little while, And He who is coming will come and will not [delay] tarry. Now the [My just one] just shall live by faith; But if anyone draws back, My soul has no pleasure in him" (Hebrews 10:36-38).*

This is the reason we must know we are a continual work-in-process, and the sanctification process God is taking us through is designed to expose any unbelief and hardness in our heart. Because of this, we should not be surprised when sin is exposed in our life, but rather be thankful it is out in the open, so we can confess it, nail it to the cross, and turn from it by the power of the Holy Spirit who gives us the strength and wisdom to do it.

Perseverance Is a Command

In *Revelation 2*, the church at Ephesus was commended for its perseverance.

> *"I know your works, your labor, your [perseverance] patience, and that you cannot [endure] bear those who are evil. And you have tested those who say they are apostles and are not, and have found them liars; and you have persevered and have patience, and have labored for My name's sake and have not become weary"* (Revelation 2:2-3).

The church at Philadelphia was called the faithful church, and we are told one of the reasons why. *"Because you have kept My command to persevere, I also will keep you from the hour of trial which shall come upon the whole world, to test those who dwell on the earth"* (Revelation 3:10).

They were commended for keeping God's *"command to persevere."* This puts the word "perseverance" on the same level as a command from God, which is proof it's not optional. It even has benefits since it says at the end of the verse they will be spared from needing to pass another test the rest of the world will experience.

To persevere, we must also be confident in God, His truth, His ways, and His promises. This will inspire us to stay strong through any test or trial because we *"know that all things work together for good to those who love God, to those who are the called according to His purpose"* (Romans 8:28).

When we believe God is always going to be with us in every trial we face, and He's going to be faithfully doing His part to get us through it so we can experience the good He intended, it should greatly reduce any anxiety and fear we may still have.

We also see perseverance is one of several qualities we are to add diligently to our faith. *"But also for this very reason, giving all diligence, add to your faith virtue, to virtue knowledge, to knowledge self-control, to self-control [patience] perseverance, to perseverance godliness, to godliness brotherly kindness, and to brotherly kindness love"* (2 Peter

1:5-7).

The reason perseverance, as well as each character trait in these verses, is so important is because of what it says in the next verse. *"For if these things are yours and abound, you will be neither [useless] barren nor unfruitful in the knowledge of our Lord Jesus Christ" (2 Peter 1:8).*

Our faith will bear fruit if we develop all these character traits, which includes perseverance. As you can see, these qualities include godliness, brotherly kindness and love. When we love God, we will also trust God, because we know He is fully trustworthy. This also means we will need to be patient for things to happen most of the time.

Abraham's Example of Perseverance

Abraham is a great example in the Bible of perseverance because of the age at which he started to follow God. *"So Abram went, as the Lord had told him; and Lot went with him. Abram was seventy-five years old when he departed from Haran" (Genesis 12:4).*

Sometime after that, God promised Abram he would have a son from his own flesh and blood. Although we don't know exactly what Abram's age was when God made this promise, it appears it was within a few years after he left Haran. What we know is he didn't have this son right away, and after waiting awhile, Sarah told Abram he should sleep with her servant Hagar to see if she could have a son for Abram. Abram thought it was a good idea, and Hagar became pregnant and had a son named Ishmael. But Ishmael was not the son God promised, and when Abram was ninety-nine years old, God appeared to him again and said Sarah would bear him a son within the next year. God also changed his name to Abraham at that time. We also know by then Ishmael was thirteen years old. This means Abraham waited about ten years before he fathered Ishmael and another fifteen years before Isaac was born. So, Abraham was holding onto God's promise for a long time, even if he didn't understand how it was going to be done. The apostle Paul summarized Abraham's faith.

> *"And not being weak in faith, he did not consider his own body, already dead (since he was about a hundred years old), and the deadness of Sarah's womb. He did not waver at the promise of God through unbelief, but was strengthened in faith, giving glory to God, and being fully convinced that what He had promised He was also able to perform. And therefore "it was accounted to him for righteousness.") Romans 4:19-22).*

Abraham didn't waver in his faith, and we are not to waver in our faith either. Instead, we are to be unshakable. *Psalm 125:1* tells us how we can be unshakable. *"Those who trust in the Lord Are like Mount Zion, which cannot be moved, but abides forever."*

Trusting God has always been and always will be the key to having an unwavering and unshakable faith in Him. We waver when we don't trust God. We have an unshakable faith when we have the same confidence in God Abraham had.

> *"By faith Abraham, when he was tested, offered up Isaac, and he who had received the promises offered up his only begotten son, of whom it was said, 'In Isaac your seed shall be called,' concluding that God was able to raise him up, even from the dead, from which he also received him in a figurative sense"* (Hebrews 11:17-19).

Abraham trusted so much in God's promise, even though God was asking Abraham to do something that seemed senseless to all of us, he concluded God could raise Isaac from the dead if needed. That's the kind of faith that can get all of us through any kind of trial or test, no matter how difficult it is. One could also conclude Shadrach, Meshach, and Abed-Nego had that kind of faith when they

> *"Answered and said to the king, 'O Nebuchadnezzar, we*

> *have no need to answer you in this matter. If that is the case, our God whom we serve is able to deliver us from the burning fiery furnace, and He will deliver us from your hand, O king. But if not, let it be known to you, O king, that we do not serve your gods, nor will we worship the gold image which you have set up.'" (Daniel 3:16-18).*

Abraham has been called the "father of faith," but based on Abraham's experience and the number of verses that talk about perseverance, patience, or endurance in these scriptures as it relates to faith, it appears Abraham could also be called the "father of perseverance." Perseverance is an essential part of our faith if we are going to become like Jesus and finish strong. It's the reason we must be training and growing in our faith so we can have the spiritual strength and stamina to persevere through the tests and trials we will face in our lives.

Waiting

The writers of the Psalms talk often about waiting on God. Because many of His promises are conditional, it means certain things must happen before we can experience some promises. It could be things must be developed in us before we are ready to do something, or it could be things must be developed or happen in other people, or it could be a combination of both. Regardless, God is the only one who knows when the timing is right. This also requires perseverance as the apostle Paul wrote. *"But if we hope for what we do not see, we eagerly wait for it with perseverance" (Romans 8:25).*

We also know perseverance is required before the signs of an apostle will manifest itself. *"Truly the signs of an apostle were accomplished among you with all perseverance, in signs and wonders and mighty deeds" (2 Corinthians 12:12).*

It's very easy to be fascinated by signs and wonders, and to want God to do those things through us. At the same time, we can also be distracted by signs and wonders, and forget God's purpose in these things is to show people He can do the things we can't. God is not showing off, He's just giving us a glimpse of His power as a way to draw us to Himself. But this isn't His primary way of revealing Himself to us, since He wants to connect our heart to His through a relationship in which we can experience His love in many ways. This is why God may not immediately enable signs and wonders to be done through new Christians. They may need to grow to maturity so they can properly use this gift in ways that glorify and honor God and not themselves.

The apostle Paul gives us a list of qualities about himself in his second letter to Timothy, including perseverance, and what it ultimately led to, which was deliverance from whatever trial he was going through. *"But you have carefully followed my doctrine, manner of life, purpose, faith, longsuffering, love, perseverance, persecutions, afflictions, which happened to me at Antioch, at Iconium, at Lystra—what persecutions I endured. And out of them all the Lord delivered me." (2 Timothy 3:10-11)*.

When we read the story of Job, it's very easy to think God was putting more tests and trials on Job than necessary. At least most of us are very glad we haven't gone through something as severe up to this point in our lives. But we also see from what James wrote that perseverance was the key to Job being able to overcome all the obstacles he faced. *"Indeed we count them blessed who endure. You have heard of the perseverance of Job and seen the end intended by the Lord—that the Lord is very compassionate and merciful" (James 5:11)*.

One could conclude from reading *Job 1* he was a mature man of God. Yet we learn through the book of Job he didn't really know God as well as he needed to know Him. Therefore, God allowed Satan to inflict some pain on Job to strengthen his faith by increasing his knowledge about God's character and sovereignty. At the end of the book of Job, after God came and told Job some things about Himself he either didn't know or didn't fully appreciate, Job responded to the Lord by saying,

> "I know that You can do everything, and that no purpose of Yours can be withheld from You. You asked, 'Who is this who hides counsel without knowledge?' Therefore, I have uttered what I did not understand, things too wonderful for me, which I did not know. Listen, please, and let me speak; You said, 'I will question you, and you shall answer Me.' I have heard of You by the hearing of the ear, but now my eye sees You. Therefore I abhor myself, and repent in dust and ashes" (Job 42:2-6).

God became much larger and more awesome in Job's eyes and heart after he went through the suffering Satan inflicted on him with God's permission. And Job was blessed with double what he had before his test started (see *Job 42:12-17*).

Another important thing for us to remember is Jesus didn't start His final three years of ministry until He was thirty years old. We don't know what happened from the time He was twelve until the time He was thirty, but it would be hard to imagine Jesus was not continuing to grow and learn so He was fully trained and ready for what God was calling Him to do, and so the human part of Him would not be able to talk Him out of it. We know He was wise well beyond His age at twelve years old from what was written about Him in *Luke 2* when His parents were looking for Him after they left Jerusalem without Him. If Jesus had to still study and train for another eighteen years, it would make sense we may need at least eighteen years to be ready for what God wants to do in and through us. He must work in us before He can work through us, and a God-sized assignment is going to require that we have become like Jesus as much as possible, so God can accomplish His mission through us, and we can finish strong.

Endurance

The first three verses in *Hebrews 12* give us a good definition of endurance.

> *"Therefore, we also, since we are surrounded by so great a cloud of witnesses, let us lay aside every weight, and the sin which so easily ensnares us, and let us run with <u>endurance [emphasis mine]</u> the race that is set before us,"*
> *(Hebrews 12:1).*

This verse tells us spiritual endurance is similar to what an athlete must have to run long-distance races. Long-distance races are often called endurance races or marathons. It doesn't take much stamina to run a one-hundred-yard sprint, but to run a mile or more takes endurance in both our lungs and our legs. *"Looking unto Jesus, the author and finisher of our faith, who for the joy that was set before Him <u>endured</u> [emphasis mine] the cross, despising the shame, and has sat down at the right hand of the throne of God" (Hebrews 12:2).*

This next verse is about enduring pain and suffering. The cross for Jesus included physical, emotional, and spiritual suffering. Physical suffering is easier for us to understand, because all of us have suffered physical pain at some point in our lives. Suffering verbal abuse for doing what is right in God's eyes is something Christians can usually relate to more than unbelievers. But spiritual suffering is something Jesus experienced far more than any of us will. He was separated from God and spent three days in Hell to pay the penalty for all our sins. Jesus had never been separated from God but had lived in His presence every moment of His life. It's impossible for any of us to imagine what it would be like to experience this kind of separation from God and how much endurance it would take. But we are told one of the key things that motivated Jesus to endure all of this was *"the joy that was set before Him."* Christians need to see the same kind of joy in front of them to keep going when they are suffering. Knowing heaven is on the other side of our earthly grave has been and will continue to be the primary motivation for all Christians to endure suffering here on earth. The next verse says, *"For consider Him who <u>endured</u> [emphasis mine] such hostility from sinners against Himself, lest you become weary and discouraged in your souls"* (Hebrews 12:3).

We see the opposite of endurance in this verse. It's discouragement and weariness that can lead to the complete loss of hope. This is the most dangerous place for anybody to be in their life. Hope is what keeps us going. When we start to lose it, we start to experience depression. And when we lose hope completely, it can lead to suicide and/or hurting others. On the other hand, Jesus tells us, *"But he who endures to the end shall be saved"* (Matthew 24:12-13 – See also Matthew 10:22 and Mark 13:13).

This tells us salvation requires us to finish the spiritual race. The apostle Paul confirmed this nearing the end of his life when he wrote to Timothy.

> *"I have fought the good fight, I have finished the race, I have kept the faith. Finally, there is laid up for me the crown of righteousness, which the Lord, the righteous Judge, will give to me on that Day, and not to me only but also to all who have loved His appearing"*
> *(2 Timothy 4:7-8).*

This is what all of us need to be able to say at the end of our lives, because we are also going to be in a war against our enemy the devil, and we are going to need the spiritual stamina Paul developed to keeping running the race just like he did.

Chapter 19
What Will Be My Legacy?

In the introduction, I shared the story about Granny Brand and about the couple who retired early to Florida and spent their days cruising on a 30-foot trawler, playing softball, and collecting shells. Their lives represented two different ends of the scale on how we could finish our lives. Granny Brand finished her life by serving God, ministering to the people in India until her final breath. The life of the couple in Florida was presented as a tragedy in the making. If we take this seriously, there are two questions we could ask ourselves. First, where are we on this scale? Secondly, in what direction are we moving? We are moving in one direction or the other, whether we know it or not.

The answer to the second question is more important than the first. The answer to the first question is only important in helping us honestly evaluate where we are currently, so we know what we need to change to ensure we are moving in the right direction. My hope is as you read this book, you started to think about the answers to the question in the title of each chapter. I'm sure some chapters spoke to you more than others, because we are all at a different point on our life journey.

Our honest answers to each of these questions can help us identify things we must change in our lives to become stronger in the Lord and finish strong in the Lord. This is why we must have trustworthy friends who have earned the right to speak into our lives. They are a gift from God to help us identify the things we have not been able to see yet.

All of us are leaving a legacy, whether we realize it or not. The question is whether we are leaving a worthy one. Our families and close friends will know if our faith is cold, lukewarm, or hot by how we live out our final days on earth. Our priorities will be revealed by what we do each day. And they will know if we finished strong or not. If you have read this book up to this point, there's a good chance you want to become strong and finish your life strong. The good news is your best days can be in front of you, regardless of where you are now.

How Much of Our Legacy Will be in Our Final Years?

It's interesting to read obituaries and see what is written about a person's life. Most of the time, it's about what they did in their early years or during their work career. For most professional athletes, their glory years were when they were young. And many of them live their remaining years trying to relive those glory years. Some, fortunately, have successful careers in other fields after their careers in professional sports. But it's not often you read an obituary that focuses on the last part of a person's life. Granny Brand was the exception, because she was driven by her vision to take the gospel to seven mountain ranges in India. As a result, most of her legacy happened during her final twenty-five years. She doctored, nursed, farmed, preached, taught, and did whatever was necessary to help and teach the people about God and how to live a life that glorified Him. And she never tired of carrying out that vision because it was a God-given vision she couldn't do without Him being with her and giving her the strength and resources to do it.

Maybe each of us needs to sit down and try to write what our obituary might say based on our life up to this point and what we hope to accomplish in our remaining years. Do we want our obituary to be more about what's happened already or what's yet to happen, God willing? If we do this, it might help us know what our life priorities really are, especially if we are not sure. And hopefully, it will challenge and inspire us to make the changes needed so our obituaries will be different than what we think they might say based on our current priorities.

Final Thoughts on Our Legacy

I hope this book has challenged and encouraged you in love to be all God created you to be. As I've said before, I believe our best years should always be in front of us. I hope that perspective alone will challenge those of you who were not thinking this was the case. As I also said at the beginning of this final chapter, I hope some of the chapters in this book have spoken to your heart about what might need to change in your life so you can finish strong.

God is still not finished doing His work in us. And although we don't need to be complete for God to start working through us, there will always be some work He needs to do in us before He can accomplish His purposes through us in the future.

I pray each of you would seek God wholeheartedly to get a vision and purpose for your life, and then carry it out daily, trusting Him to lead, transform, and strengthen you, and give you the resources needed for the work He wants to do in and through you to your final breath. I know such a person will have people say about them at the end of their lives what David Lister said about Granny Brand.

"She was happier and more alive than anyone I had ever met," he was to confess later. "When she looks at you, it's as if she could see right through you." [13]

---

[13] Granny Brand Her Story, Dorothy Clarke Wilson, Paul Brand Publishing, Seattle WA, 1976, Page 198

About the Author

Mike Garst has worked as an engineer and engineering consultant for Lennox International in the HVAC business for fifty years, and has no plans to retire. He considers his workplace and his neighborhood not only to be places to work and live, but also to be mission fields to share and show the love of Christ. He went to Costa Rica on his first mission trip in 1997, and that experience altered his life forever.

He still travels there regularly to encourage his spiritual sons and daughters, and to make devoted disciples of Jesus Christ. He went on his first mission trip to Germany in 2001 to help lead a Baseball Camp for Jesus, and that also impacted his life forever. Seven years later God worked through Mike to start the first of three yearly one-week Baseball Camps for Jesus in Germany (Aurich, Vechta and Osterholz-Scharmbeck) and has given him a vision for the rest of his life to start new camps as God opens the doors in Germany and other countries in Europe or around the world. Through these camps, he has become a spiritual father, friend and mentor to many in Germany.

Mike has been married to his wife Susie since 1977, and they currently live in Dallas, Texas, where they are blessed to spend time with and invest in the lives of their two married children, their spouses, and six grandchildren.

Acknowledgments

Writing is not a natural gift for me, so writing a spiritual book had to be a spiritual gift. I want to thank two dear brothers in Christ who invested in me by giving me opportunities to grow in my faith, so I could recognize God's voice when He led me to write this book. The first man, pastor Bud Miller, gave me opportunities to preach and teach God's Word, and taught me how to lead mission trips and be a spiritual mentor. The second man, Paul Foss, the head and visionary of Waterboyz for Jesus, gave me opportunities to lead men in ministry, went on mission trips with me to Germany, inspired me to memorize scriptures, and also taught me how to be a spiritual mentor.

Dear friends and fellow believers, Bill Moore and Mary Anne Davis, were faithful to read all the first drafts of this book and give me valuable feedback, which helped me refine what I had written initially. Mary Anne, who has been a great encourager to me for twenty-five years, was also the person who connected me to the Roaring Lambs ministry for writing and publishing books and paid for me to go to the writer's conference they put on in 2023, which connected me with the right people in that ministry. Marji Laine and Frank Ball made this book possible. Marji has been the key person in taking my manuscript and turning it into a book that can be offered to the public. Roaring Lambs was the answer to my prayer on whether I would ever publish this book.

Bob Van Horn, one of my college roommates more than a half a century ago, invested the most time in reading, editing, and providing me valuable and honest feedback, not only on my initial drafts of each chapter but also the final drafts. When you consider Bob and I don't share the same beliefs, this helped me see what I had written from a different perspective. It's also a great testimony of what good friends do for each other, regardless of what we believe.

www.ingramcontent.com/pod-product-compliance
Lightning Source LLC
LaVergne TN
LVHW051224080426
835513LV00016B/1395